Data Journalism
Past, Present and Future

EDITED BY

JOHN MAIR, RICHARD LANCE KEEBLE,
MEGAN LUCERO AND MARTIN MOORE

Published 2017 by Abramis academic publishing

www.abramis.co.uk

ISBN 978 1 84549 714 9

Printed and bound in the United Kingdom

Typeset in Garamond

Abramis is an imprint of arima publishing.

arima publishing
ASK House, Northgate Avenue
Bury St Edmunds, Suffolk IP32 6BB
t: (+44) 01284 700321

www.arimapublishing.com

Contents

Acknowledgements

These books are never solo efforts. The editors work like Trojans to identify, commission, chase and edit authors' contributions. Nobody, especially not the editorial quartet, is paid a penny. We continue to be impressed by the willingness of our colleagues in the academy and media industries to share and advance knowledge. The designer of the superb book cover, Dean Stockton, deserves praise too. As ever, our publishers Richard and Pete Franklin at Abramis make it happen in record time and with little fuss.

We thank them all.

John Mair, Oxford
Richard Lance Keeble, Withcall, Lincolnshire
Megan Lucero, London
Martin Moore, London

The editors

John Mair has taught journalism at the Universities of Coventry, Kent, Northampton, Brunel, Edinburgh Napier, Guyana and the Communication University of China. He has edited 20 'hackademic' volumes over the last seven years on subjects ranging from trust in television, the health of investigative journalism, reporting the 'Arab Spring' to three volumes on the Leveson Inquiry. He and Richard Lance Keeble invented the sub-genre. John also created the Coventry Conversations which attracted 350 media movers and shakers to Coventry University; the podcasts of those have been downloaded six million times worldwide. Since then, he has launched the Northampton Chronicles, Media Mondays at Napier and most recently the Harrow Conversations at Westminster University. In a previous life, he was an award-winning producer at the BBC, ITV and Channel Four.

Richard Lance Keeble, chair of The Orwell Society, is Professor of Journalism at the University of Lincoln and Visiting Professor at Liverpool Hope University. He has written and edited 36 books on a wide range of topics: including newspaper reporting skills, media ethics, peace journalism, investigative reporting, literary journalism, humour and journalism, profile writing and the links between Fleet Street and the secret state. In 2011, he was given a National Teaching Fellowship, the highest award for teachers in higher education in the UK, and in 2014 he received a Lifetime Achievement Award from the Association for Journalism Education. He is joint editor of *Ethical Space: The International Journal of Communication Ethics* and *George Orwell Studies*.

Megan Lucero is the Director of the Bureau Local, a data journalism unit at the Bureau of Investigative Journalism dedicated to uncovering local public interest stories in the UK. Megan, formerly the Data Editor at *The Times* and *Sunday Times*, was part of the first data journalism team at The Times and led its development from a small supporting unit to a key component of investigations. She spearheaded the newspaper's political data unit ahead of the 2015 General Election – making it the only one in the industry to reject polling data ahead of the vote. Using computational method, her team brought many issues into the public eye and won awards for revealing the widespread use of blood doping in the Olympics.

Martin Moore is Director of the Centre for the Study of Media, Communication and Power at King's College London and a Senior Research Fellow in the Policy Institute at King's. He teaches courses on media, technology and politics. His research focuses on political communication during election and referendum campaigns and on the civic power of technology platforms. Before teaching and researching at King's he was Director of the Media Standards Trust. He is the author of *The Origins of Modern Spin* (Palgrave MacMillan, 2006).

Foreword:

'Data journalism has become just part of what journalists do'

Simon Rogers

'A blog about data? Who on earth would want to read that?' That was the incredulous response from a senior editor when I suggested putting together a blog about data.

That was 2009 and it probably seems quaint now. It was pretty simple as ideas go: we'd call it the Datablog and it would be a way for us to publish the datasets I'd accumulated working with the graphics team at the *Guardian*. Looking for GDP data, or carbon emissions ratings? Tired of numbers buried on PDFs (where data goes to die)? We would liberate those datasets and make them available for people to use. This was the *Guardian* Datablog – to become the first major national news data website at the start of the new data journalism boom.

My journey into data journalism had actually started a couple of years earlier when I was working with the graphics team as a news editor on the *Guardian*. It coincided with the 'Berliner'-sized paper, with more space devoted to visuals and graphics. The idea had been to have an editor working with the head of graphics, Mike Robinson, to help bridge the gap between the newsroom and the graphics team. A side-effect was that I started collecting data – lots of it. We launched the Datablog with 250 datasets, published on Google Docs.

We'd actually started using Google Docs because we didn't have the resources to build out a proper database. In the end, it meant we had a robust way of organising the thousands of datasets we published over the years.

As anyone who knows my academic record will be aware, maths had never been my natural forte at school. I had gone into journalism as a way to tell stories and I had imagined that would be primarily with, you know, words.

But journalism has changed a lot. When I left City University's newspaper journalism course in 1992, the idea was to go work for a local paper, then get one of the magical jobs in a national newspaper (note the use of the word 'paper').

1

The new thing then was for reporters to be specialised in a subject, such as finance or crime. But my entry into a national newspaper was through its website, as the launch news editor of the *Guardian Unlimited* network of websites.

As journalists know, your work is more akin to an output: the resulting story being told in pictures, words, graphics, audio, video, VR. … Journalism is always at the edge of what's technologically possible – data journalism even more so. And just as 'internet journalism' was an actual field of reporting in the late 1990s, data journalism has become a field of reporting now, in a way which will probably seem pretty quaint to a working reporter in the next decade when it becomes just part of what they do.

For me, it was a journey I just hadn't been expecting. I had been a news editor, edited a weekly science section and launched a website. The idea of working with data every day had never even been a possibility. In particular, there were some things that now seem significant but hadn't at the time. At one point, in an editorial meeting about workflows, I realised that I was increasingly not only dealing with how things work, but also in collating data to give those visuals more depth.

There was also something else: trust. Increasingly, journalists fight hard to gain reader trust. It's a huge challenge for the ways we work, day to day. By putting the raw data out there, by bringing that transparency to the ways we work, suddenly that trust is earned. Not only are we telling you a story but here is the background to it. There's a crucial openness to data journalism and a recognition that we are not always *the* expert in a particular story. But if we open up that data, we can learn more about it simply from the experts in the field.

There were certainly key moments in the newsroom acceptance of data journalism. For instance, the Iraq and Afghanistan war logs, leaked to WikiLeaks, MPs' expenses' crowdsourcing were all stories it would have been very difficult to tell without some kind of data analysis. But at least as important was the rolling drumbeat of daily data journalism: the idea that this could be another part of a reporter's arsenal and that every day we could have something to contribute was new then, as now it has become accepted and normal.

At a time when facts themselves are up for debate, data journalism has never been more important. Today, data journalism has become the closest to mainstream it has ever been, arguably since before the Data Journalism Award days of Philip Meyer's *Precision Journalism*. This year saw almost 500 entries from around the globe. No longer a preserve of the West nor of organisations with huge bank accounts, data journalism has become just part of what journalists do.

Maybe one day it will be seen as funny that there was ever anything such as a 'data journalist'. But data journalism will be alive and well and as vital as it ever was.

Section 1:
Calling all journalists

Megan Lucero

When I was first asked to contribute to this book in 2015, I thought it kind of odd. Why publish something in printed text on data journalism when it is changing so rapidly? Anything published must surely be instantly out of date. It merely took a moment's pause to recognise that the answer is: because we must. If we want to take part in shaping the future of data journalism, we must stop and understand the trajectory of change and what it means for journalism itself.

Technology is advancing rapidly. Information is being digitised at an ever-growing speed. Data points are stacking up in front of journalists at a rate that a human cannot possibly compute. These data points represent crime rates, pollution measures, GCSE results – and so on. Hidden in this sea of data is evidence of systemic wrongs, institutional progress and lives lived. In these data points are the stories of our communities. And it is the job of journalists to tell those stories. To do so, we need to learn how to navigate the technology that captures them.

The challenge of tackling vast quantities of data comes at a time when the industry is having to rethink its digital business model and how it publishes. But the onus to change is not on employers alone. Journalists must find new ways to find and tell stories. This is no small challenge. It is tempting to believe that every latest piece of tech is a silver bullet, or to chase down a start-up that promises to have all of the answers. Conversely, to slow down and question what is in front of us or to learn from others takes a bit more work, a bit more commitment. But to innovate successfully, it's the necessary task.

The first section of this book will help you to do exactly that. Five authors give us the learning, perspective and inspiration to understand how to find stories faster, dig deeper and unearth complexity in ways we have never been able to do before. The book opens with the Director of Interactive and Newspaper Journalism at City, University of London, Jonathan Hewett, rooting the text in the history of data journalism in the UK. He chronicles the influence of the US's computer assisted reporting (CAR) movement and the beginnings and reach of the London-based Centre for Investigative Journalism. He tackles the fight for freedom of information and the launch of *data.gov.uk*. He tells of the journalism and tech scenes that have formed as a result of this series of innovations. He reminds us that data journalism was once considered something of a niche, the preserve of financial journalists, but is now recognised to have permeated every strand of the industry.

Next, Mar Cabra, head of the Data and Research Unit at the International Consortium of Investigative Journalists, takes us behind the scenes of the largest collaborative investigation in journalism history, the Panama Papers. In breaking the story, Cabra, didn't just wrangle 2.6 terabytes of data (11.5 million files from the Panama-based law firm and corporate service provider Mossack Fonseca), but worked with nearly 400 journalists to produce more than 4,700 articles worldwide. She doesn't just awe and inspire in this piece, she lays out a blueprint for the sustainability of journalism through collaboration.

And then we tackle trust. Joseph O'Leary, senior researcher at *Full Fact*, discusses the importance and role fact-checking plays in the current political climate. He shows us how easy it is for journalists, politicians and the public to slip up with numbers, the damage that it can do and how hard it can then be to set the record straight. Building trust and doing it rigorously is a complex challenge for 2017 and beyond. O'Leary's key message is that the responsibility to report the truth isn't just for fact-checkers. All journalists must lead by example.

Aasma Day brings a fresh perspective to this section. She invites us to look beyond the London-centric bubble and challenges us to think not just about whose stories we are telling, but about who is telling the stories. Investigative reporter and Lifestyle Editor at the *Lancashire Post*, Day argues that being on the cutting edge isn't all about the tech. If the data journalism industry wants to lead in innovation, it should also be leading in inclusion. Day tells us that we need diversity in the ethnicity, education, location, social background, gender, age, sexual orientation and disability amongst both reporters and the voices heard in the media. She argues that breaking up the homogeneity of newsroom practices will not just make journalism more innovative and creative, it will ensure the data in our journalism better reflects the world we report.

The section ends with a grounding call to make data more human. Simon Rogers, Data Editor at Google and former Editor of the *Guardian* Datablog, sets journalists a challenging but important task – make data accessible. Now that we know of the power of data, we need to democratise it. We need to find a way to ensure readers can see for themselves the art, beauty and humanity of every data point. Rogers argues that if journalists do it right, they become better reporters by bringing the data closer to their readers and to themselves.

I hope, like me, you find that these authors provide a necessary pause for reflecting on the exciting state of data journalism and the steps journalists must take collectively to shape its future.

Collaborative learning: From CAR to data journalism and Hacks/Hackers

Data journalism in the UK grew out of computer-assisted reporting (CAR) in the USA. But how did it cross the Atlantic and also feed into journalism education in Britain? Jonathan Hewett traces the development and teaching of data journalism in the UK

We have come a long way since Tim Berners-Lee, the inventor of the world-wide web, declared 'data journalism is the future' in 2010 (Arthur 2010). By then the term was only beginning to become recognised outside specialist circles and 'data journalist' was a designated role in few newsrooms. Reporters and others were working with data, typically to source stories – notably in financial journalism. Some were familiar with spreadsheets and databases, of course, and a few with computer-assisted reporting (CAR), particularly if they had come across the latter in US investigative journalism. A similarly low level of recognition would probably have been evident at many university journalism departments in the UK.

A few years later, however, data journalism was appearing in job advertisements, conferences, university courses, discussions about the future of journalism and research projects. Its rapid and diverse evolution meant that data work was found among almost every strand of journalism, from local newspapers and hyperlocal bloggers to international news agencies, broadcast, investigative and specialist journalists and beyond.

This chapter explores both how this shift happened, including the US influence on data journalism's emergence in the UK, the role of freedom of information and the development of data-focused courses within journalism education. It draws on interviews with some of the key players and documentary research.

Tough times for investigative work

One factor underlying the relative lack of computer-assisted work in UK journalism at a time when it was well-established in the USA involved the challenges faced by investigative journalism, the main focus for CAR. 'Many would argue that the glory days of investigative journalism in the UK are well beyond us now,' Arjan Dasselaar suggested (2005: 221), attributing this to cuts in editorial budgets, fierce competition and legal liabilities. David Leigh, then-investigations editor at the *Guardian*, bemoaned 'difficult and frustrating times for investigative journalism in Britain' (Meek 2005).

Dasselaar's survey noted also 'some distrust towards new methods of information gathering, such as the internet'. While the BBC's *Panorama* programme employed 'computer researchers, journalists seem to consider going out and talking to people as superior to using Google'. Others felt that 'information on the internet must be untrue, for otherwise it would have been picked up already' (ibid: 224) – a point well made, given recurring errors attributable to 'facts' taken from websites apparently without checking (Orlowski 2007).

Signs of change were already evident in 2005, as more journalists grasped the opportunities offered by the internet, particularly financial reporters accessing records: 'The advent of the internet has revolutionised this branch of journalism,' noted Dasselaar (op cit: 224). Even so, few could have anticipated the scale of a shift that led five years later to news organisations such as the *Guardian* dealing with huge volumes of data requiring detailed analysis. These included the Afghan war logs (92,201 rows of data), the Iraq war logs (391,000) and the US embassy cables (251,287) – all released through WikiLeaks (Rogers 2013a: 71).

Nerds plus words add up in the USA

Journalists on the other side of the Atlantic were far ahead of their UK counterparts. Already by 1999, a growing network of reporters, editors and journalism educators could look back on substantial developments in CAR over the previous ten years (Paul 1999). *When Nerds and Words Collide* reviewed progress since the 1989 creation of the National Institute for Advanced Reporting and the Missouri Institute for Computer-Assisted Reporting (which became the National Institute for CAR, NICAR). Education and training formed a recurring theme in that report: notably how to train practising journalists and integrate CAR into journalism education at universities.

The resistance to change among the latter has been documented extensively (Hewett 2016). It is linked to another long-standing debate on the stance of journalism education towards employers; some critics attribute a lack of innovation partly to it having been a 'handmaiden to industry, not its critic or visionary guide' (Dennis 1983: 3). In any case, it is hard to disagree with Folkerts that 'journalism education has, to a great degree, ignored the larger contours of the digital age' (2014: 63).

Even by the mid-2000s, the lack of UK networks such as NICAR in the USA for sharing ideas, skills and discussions was a pointed contrast with the situation not only across the Atlantic but also with many other European countries such as the Netherlands, Denmark, Sweden and Germany. Again, this may have reflected the state of investigative journalism in the UK which provided only 10 out of

450 delegates at the Global Investigative Journalism Conference in Amsterdam in 2005 (Meek 2005).

Some CAR training was taking place in the UK, however, particularly through the Centre for Investigative Journalism (CIJ). Established in 2003, it had close links with the USA – hardly surprising as it was founded by a journalist from the States. Gavin MacFadyen had worked as a producer of investigative documentaries on both sides of the Atlantic – including on *World in Action*, Granada Television's campaigning series – and became the CIJ's director. The CIJ's first summer school in July 2003 offered what may have been the first intensive training conference in the UK (albeit with participants from outside the UK, too) on investigative techniques for journalists. It included a half-day introductory CAR course, plus advanced classes, explaining: 'CAR is an increasingly important tool that enables journalists to add depth to their stories by accessing, making sense and presenting relevant government, financial, and social statistics' (CIJ 2003).

Transatlantic training triumphs

The influence of US journalism's experience in CAR was clear from the seven trainers who led the CIJ sessions. They all came from or had close links with NICAR and/or its parent body, Investigative Reporters and Editors (IRE), and included already experienced data practitioners such as Brant Houston, Aron Pilhofer and Jennifer LaFleur. The leading role played by NICAR can be inferred from the 40 to 50 seminars a year it ran over the period 1994-1999, and the estimated 12,000 journalists who attended its 300 conferences and seminars in its first ten years (Houston 1999: 7).

Houston became managing director of NICAR in 1993 (before it gained that name), having been database editor at the *Hartford Courant* and won awards for his investigative work. His book *Computer-Assisted Reporting: A Practical Guide*, into a third edition by 2003 (Houston 2003), became a key resource, drawing on 'what many of us had learned about training' and providing 'at least one road map for classes in newsrooms and journalism schools' (Houston 1999: 6).

Pilhofer was working as database editor at the Center for Public Integrity, in Washington DC, and later led the development of data and interactive journalism at *The New York Times*. LaFleur had worked as database editor at the *San Jose Mercury News* before becoming IRE's first director of training. She went on to be CAR editor at the *Dallas Morning News* and director of CAR at non-profit investigative newsroom *ProPublica*. As early as 1989, she had analysed the use of computers as part of her Master's degree at the University of Missouri School of Journalism (home to IRE and NICAR) (LaFleur 1999: 25).

The beginner's CAR workshop at the 2003 CIJ summer school focused on 'more effective searching techniques, resources and data on the internet, downloading data, and doing basic analyses using spreadsheet software such as Microsoft Excel'.

An 'intermediate track' involved moving 'from filtering and sorting data in Excel to calculating rates and ratios for news stories, cross-tabulating data and generating graphics' before 'showing how to select and filter information in a database manager and introducing users to summarising data effectively to find trends and story ideas' (CIJ 2003).

More complex techniques of data analysis were covered in an 'advanced track' with 'techniques of summarising data and using relational databases to compare different files of information to see connections that could lead to new stories', and used Microsoft Access. It also offered participants the opportunity to 'learn how to build their own databases when there is no electronic information or when governments or businesses refuse to release electronic data. Lastly, the track will include an overview of the new and increasing use of mapping (GIS) software to visualise the results of data analysis' (ibid).

Freedom of information, better journalism?

Such CAR training became a core feature of CIJ summer schools, along with another theme relevant to the emergence of data journalism: the use of freedom of information (FoI) legislation. Passed in 2000, the FoI Act came properly into force on 1 January 2005 and was fundamental to the development of data journalism in the UK. For the first time, journalists had a legal right to request information held by public bodies, which now had to respond (although not necessarily by providing the information requested). This was a huge advance on the preceding code of practice on access to government information, introduced in 1994 as an alternative to FoI legislation (Brooke 2004). Drawing on her background as a reporter in the USA, Heather Brooke wrote a pioneering book on using FoI in the UK, *Your Right to Know*, partly out of her 'frustration with the relationship between the citizen and the state in Britain, which was not as egalitarian as in America' (Brooke 2013). Primarily because a culture and legislative framework enabled access to information there, data and CAR techniques were becoming well-established among US investigative reporters in the 1990s, Brooke says:

> The main reason was that the datasets were available. A typical story was to get hold of a list of school bus drivers and cross-reference it with a list of sex offenders or other offences. They are both public records in America, with no privacy law, so you could find out whether any of the school bus drivers were paedophiles or had other convictions (ibid).

The appliance of science to reporting

In contrast to the UK – and its lack of public data – the US federal FoI Act had operated since 1967. The timing seems coincidental, but it was same year in which Philip Meyer and colleagues at the *Detroit Free Press* produced a Pulitzer Prize-winning investigation into the causes of riots in the city, often cited as the beginning of CAR. Meyer saw the potential to apply social science techniques to journalism, having studied them the previous year while on a Nieman fellowship at Harvard. A course he took there also introduced him to computing in the form of an IBM 7090 mainframe machine (Meyer 1999: 4). In Detroit, Meyer deployed quantitative survey research, helped by two university professors, a team of 30 interviewers for field work – and a computer programmer. (This was not the first use of computing in support of journalism, however: in 1952, a Remington Rand Univac machine was used to help US television network CBS predict election results; see Chinoy 2010.)

Having demonstrated 'the application of the scientific method to the practice of journalism' (Meyer 1999: 4), he started to pass on his skills to other reporters in the same newspaper group as he developed his statistical and computing abilities. Published in 1973, his *Precision Journalism* – subtitled *A Reporter's Introduction to Social Science Methods* (Meyer 1973) – and its 1991 successor became landmarks in CAR. Meyer did not use public records in his investigative journalism until 1972 (Meyer 1999: 4), but his work converged with FoI in the use of computing tools and statistical techniques for analysis. As computers and software became more ubiquitous and easier for non-specialists to use, so US news organisations began to appoint dedicated database editors.

Grappling with hygienic spreadsheets

Interest in the UK appears to have remained very limited until more journalists began to realise the opportunities provided by FoI. From 2005, Heather Brooke trained hundreds of journalists in FoI techniques with the National Union of Journalists and elsewhere – and while she mentioned the value of obtaining information in the form of spreadsheets, she was not teaching analysis using them (Brooke 2013). She was also putting FoI through its paces herself as a freelance journalist – and learning CAR techniques to deal with the resulting data. One striking success published during the first year of FoI was an investigation with *The Times*. The resulting 'justice by postcode' story, published on the front page, revealed huge disparities in conviction rates around the UK (O'Neill, Gibb and Brooke 2005). It also highlighted the greater experience in data analysis that journalists elsewhere in Europe had developed.

'I talked to the FoI officer at the Crown Prosecution Service about when they switched to electronic data. I got three years' worth of data in Excel spreadsheets – which was great, but it was 42 different sets of records from different CPS areas,' Brooke recalls (2013; O'Neill and Brooke 2005). To help with the analysis, she turned to Tommy Kaas who had run CAR training sessions at CIJ summer schools. He had set up the Danish International Center for Analytical Reporting (DICAR) which evolved from the Association of CAR in Denmark, set up in 1997 with other CAR pioneers such as Nils Mulvad, who taught CAR at the Danish School of Journalism.

A tipping point for CAR and UK data journalism

The fourth CIJ summer school (2006) was a turning point for CAR and data training. CIJ director Gavin MacFadyen noted a 'surge in interest in computing. The rooms where those skills were being taught were packed and that's the first time that's happened. ... The whole landscape has changed and journalists see the value of using electronic tools that we've taken for granted and don't really know much about' (Brooke 2006). CAR trainers at the summer school – as previously, mostly from the USA – were starting to use data about the UK, obtained from UK public bodies under UK FoI legislation, to demonstrate what could be done:

One of my very first FoI requests was for London councils' inspection reports on restaurant hygiene. Most of them were electronic datasets, which I didn't really know how to handle properly. It was around that time that Aron Pilhofer was over, and I gave him my restaurant inspection data. 'This is really great for teaching,' he said. 'I'm going to use this for our CAR classes in London.' He showed us different ways of analysing it using Excel – but also what the limits were and how you could switch over to Access and write SQL queries to drill down into the data and find out specifically which were the dirtiest restaurants in London. 'I think that was a real transitional point because it was teaching using real data from this country rather than America, and obtained from FoI' (Brooke 2013).

Another US CAR trainer, David Donald (then training director of IRE), was encouraged: 'I think you'll begin seeing many more in-depth investigative stories that will be based on using CAR,' he said (Brooke 2006). To support that growth and to share tips and ideas among interested journalists in the UK, a mailing list called BICAR emerged – inspired by the successful equivalents at DICAR in Denmark and NICAR in the USA. It was set up by Martin Stabe, then at journalism weekly *Press Gazette*, after post-CIJ summer school discussions in a pub with Brooke and freelance investigative journalist Stephen Grey. Alas, their enthusiasm seemed to outrun the wider interest among journalists for such a project, as Stabe recalls:

It never really amounted to much – there were almost no messages and it fizzled out quickly. There just wasn't the volume of material or people to make that viable, and I seemed to spend more time administering the server it ran on than actually having any content. I like to think that it was just ahead of its time (Stabe 2013).

Journalism education and training

Data-related work was also developing at City, University of London, where the CIJ was based and Brooke had become involved in teaching. I introduced FoI as part of the postgraduate Newspaper Journalism course at City in 2005; every student researched an FoI project to generate their own original story for publication. Some City students also worked with Brooke on other FoI/data projects, too. They included Elena Egawhary (BBC *Newsnight* and *Panorama*), James Ball (later data editor at the *Guardian*) and Alex Wood (who worked as a data journalist at the BBC World Service).

FoI became important not only for the data it enabled journalists to access (for data journalism stories and projects); it also acted as a gateway for students – a valuable bridge from more conventional reporting to data journalism. Many characteristics of journalistic FoI work – from spreadsheets and the analysis of changes over time, to patterns and statistics – underlie data journalism, too. Arguably FoI serves as a useful introduction to computational thinking (Hewett 2014a), which underlies the pedagogy of some data journalism education – and the introduction of coding – in universities.

A stuffy computer room hosted a dozen or so participants for a key training event for UK data journalism in July 2007. Two hugely experienced trainers, Aron Pilhofer (then database editor at *The New York Times*) and David Donald (by then data editor at the Center for Public Integrity, in Washington) ran an intensive three-day 'training the trainers' programme at City. Subtitled 'How to teach computer-assisted reporting', the course – arranged through MacFadyen and the CIJ – aimed to 'show how CAR is successfully taught so that more CAR training can take place here and more home-grown, UK-based journalists can take advantage of these skills'. An outline of the course noted not only the importance of CAR – but also the lack of training in data-related skills and stories in the UK:

> Computer-assisted reporting (CAR) has led many reporting advances over the past 20 years in the United States, Europe and elsewhere. It's both a method to discover stories that otherwise would go unreported and a way of adding depth and context to existing stories. Historically, the United Kingdom has offered little training in these techniques for experienced journalists and novices alike (CIJ 2007).

What may have been the first such course in the UK – geared explicitly towards increasing the teaching of CAR and of working with data, and their future development – brought together a number of people who were making their mark in data journalism and its training or education, or were to do so subsequently, including:

- James Anslow – then a lecturer on BA Journalism at City; later developed modules with a more digital focus.

- Heather Brooke – FoI expert; went on to teach CAR and data at City, University of London.

- Elena Egawhary – then completing the Newspaper Journalism course at City; later became BBC researcher on *Panorama* and *Newsnight*, and data trainer.

- Stephen Grey – freelance investigative reporter; former editor of *The Sunday Times* Insight team; had investigated the CIA's secret 'extraordinary rendition' programme, analysing the details of more than 12,000 flights. Later he became special investigative correspondent at Reuters.

- Jonathan Hewett – then (and now) leading the MA Newspaper Journalism programme at City; later set up the Interactive Journalism MA with dedicated modules on data journalism.

- Mike Holderness – freelance journalist; ran training courses in online publishing and databases with the NUJ.

- Francis Irving – then a programmer with innovative NGO MySociety; main developer of its FoI site *WhatDoTheyKnow*, and later chief executive of *Scraperwiki* (which helps organisations to collect and analyse data).

- Adrian Monck – then head of the Journalism Department at City, encouraged the development of the MA Investigative Journalism. Later, managing director, head of communications and media, at the World Economic Forum.

- Cynthia O'Murchu – *Financial Times* reporter; later, investigative reporter on stories such as the data-intensive exposé of the EU Structural Funds (jointly with the Bureau of Investigative Journalism), and deputy interactive editor.

- Martin Stabe – then new media editor at *Press Gazette*; later head of interactive news at the *Financial Times*.

Also that summer, two university courses for postgraduates were preparing to welcome their first investigative journalism students. Both included the use of CAR techniques and elements – such as data-mining or scraping – of what one might now call data journalism, and were led by experienced investigative journalists (Waterhouse 2011; O'Neill 2011a). At the University of Strathclyde, in Glasgow, Eamonn O'Neill set up an MSc Investigative Journalism after studying the development of courses at universities in the USA. Investigative classes had been 'available on American campuses since at least the 1950s and possibly earlier' (O'Neill 2011b).

The Investigative Journalism MA at City, University of London, was run by Rosie Waterhouse, formerly with BBC *Newsnight* and *The Sunday Times*. She was able to build also on the teaching experience at City, including the CIJ and its director, Gavin MacFadyen; the investigations editor of the *Guardian*, David Leigh; David Lloyd, former head of news and current affairs at Channel Four, and Heather Brooke. While these two courses represented an important step in journalism education in UK universities, and were followed by a BA in Investigative

Journalism at the University of Lincoln, it would be misleading to suggest that investigative journalism had previously been absent from the curriculum.

At Sheffield University, for example, Mark Hanna had developed an investigative module for journalism undergraduates, the first to include a requirement to use FoI (Hanna 2008). At City, some courses included investigative research techniques and FoI, and Leigh and MacFadyen had already run a specialist investigative option. But such developments were relatively recent; O'Neill suggests that the UK 'did not offer investigative journalism classes until the mid-late 1990s' (2011b). An earlier Investigative Journalism MA, at Nottingham Trent University, had been launched in 1997 (Hanna 2000) but ran into difficulties Adams 2001).

More online, more open data

Journalism education was also reflecting the industry's shift to the web, which was another factor that enabled data journalism to take off. Some courses focused specifically on online, such as the Online Journalism MA started by Paul Bradshaw in 2009 at Birmingham City University. He had noted data's significance for journalists, and had been teaching students to use Yahoo Pipes to aggregate, filter, mash and map since 2006. By 2010 he was also teaching data journalism to established reporters and news organisations' trainees (Bradshaw 2013), and made an introduction to data part of the core MA journalism curriculum at City.

The timing probably helped the later courses to thrive. Online tools and web publishing were making new forms of storytelling possible. FoI was becoming better established and continuing to help journalists break stories. It was also at the heart of one of the biggest stories of the period in 2009, on MPs' expenses, even though the core material was ultimately leaked before it was due to be released (with redactions) under FoI legislation.

Although the MPs' expenses files were obtained electronically, it was not a database that the *Telegraph* obtained – it was a mass of PDF files. That meant the investigating journalists 'could mostly still operate like old-style reporters', says Brooke (2013), cross-referencing names, addresses and other details – even if spreadsheets were involved (Winnett and Rayner 2009: 220).

The open data movement was gathering pace, too, emphasising the importance of publishing data resulting from publicly-funded work, and in accessible formats. Technology journalists Charles Arthur and Michael Cross had kicked off a 'Free Our Data' campaign aimed at changing government policy (Arthur and Cross 2006). The *data.gov.uk* site eventually followed in January 2010, expanding to offer more than 9,000 datasets by October 2013. Spurred on also by the commercial possibilities, David Cameron made a series of commitments on open data after he became prime minister in May 2010 – complementing the momentum that FoI had provided for data journalism.

Dealing with data from FoI requests had been an essential part of James Ball's route towards data journalism in 2007-2008, when he worked with Brooke as a student on the pilot Investigative Journalism course at City:

> Lots of the early stuff I was doing was standardising FoI responses, getting them into a spreadsheet, and doing ... everything the hard way actually, because I hadn't been taught lots of things that I would now do to make the process easier. ... But this was before anyone was interested in data journalism (Ball 2013).

WikiLeaks – and a journalism MA goes interactive

In 2010, the year after MPs' expenses, and more significantly for data journalism, came the huge WikiLeaks releases of war logs from Iraq and Afghanistan, and of cables from US embassies around the world. 'It was a big deal for us – and it also made newsrooms see data people differently,' says Simon Rogers who had launched the *Guardian*'s Datablog the previous year (Rogers 2013b).

Working on the war logs and cables also proved formative for Rogers' successor as data editor, Ball, first at the Bureau of Investigative Journalism and then at WikiLeaks (Ball 2013). Ball was soon teaching his successors at City, first on the MA Investigative Journalism. Data experience from the course helped Conrad Quilty-Harper gain a job at the *Telegraph* in 2010, when he became interactive news editor. The next step in data journalism at City was the MA Interactive Journalism, which I set up in 2011. This included a separate module dedicated to data journalism, led by Ball and Bradshaw, with input from Rogers – at the same time as his team grappled with data from the riots that took place in London and other cities that August.

Out of the first 36 graduates, 11 went on to work as data journalists and a further eight in data-related roles (Hewett 2014b). These alumni went on to work at the BBC, *The Times* and *Sunday Times*, the *Guardian*, *Telegraph*, *Financial Times*, *Manchester Evening News*, *CityAM*, *Property Week*, investigative site *Exaro* and Trinity Mirror's data journalism team. From the start, the course also included a specialist module on strategic social media and online engagement – where data is also relevant, e.g. in analytics – and many alumni went on to work in this area as well as in more traditional reporting or editing roles.

Professional network for collaboration

More journalism courses were including data journalism in their curricula, too, notably at Birmingham City University, University of Central Lancashire, Cardiff and Goldsmiths, partly in response to the rise in prominence of data in the journalism industry (and more widely). Beyond universities, too, pioneering practitioners were getting together – often internationally -- to share emerging good practice, ideas for projects and to develop their own initiatives in Europe

(Lorenz 2010). Moreover, an international project produced the *Data Journalism Handbook* (Gray et al. 2012), supported by the European Journalism Centre and Open Knowledge Foundation. In addition, several massive open online courses (MOOCs) focused on data journalism (Howard 2013), and other organisations developed their own training courses.

Data teams at newspapers, the BBC and elsewhere were assembling or expanding their data teams, while other publishers looked to integrate elements of data journalism within their existing structures. In 2013, Trinity Mirror set up a central data journalism unit to work with its regional newspapers and the *Daily Mirror* – and it also piloted a fresh approach to data journalism with its standalone *ampp3d* project. With its rapid response to news events, tabloid-style approach, high-impact graphics and interactivity, produced for mobile access and social sharing, the site reached places (and audiences) that few data projects had tried to go. Although it closed after 18 months, *ampp3d*'s impact was felt widely (Bradshaw 2015) and Trinity Mirror's data journalism unit continued, later expanding to ten-strong (Southern 2016).

At a number of news organisations, developers and journalists were starting to get used to working together on specific projects or ongoing teams – but wider, more open networks for collaboration were playing an increasingly important role, too. In March 2010, some coders and journalists, including James Ball and Joanna Geary (then web development editor, business, at *The Times*), held the first of a series of 'Ruby in the Pub' meetings to explore areas of mutual interest – and to help the journalists to learn Ruby (Goodchild 2010). This soon evolved into Hacks/ Hackers London, coordinated by Geary and launching in August 2010 as part of the international Hacks/Hackers network that was founded in San Francisco less than a year earlier to become the most prominent example of computing-journalism collaboration (Lewis and Usher 2014).

Taking a slightly wider focus than journalism and coding – to embrace media-related start-ups and entrepreneurial/tech initiatives – the monthly meetings of Hacks/Hackers London quickly outgrew the basement bar in which it had begun. Despite – or because of – moving to larger venues (often at tech/media companies' offices), with corporate sponsorship and online bookings, its meetings are consistently oversubscribed. Indeed, it has become one of the prime networking events for those working at the intersection of media and technology in London, attended by several hundred people, and sister groups elsewhere in the UK.

This left room for another group, Journocoders, to take a more explicit focus on learning technical skills for use in journalism. With a lower profile and smaller informal meetings, it began in London in December 2014 (Bentley 2014). The monthly sessions typically take a hands-on approach, with participants bringing laptops to work on, focused on sharing and learning journalistic uses of coding.

Within university journalism education the picture remained mixed, despite growing interest. As late as 2014, one journalism educator concluded that 'the route into data journalism is not an obvious one and a period of studying journalism at a UK university certainly doesn't seem to be part of that route' (Hannaford 2014). Most journalism schools 'don't get it', said the head of interactive news at the *Financial Times* (Tinworth, 2014). This may reflect the particular complexities of running data journalism courses, which include ensuring its currency; the 'million-dollar question' (McKerral 2013) of who will teach it; technical and statistical demands; and – in a market-oriented HE system – the need to attract students who may not be familiar with data journalism (Hewett 2016). Studies of data journalism education around the world have identified similar issues (e.g. Berret and Phillips 2016; Yang and Du 2016; Davies and Cullen 2016; Treadwell, Ross, Lee et al 2016).

Some British educators were starting to respond more fully, however, incorporating data journalism into textbooks for university courses, for example (e.g. Hill and Lashmar 2014; Holmes et al. 2013; Bradshaw and Rohumaa 2011)..

Data, coding and computational thinking

One key feature of their recent evolution has been the introduction of coding as a core element of journalism programmes. An additional data and coding module was introduced at City, University of London, in 2015 as part of the MA Interactive Journalism, for example; Cardiff launched an MSc in Computational Journalism in 2014; coding forms part of Goldsmiths' Digital Journalism MA/MSc and of the Data Journalism MA that starts at Birmingham City University in 2017/18.

How far journalism students – and established journalists – need to learn to code has been a point of discussion for some years, particularly since the emergence of newsroom developers or 'programmer-journalists' alongside data journalists (Royal 2010; Parasie and Dagiral 2012; Taylor 2009). Learning coding, in this context, means going far beyond mark-up and styling with HTML and CSS. Data journalism programmes in the UK have concentrated on developing relevant skills and understanding of Javascript, R and Python, and in some cases D3 and/or SQL.

Typically – and importantly – programmes tend to involve more than technical skills alone. The aim is also to enable students to develop computational thinking, for example (Wing 2006). This approach seeks to tackle problems by drawing on key concepts from computer science, such as automation and modularity. 'Most fundamentally it addresses the question: what is computable?' (ibid: 33). In many ways, computational thinking is about unpacking and understanding the processes of computing and applying critical thinking and reflective practice to these to design solutions – here, in the context of journalism (Meza 2016).

Data journalism has spread, evolved and diversified over the past decade. This 'quantitative turn' in journalism (Petre 2013) has prompted more research, including a typology that seeks to differentiate CAR, data journalism, and computational journalism – while recognising that this interests scholars more than practitioners (Coddington 2014). Regardless of such delineations, the increasing ubiquity and availability of data in many fields makes it hard to ignore – particularly for anyone concerned with the future of journalism. Data underlies many current media trends, from verification and automation to networked investigations and personalisation (Newman 2017), while data-driven processes appear essential for successful innovation in digital news (Küng 2015).

This rise of data makes a compelling case for journalism students to learn to handle data competently, at least at a basic level, and to understand its increasing strategic and range of uses. At a more advanced level, the position of data journalist remains largely a specialist role in the industry – and of limited appeal to many journalism students, it appears (Yang and Du 2016; Hewett 2016). But other positions in journalism now also rely on data as essential inputs to editorial decision-making – in social media and audience development roles, for example (Thurman 2016). The central place in journalism of data analysis (and coding) is suggested in their appearance among criteria for UK news organisations' journalism trainee schemes in recent years (Hannaford 2015).

The importance of including data work in university journalism programmes appears to be confirmed, in broad terms, by an international survey of data journalists (Heravi 2017). Initial findings indicate that many more (62 per cent) had a degree in journalism than one in a data-related or technical discipline (12 per cent). The majority were also relatively new to journalism, having 1-4 years' experience (41 per cent) or 5-9 years (26 per cent).

Where now – and where next?

While data journalism remains a specialist pursuit for most people in the media, its profile and authority are arguably higher than ever. It is becoming well established in most areas of journalism and can look to both thriving professional networks that involve developers as well as journalists, and a range of university journalism programmes offering data and coding courses to students in HE. In many ways, the demand for training and professional networking reflects the 'mainstreaming' of digital journalism and specific areas such as data (Tinworth 2016).

Back in 1999, Philip Meyer lamented that CAR was 'an embarrassing reminder' that journalism was 'the only profession in which computer users feel the need to call attention to themselves' (1999: 4). Nearly 20 years later, can we look forward to the day when journalists will no longer feel the need to call attention to themselves as users of data?

References

Adams, Catherine (2001) Inside story, *Guardian*, 13 March. Available online at http://www.theguardian.com/education/2001/mar/13/highereducation.uk, accessed on 30 October 2013

Arthur, Charles (2010) Analysing data is the future for journalists, says Tim Berners-Lee. *Guardian*, 22 November. Available online at http://www.guardian.co.uk/media/2010/nov/22/data-analysis-tim-berners-lee, accessed on 3 September 2015

Arthur, Charles and Cross, Michael (2006) Give us back our crown jewels, *Guardian*, 9 March. Available online at http://www.theguardian.com/technology/2006/mar/09/education.epublic, accessed on 30 October 2013

Ball, James (2013) Interview with Jonathan Hewett, 25 October 2013, London

Bentley, Elliot (2014) Journocoders inaugural [sic] meetup, *Meetup.com*. Available at https://www.meetup.com/Journocoders/events/219005707/

Berret, Charles and Phillips, Cheryl (2016) *Teaching Data and Computational Journalism*. Columbia Journalism School. Available online at https://journalism.columbia.edu/system/files/content/teaching_data_and_computational_journalism.pdf

Bradshaw, Paul and Rohumaa, Liisa (2011) *The Online Journalism Handbook: Skills to Survive and Thrive in the Digital Age*, Harlow: Longman

Bradshaw, Paul (2013) Interview with Jonathan Hewett, 14 October 2013, London

Bradshaw, Paul (2015) The legacy of Ampp3d, UsVsTh3m and Row Zed, 13 May. Available online at: http://onlinejournalismblog.com/2015/05/13/the-legacy-of-ampp3d-usvsth3m-and-row-zed/, accessed on 15 September 2015

Brooke, Heather (2004) *Your Right to Know*, London: Pluto Press

Brooke, Heather (2006) Investigate! *Journalist*, August/September, National Union of Journalists. Available online at http://heatherbrooke.org/2006/article-future-of-investigative-reporting/, accessed on 27 October 2013

Brooke, Heather (2013) Interview with Jonathan Hewett, 18 October 2013, London

Centre for Investigative Journalism (2003) Programme for CIJ Summer School, 18-20 July 2003, London

Centre for Investigative Journalism (2007) Programme for Training the Trainers: How to Teach Computer-Assisted Reporting, 23-25 July, London

Chinoy, Ira (2010) *Battle of the Brains: Election-Night Forecasting at the Dawn of the Computer Age*, Dissertation: University of Maryland. Available online at http://drum.lib.umd.edu/bitstream/handle/1903/10504/Chinoy_umd_0117E_11395.pdf;jsessionid=F52BCFE72351DABAE91D0418D470E70C?sequence=1

Coddington, Mark (2014) Clarifying journalism's quantitative turn: A typology for evaluating data journalism, computational journalism, and computer-assisted reporting, *Digital Journalism*, Vol. 3, No. 3 pp 331–348

Dasselaar, Arjan (2005) United Kingdom, Van Eijk, Dick (ed.) *Investigative Journalism in Europe*, Amsterdam: Vereniging van Onderzoeksjournalisten pp 213-226

Davies, Kayt and Cullen, Trevor (2016) Data journalism classes in Australian universities: Educators describe progress to date, *Asia Pacific Media Educator*, Vol. 26, No. 2 pp 132-147

Dennis, Everette E. (1983) An exchange. Journalism education, *Planning for Curricular Change in Journalism Education*, Eugene: School of Journalism, University of Oregon

Folkerts, Jean (2014) *History of Journalism Education: Journalism & Communication Monographs*, Thousand Oaks, CA: SAGE Publications

Goodchild, Dave (2010) Developers and journalists forging common ground, *Journalism.co.uk*, 17 May. Available online at https://blogs.journalism.co.uk/2010/05/17/developers-and-journalists-forging-common-ground

Gray, Jonathan, Bounegru Liliana and Chambers, Lucy (eds) (2012) *The Data Journalism Handbook*. Sebastopol, CA: O'Reilly Media. Available online at http://datajournalismhandbook.org/1.0/en/

Hanna, Mark (2000) *British investigative journalism: Protecting the continuity of talent through changing times*. Paper presented to the International Association for Media and Communication Research, Singapore, 18 July

Hanna, Mark (2008) Universities as evangelists of the watchdog role: Teaching investigative journalism to undergraduates, De Burgh, Hugo (ed.) *Investigative Journalism*, Abingdon and New York: Routledge, third edition pp 157-173

Hannaford, Liz (2014) *Data Journalism: A Modern Day Bletchley Park*? Available online at http://www.lizhannaford.com/data-journalism/data-journalism-a-modern-day-bletchley-park/, accessed on 8 October 2014

Hannaford, Liz (2015) Computational journalism in the UK newsroom, *Journalism Education* Vol. 4, No. 1 pp 6-21

Heravi, Bahareh R. (2017) The state of data journalism globally, *Proceedings of the European Data and Computational Journalism Conference,* Dublin, 6-7 July

Hewett, Jonathan (2014a) *Engaging with Data: Reflections on Developing a Data Journalism Course.* Paper presented to Computation + Journalism symposium, 24-25 October, New York

Hewett, Jonathan (2014b) Growing data journalism in the UK, *American Journalism Review*, 13 November. Available online at http://ajr.org/2014/11/13/growing-data-journalism-uk/, accessed on 15 September 2015

Hewett, Jonathan (2016) Learning to teach data journalism: Innovation, influence and constraints, *Journalism*, Vol. 17, No. 1 pp 119-137

Hill, Steve and Lashmar, Paul (2014) *Online Journalism: The Essential Guide,* Los Angeles, CA: SAGE

Holmes, Timothy, Mottershead, Glyn and Hadwin, Sara (2013) *The 21st Century Journalism Handbook: Essential Skills for the Modern Journalist*, Harlow: Pearson

Houston, Brant (1999) Changes in attitudes, changes in latitudes, Paul, Nora (ed.) *When Nerds and Words Collide: Reflections on the Development of Computer Assisted Reporting*, St Petersburg, Florida: Poynter Institute for Media Studies pp 6-7

Houston, Brant (2003) *Computer-Assisted Reporting: A Practical Guide*, Boston: Bedford/St Martin's, third edition

Howard, Alexander (2013) Data journalism MOOCs offer new options for distributed learning, *towcenter.org/blog*. Available online at http://towcenter.org/blog/data-journalism-moocs-offer-new-options-for-distributed-learning/

Küng, Lucy (2015) *Innovators in Digital News*, London/New York: I. B. Tauris

LaFleur, Jennifer (1999) Evangelizing for CAR, Paul, Nora (ed.) *When Nerds and Words Collide: Reflections on the Development of Computer Assisted Reporting*, St Petersburg, Florida: Poynter Institute for Media Studies pp 25-27

Lewis, Seth C. and Usher, Nikki (2014) Code, collaboration and the future of journalism, *Digital Journalism*, Vol. 2, No. 3 pp 383-393

Lorenz, Mirko (2010) *Data Driven Journalism: What is There to Learn?* Paper on the Data-Driven Journalism Roundtable, Amsterdam, 24 August

McKerral, Mac (2013) Steering data journalism into the curriculum. *Quill*, Vol. 101, No. 4 p. 24

Meek, Colin (2005) Analysis: Computer-assisted reporting leaves UK journalists in the slow lane, *Journalism.co.uk*, 5 October. Available online at http://www.journalism.co.uk/news/analysis-computer-assisted-reporting-leaves-uk-journalists-in-the-slow-lane/s2/a51543/, accessed on 25 October 2013

Meyer, Philip (1973) *Precision Journalism: A Reporter's Introduction to Social Science Methods*, Bloomington and London: Indiana University Press

Meyer, Philip (1991) *The New Precision Journalism*, Bloomington and Indianapolis: Indiana University Press

Meyer, Philip (1999) The future of CAR: Declare victory and get out, Paul, Nora (ed.) *When Nerds and Words Collide: Reflections on the Development of Computer Assisted Reporting*, St Petersburg, Florida: Poynter Institute for Media Studies pp 4-5

Meza, Radu (2016) Computational thinking and journalism education, Singla, Carles da Rocha, Irene and Ramon, Xavier (eds) *Shaping The Future Of News Media*, Integrated Journalism in Europe pp 179-206

Newman, Nic (2017) *Journalism, Media, and Technology Trends and Predictions 2017*, Oxford: Reuters Institute for the Study of Journalism

O'Neill, Eamonn (2011a) Digging deeper: Reflecting on the development and teaching of investigative journalism in a university setting in the United Kingdom, Mair, John and Keeble, Richard Lance (eds) *Investigative Journalism: Dead or Alive?* Bury St Edmunds: Abramis pp 291-307

O'Neill, Eamonn (2011b) Written evidence, *The Future of Investigative Journalism*, London: House of Lords Select Committee on Communications pp 425-429

O'Neill, Sean and Brooke, Heather (2005) Prosecutors in dock over disparity in convictions, *The Times*, 23 November p. 6

O'Neill, Sean, Gibb, Frances and Brooke, Heather (2005) Justice by postcode: The lottery revealed, *Times*, 23 November p. 1

Orlowski, Andrew (2007) Braindead obituarists hoaxed by Wikipedia: Only fools and journos, *Register*, 3 October. Available online at http://www.theregister.co.uk/2007/10/03/wikipedia_obituary_cut_and_paste/, accessed on 30 October 2013

Parasie, Sylvain and Dagiral, Eric (2013) Data-driven journalism and the public good: 'Computer-assisted reporters' and 'programmer-journalists' in Chicago, *New Media & Society*, Vol. 15, No. 6 pp 853-871

Paul, Nora (ed.) (1999) *When Nerds and Words Collide: Reflections on the Development of Computer Assisted Reporting*, St Petersburg, Florida: Poynter Institute for Media Studies

Petre, Caitlin (2013) *A quantitative turn in journalism?* Tow Center for Digital Journalism, October 30. Available online at http://towcenter.org/blog/a-quantitative-turn-in-journalism/

Rogers, Simon (2013a) *Facts are Sacred: The Power of Data*, London: Faber and Faber/Guardian Books

Rogers, Simon (2013b) Interview with Jonathan Hewett, 22 October 2013, San Francisco/London (via Skype)

Royal, Cindy (2010) The journalist as programmer: A case study of *The New York Times* interactive news technology department, *International Symposium on Online Journalism*. Available online at https://www.semanticscholar.org/paper/The-Journalist-as-Programmer-A-Case-Study-of-The-N-Royal/b77a51be50f449ef821e84c07848854a0cdc211f

Silver, Nate (2014) What the fox knows, *FiveThirtyEight*, 17 March. Available online at http://fivethirtyeight.com/features/what-the-fox-knows/, accessed on 15 September 2015.

Southern, Lucinda (2016) Inside Trinity Mirror's data-visualization unit, 8 December. Available online at: https://digiday.com/uk/trinity-mirror-data-visualization/

Stabe, Martin (2013) Email exchange with Jonathan Hewett, 30 October 2013, London

Taylor, Megan (2009) How computer-assisted reporters evolved into programmer/journalists, *MediaShift*, 7 August. Available online at http://mediashift.org/2009/08/how-computer-assisted-reporters-evolved-into-programmerjournalists219

Tinworth, Adam (2014) *Data Journalism:Buzzword or Baseline Skill?* Available online at http://www.onemanandhisblog.com/archives/2014/01/data_journalism_-_buzzword_or_baseline_s.html

Tinworth, Adam (2016) Hacks/hackers London: It's only going to get harder to get a ticket – and that's just how it should be. Available online at https://www.onemanandhisblog.com/archives/2016/03/hhldn-tickets-attendance-growth-mainstream-digital-journalism.html

Thurman, Neil, Cornia, Alessio and Kunert, Jessica (2016) *Journalists in the UK*, Oxford: Reuters Institute for the Study of Journalism

Treadwell, Greg, Ross, Tara, Lee, Allan, Lowenstein, Kelly, Jeff (2016) A numbers game: Two case studies in teaching data journalism, *Journalism & Mass Communication Educator*, Vol. 71, No. 3 pp 297-308

Waterhouse, Rosie (2011) Can you teach investigative journalism? Methods and sources, old and new, Mair, John and Keeble, Richard Lance (eds) *Investigative Journalism: Dead or Alive?*, Bury St Edmunds: Abramis pp 284-290

Wing, Jeanette M. (2006) Computational thinking, *Communications of the ACM*, Vol. 49, No. 3 pp 33-35

Winnett, Robert and Rayner, Gordon (2011) *No Expenses Spared*, London: Random House

Yang, Fan, and Du, Ying Roselyn (2016) Storytelling in the age of Big Data: Hong Kong students' readiness and attitude towards data journalism, *Asia Pacific Media Educator*, Vol. 26, No. 2 pp 148-162

Note on the contributor

Jonathan Hewett is Director of Interactive and Newspaper Journalism at City, University of London. His research interests include social media, data journalism and the teaching and learning of journalism. Jonathan has led and taught on journalism programmes since 1997. He welcomes suggestions, corrections and other constructive feedback, plus offers of help, funding, coffee and chocolate to J.C.Hewett@city.ac.uk or @jonhew.

Panama Papers – the largest collaborative investigation in journalism history – and more

Mar Cabra tells the extraordinary story of how the award-winning International Consortium of Investigative Journalists went from having no data team to being a tech-driven media organisation

In April 2015, I had a conference call with my boss, the director of the International Consortium of Investigative Journalists, Gerard Ryle. He didn't want to tell me the purpose of the call in writing. When we started talking, he spoke to me in code language to avoid naming names. The bottom line was that *Süddeutsche Zeitung*, a German newspaper with which we had worked in the past, had a leak of about one terabyte, too big for them to handle. They wanted ICIJ's help, and Gerard was seeking my advice as the editor of the data team on how to proceed.

'How on earth are we going to do this?' I thought, but I didn't tell that to him. Even though I felt a bit overwhelmed by the situation, I knew I had a great team I could count on to tackle this challenge. What I didn't imagine at that time was how big of a role we, and our technology, would play in what became at the time the largest collaborative investigation in journalism history.

The so-called Panama Papers exposed like never before a system that enables crime, corruption and wrongdoing, hidden by secretive offshore companies. It had historic global effects. At least 150 inquiries, audits or investigations were announced in 79 countries around the world due to its revelations. There were resignations from high-ranking officials, including the prime minister of Iceland. The prime minister of Pakistan was removed from office. ICIJ won almost twenty awards, including the Pulitzer Prize and the Data Journalism Award.

We were lucky that such a request for help by *Süddeutsche Zeitung* came to us at that point in time. ICIJ was founded in 1997 as a global network of investigative journalists who collaborated on in-depth investigative stories but it was not until 2014 that it incorporated a data team for its newsroom. That doesn't mean data had not been important to investigations before. Data was key in a two-year series on overfishing called *Looting the Seas* (2010-2012) and also to *Skin & Bone* (2012), an exposé on the human tissue trade. However, the project where its relevance became more evident was *Offshore Leaks* (2013).

Power data Journalism

Exposing the secrecy of the offshore economy

When Gerard became ICIJ director in the fall of 2011, he brought a hard drive with 260 gigabytes full of documents that exposed the secrecy of the offshore economy. The investigation was not easy on many levels. One of the most difficult parts was making the data available to partners around the world. Seeing that assisting all of them would be too labour intensive, we resorted to technology to help us. We ended up putting the documents in the cloud and making them searchable securely on the web; we had an online forum to share leads and discuss the research, and we created a public website for our readers to explore the names of the people with companies in tax havens. Freelances – including myself – and the data team at *La Nación* newspaper in Costa Rica, with which ICIJ collaborated, did most of the data work.

One of the lessons learned from *Offshore Leaks* – and its sequel, *China Leaks* – was that ICIJ needed data journalists and programmers in-house. When we started the next project, ICIJ hired two of the developers we had worked with before, Rigoberto Carvajal and Matthew Caruana Galizia, and ICIJ put me in charge of the team. In April 2014 – one year before that call from my boss – the ICIJ data team was created.

Our first year was hectic. ICIJ published three investigations over that period and a fourth was being reported – many more than the average the organisation had been doing in recent years. Our team's mission was nothing short of ambitious: 'to add a data component to every project ICIJ does right from the start and not as an afterthought.'

The projects that took most of our time were those connected to leaks. Our first task was dealing with more than 1,000 image PDFs of secretive tax agreements between corporations and the Luxembourg government. We needed to make them searchable and available to reporters worldwide. It was a similar problem to the one we faced in *Offshore Leaks*, but this time we wanted to use open-source tools that would allow us to keep improving the system as the need grew. Matthew had the brilliant idea of using a software called Project Blacklight, originally created for library catalogues, to allow reporters to search documents remotely. To improve the virtual newsroom where journalists interacted on a regular basis, Rigoberto proposed to repurpose Oxwall, an open-source social networking software meant for dating – among other things.

As we were working on this, the French newspaper, *Le Monde*, shared with ICIJ 60,000 leaked files from the bank HSBC. They were mostly spreadsheets with names of people connected to accounts in its Switzerland subsidiary and the amounts of money in those accounts – in many cases, hidden from the tax authorities. We also used Blacklight and Oxwall in this project and executed an agreement with a French company to use its software, Linkurious, to visualise connections and follow the money more easily. In these two projects, we created the base of the stack that would later allow us to move quickly on the Panama Papers.

As our tools and platforms solidified, the number of journalists working on ICIJ projects and their engagement grew. *LuxLeaks* (2014) involved more than 80 reporters in 26 countries. *Swiss Leaks* (2015) more than 140 reporters in 45 countries.

On top of helping reporters secure access to the documents, we performed data analysis – the key to strengthening the articles – and created interactive applications that were among the most viewed items in ICIJ's website.

Becoming essential to ICIJ's investigations

Leaks were not the only type of data we worked on. In *Evicted & Abandoned*, a project about how the World Bank regularly failed to protect people displaced by development, we estimated 3.4 million people had been affected in a decade and created a unique database of projects using public data. In *Fatal Extraction*, we combed corporate data and combined it with information from our reporters in the field to reveal deaths, injuries and community conflicts linked to Australian mining companies across Africa.

Within a year, we had grown to a team of five and were around half of the people in ICIJ's small newsroom. We added Emilia Díaz-Struck as research editor and hired then-intern Cécile Schilis-Gallego as a data journalist. This is the team I was counting on to help me solve the Panama Papers data challenge after the director called me.

Firstly, we travelled to Munich to get the data. Rigoberto flew in from San José, Costa Rica, and I from Madrid, Spain. We stayed in an Airbnb apartment which we converted in our base camp to copy encrypted hard drives. During the first meeting with our German colleagues, we discovered the complexity of the data, and one of my first comments to my bosses was: we need to hire an extra developer for the team. A few weeks later, Miguel Fiandor joined us from Spain.

The data included mostly emails, but it had millions of PDFs and images that needed to be made machine-readable. We used more than 30 servers in the cloud to process them in parallel to make the first batch of data ready for reporters in less than two months. That was the most difficult part, because after the data was searchable, we used the same tools we had created for the previous projects. In late June, ICIJ had its first meeting with a small group of reporters in Washington, D.C. to kick-off the project, although most journalists joined in September after a meeting in Munich.

As the months progressed, the leak grew to be 2.6 terabytes and contain 11.5 million files, which meant we had to continue processing data throughout the whole project. The number of reporters involved also skyrocketed – we had almost 400 when the investigation went live in April 2016. They produced more than 4,700 articles.

With more reporters, more needs appeared: we had to create a 'support team' to help them with problems over our platforms; we created manuals and conducted training in three languages for people on four continents, and we kept improving our tools until publication. For example, we incorporated a popular feature to search for lists of individuals and know, in one go, if there were any hits. We also updated the public database of offshore companies (https://offshoreleaks.icij.org/), making it the most-used product in the history of the ICIJ. Today, it is used by reporters, investigators and authorities around the world to chase tax evaders.

Conclusion

It's impossible to know how the Panama Papers would have been without the work of ICIJ's data team but, for sure, we could not have had so many reporters working on it. We would have missed many stories and would have had less impact. Technology and data worked together to make the Panama Papers become part of history.

As we move into the future, three things are clear to me. One is that massive leaks are the new standard, and we'll see more – and bigger – leaks. Second, global collaboration is the only way to deal with the complex world in which we live. And finally, data journalism is here to stay. If you don't believe it, let me share just one more fact: almost three years and half into its creation, ICIJ's data team now has 11 people.

Note on the contributor

Mar Cabra is head of the Data and Research Unit at the International Consortium of Investigative Journalists. She has been an ICIJ staff member since 2011 and is also a member of the network, participating in projects that have won more than two dozen awards, including the Pulitzer Prize and the Data Journalism Award twice. She also received the Spanish Larra Award in 2012 for the country's most promising journalist under 30. Mar fell in love with data while being a Fulbright Scholar and Fellow at the Stabile Center for Investigative Journalism at Columbia University in 2009/2010. Since then, she has promoted data journalism in her native Spain, co-creating the first-ever Master's degree on investigative reporting, data journalism and visualisation and the national data journalism conference. She previously worked in television – and her work has been featured in the *International Herald Tribune*, the *Huffington Post*, PBS, *El País*, *El Mundo* and *El Confidencial*, among others.

Spreading falsehoods with real data

Joseph O'Leary explores how current insights and new technology can make fact-checking data faster and better than ever before

It's late evening on 21 April 2015, barely a fortnight away from the general election. The BBC's *Newsnight* has just led with the claim that, last year, more than a million people used food banks run by the Trussell Trust charity. Actually, the charity had not recorded a million people using its banks, it was more like a million uses by about half as many people (*Full Fact* 2015). Towards the end of the same show, the presenter issued a correction.

Fact-checking did that. At its heart, this was about spotting and understanding the distinction between users and uses of food banks. But simply knowing that doesn't help hundreds of thousands of *Newsnight* viewers who have just been told something that isn't true. Fact-checking is valuable not just for what it unearths about the big claims but for what happens as a consequence. One call to a BBC producer and less than an hour later, the claim was corrected.

There's an obvious lesson from this: fact-checking has to be fast to be effective. This should not be news to any of us: after all, over two centuries ago, Thomas Francklin famously wrote: 'Falsehood will fly, as it were, on the wings of the wind, and carry its tales to every corner of the earth, whilst truth lags behind: her steps, though sure, are slow and solemn, and she has neither vigour nor activity enough to pursue and overtake her enemy' (Francklin 1787).

This is a race we're still running. Any tweet or Facebook post is just a few clicks away from notoriety, and rebuttals are needed quickly, especially ahead of a big public decision.

Tough on the causes of fact-checking

As fact-checkers and journalists, we also need to care as much about how falsehoods come into being as about rebutting them quickly.

At the end of the election, we fact-checked a poster listing economy and public spending metrics, comparing what they were in 2010 with what they are now (*Full Fact* 2017a). They were, as we put it 'big, meaningless numbers', often wrong or inconsistent and always presented with little context. The curious thing about this poster wasn't so much the context, which is easy to miss when you are quoting snapshot figures. It was the fact that so many of the numbers were just wrong, or not comparing like-with-like. Even so, it's difficult not to have some sympathy with the author of such a poster when you try to find the numbers for yourself.

When you visit the Treasury's public spending statistics, you are greeted with thousands upon thousands of numbers. It's not like a dictionary, where you can just look up in index form what you want to find out. If I want to know about education spending, I've got a selection box to choose from – provided I know what chapter even gets me this far. Do I want the Department for Education's resource spending, capital spending, total 'departmental expenditure limit', total 'annually managed expenditure', 'total managed expenditure', or education spending as a function of public spending?

It's often neither useful nor fair to place all the blame on the people who actually share misinformation, and I would challenge anyone who disagrees to explore the wonders of public spending statistics for themselves. But producers and publishers of information don't just need to make their data easier for human fact-checkers to read. This centuries-old race has already gone way past the point where traditional, manual journalism is enough. We need automated fact-checking to be able to spot those 'zombie statistics' that never die but continue to bamboozle us – like the million food bank users. And we need to be able to spot tomorrow's zombies too, so that journalists have the facts to hand while the news cycle is still fresh. In their early forms, these kinds of tools are close to becoming reality (*Full Fact* 2016a).

Even while exciting tools like these are being developed, they won't help us in the race unless we understand *how* they help us. It's not enough just to have accurate, easily-accessible data at your fingertips in seconds, because a great deal of misinformation is based on accurate data. So to train properly for the next phase of the race, we need to understand a lot more of the lessons that fact-checking teaches us.

Torturing numbers

Fact-checking isn't just about numbers. If it were, we would be happy saying that crime is rising, that zero hours contracts are soaring, or that 92 per cent of Brits want to quit the EU. There are numbers out there that will tell you all these things. But these claims either overstate the available evidence (*Full Fact* 2017b), ignore it (*Full Fact* 2017c) or make no sense whatsoever (*Full Fact* 2016b).

Experienced fact-checkers are not just quicker than new ones because they know where to find the information. They have learned to recognise the patterns: the ways in which numbers can be 'tortured so they'll confess to anything'. The challenge is to mould that experience into something teachable to both humans and computers.

It starts by recognising that data can be a victim as well as an offender. Almost every problematic claim I have encountered is the result of at least one of these major factors:

1. There's no obvious or accessible source.

2. The source is flawed in some way.

3. The source has been miscommunicated.

4. Important context is missing.

Sometimes, all four come up at once. Take the case of *The Times* which once printed the headline: '400 patients thrown out of hospital beds every night' (*The Times* 2014). The first port of call for a fact-checker is the source. The trouble is, there are actually hundreds of sources, and not all of them are published. The story was based on Freedom of Information requests, sent by *Sky News*, to hospital trusts across England, asking them how many patients were discharged in the early hours (*Full Fact* 2014a). The only way you have a hope of evaluating whether '400' are being 'thrown out' is to have the research which compiled the responses, unless you care to trawl through some 150 PDFs and spreadsheets yourself. So we had to find samples of responses from hospital trusts that published them, and that's when things got interesting.

It turned out that hospitals' discharge data was, in many cases, horribly unreliable. Some trusts were recording huge spikes in patients being discharged at precisely 12 midnight. As you might expect, this wasn't because swathes of people across England were rushing out of hospitals before they turned into pumpkins. It was actually a feature of the systems that staff use to record the discharge times. One trust confirmed that, where there isn't a discharge time entered on its system, it defaults to midnight.

So as it happened, some of these 400 patients a night may not have left the hospital overnight at all. The data says so, but in reality we don't actually know, and can probably expect the figure to be somewhat smaller.

The story doesn't end there. The reporting didn't just do a bad job because they ignored or didn't know about the data quality issues. The data could have been pristine, shown an average of 400 discharges a night, and the report would still have been wrong.

That's because of problem number three: even if you point to the data and the data is accurate, you can still mistranslate it. Reading *The Times*'s headline almost conjures up images of patients being dragged kicking and screaming out of hospital in the early hours or, at the very least, leaving against their will. The 400 (minus the midnight pumpkins) certainly didn't represent that. If you actually look at discharges data, you realise that 'discharges' and 'thrown out' aren't really in the same league at all. To count as 'discharged', you could have discharged yourself voluntarily. You could have been discharged by relatives. And, remarkably, you could even have died.

So badly sourced, badly collected and badly reported data. And still there's the fourth point to consider: context. How big is 400 people? In one sense, the context isn't everything – it's still 400 people (minus the many non-thrown-out cases) too many. But if the same figure a year earlier was three times the size, or paled in comparison to daytime discharges, you'd probably look at the story a bit differently.

Fact-checkers have demonstrated time and again how to do a comprehensive job on claims like this – the big question now is how we can all make it quicker and easier for humans and computers to do, without sacrificing quality.

Upping our game

Here are four ways we can respond to each of the themes discussed. First, tackling the problem of unsubstantiated claims starts with leading by example. It's difficult not to applaud the sentiment of transparency when it comes to evidence, but it seems all too easy to forget that this also applies to the rest of us as well. How many times have you read factual statements in the news or on your social media feeds, with no links and no references? How many times have you written about facts and left it to your readers to take your word for it? We are all well within our rights to suspend final judgment when we aren't being told where something is from. In order to place our trust, we need both information and the means to judge that information (O'Neill 2002).

Second, checking data quality in detail is sometimes burdensome, but we don't always need to reinvent the wheel. We need help from experts and trusted institutions to have a hope of rapidly rebutting claims that use complex data.

Opinion polls, for example, throw up both simple and complex questions about the data. The sample size is simple – you know it needs to be a certain size to be worth looking at. The representativeness of the sample isn't – there's a lot that can be done to the data to make it an accurate reflection of what the population thinks.

But fact-checkers rarely need to answer tough questions from scratch. Member organisations of the British Polling Council are required to meet certain standards in all the research they produce, including having sufficiently representative samples of the populations they are purporting to measure (British Polling Council 2017). As long as that institution is effectively upholding such standards – and that part can't be stressed enough – it gives the rest of us a valuable fall-back. By extension, if a poll has been conducted by a non-member organisation, we need to ask more questions. Non-membership of the BPC certainly doesn't make the polls that are produced dodgy, it just requires us to place more caution before we draw conclusions from their findings.

Thirdly, we need to recognise that this kind of institutional quality mark can still only give us the broadest of steers and should not make us any less vigilant about how specific parts of the data are being used. In order to communicate data quickly, fairly and accurately, we need to know whether the conclusion we are trying to draw reflects what the data is actually saying.

Following the Scottish referendum in 2014, it was claimed widely on Twitter that 71 per cent of 16 to 17-year-olds voted in favour of independence. That was based on a perfectly rigorous poll conducted using all the right methods (*Full Fact* 2014b). It was still a bogus claim. The claimants presumably hadn't noticed that while more than 2,000 people were involved in the poll as a whole, only 14 were aged 16-17, 10 of whom said they had voted Yes to independence. To give that figure some context, polling expert Anthony Wells, of YouGov, has said that, as a rule of thumb, any poll with a sample size of under 100 should be treated with extreme caution and under 50 should be ignored (Wells 2012). A sample of 14, then, belongs in a comedy sketch.

Structured data brings two key benefits for fact-checking. It allows for standardising the way that data is presented and communicated. One of the challenges of fact-checking is how to present conclusions consistently and which are fair to the underlying data. Should I stress this is an 'estimate' or not? Do I need to mention the change in measurement practice a few years back when comparing over time? And it opens the door for machines to be able to use data intelligently. If a newspaper wants to scrape data on crime over time for a chart, how is it going to cope with the fact the police data has changed counting methods over time, that its quality is known to have drifted in the noughties and improved in recent years, and that the data switches on occasion from calendar to financial years? A list of numbers just isn't going to cut it, nor is writing those caveats out descriptively with asterisks alongside the data as, remarkably, you see in some official datasets.

Fourthly and finally is the challenge of providing appropriate context, and in many ways this is the most difficult. We can't nestle snugly in one dataset, assuming a spreadsheet entitled 'Poverty in the UK' actually tells us everything we need to know about poverty. Again, polling offers the most vivid case studies. A poll once found that 82 per cent of the UK public supported keeping the monarchy (*Full Fact* 2012). That was a robust poll, and that's exactly what it found, allowing for some margin of error. But five other polling companies also asked about the monarchy around the same time: they all posed different questions, and came up with different answers. All but one still found at least two-thirds popular support for the monarchy. The sixth had it at barely over half. The key difference was that while the other five polls gave people the option to agree, disagree or say they didn't know, the sixth added the extra option of 'makes no difference to me'. That one option unearthed a quarter of the public who apparently didn't care whether the monarchy kept going or not. So you don't get the full facts by looking at one poll in isolation.

I think there are ways of applying structured data here too, where different datasets are similar to one another. When you go shopping online, most websites suggest 'similar items' to the ones you have just bought. Similarly, if a computer finds data on relative poverty, it's also going to need the absolute poverty data too

– and the derived sets which convert the proportions into numbers, or vice-versa. Often – but not often enough – context is built into datasets too. Whenever you see denominators – per person, per household, as a proportion of a whole – you're getting numbers that actually mean something to people who will eventually be consuming that data.

We need help from institutions here too: from a user's perspective, it's a nonsense that statistics on A&E exist in different forms in different places, some held by NHS England, some held by NHS Digital. On topics like these, we rely on the work of organisations such as the House of Commons Library to bring it all together in one place, to give an overall narrative.

Conclusion

If there's one thing that ties all these strands together, it's that fact-checking can't just be for fact-checkers. If we had to go out and find every source because nobody cites them; if we had to critique every research report and dataset because nobody quality assures them; if we had to go out and find all the context and background because no one had done the analysis, public debate would be poorer for it. So journalists, campaigners and producers of information who care about having a quality debate all need to play their part. We're all in this race together.

References

British Polling Council (BPC) (2017) Objects and rules. Available online at http://www.britishpollingcouncil.org/objects-and-rules/, accessed on 19 June 2017

Francklin, Thomas (1787) Sermons on various subjects, and preached on several occasions, Printed for T. Cadell, in the *Strand* p. 233

Full Fact (2012) How strong is public support for the monarchy? 1 June. Available online at https://fullfact.org/news/how-strong-public-support-monarchy/

Full Fact (2014a) Are hundreds of patients being 'thrown out' oh hospital beds overnight? 22 May. Available online at https://fullfact.org/health/are-hundreds-patients-being-thrown-out-hospital-beds-overnight/

Full Fact (2014b) 71% of 16 and 17 year olds voted yes – based on 14 responses, 19 September. Available online at https://fullfact.org/news/71-16-and-17-year-olds-voted-yesbased-14-responses/

Full Fact (2015) More than one million people used food banks last year: that's not what the evidence shows, 24 April. Available online at https://fullfact.org/economy/more-1-million-people-used-food-banks-last-year-s-not-what-evidence-shows/

Full Fact (2016a) The state of automated fact-checking. Available online at https://fullfact.org/media/uploads/full_fact-the_state_of_automated_factchecking_aug_2016.pdf

Full Fact (2016b) Poll does not prove Brits want to quit the EU, 11 February. Available online at https://fullfact.org/europe/poll-does-not-prove-brits-want-quit-eu/

Full Fact (2017a) Big meaningless numbers: the viral economy infographic, 7 June. Available online at https://fullfact.org/economy/big-meaningless-numbers-viral-economy-infographic/

Full Fact (2017b) The facts about zero hours contracts, 26 May. Available online at https://fullfact.org/economy/facts-about-zero-hour-contracts/

Full Fact (2017c) Is crime up under the Conservatives?, 4 May. Available online at https://fullfact.org/crime/crime-under-conservatives/

O'Neill, Onora (2002) Reith lectures: A question of trust, Lecture 4: Trust and transparency. Available online at http://downloads.bbc.co.uk/rmhttp/radio4/transcripts/20020427_reith.pdf

The Times (2014) 400 patients thrown out of hospital beds every night, 22 May

Wells, Anthony (2012) How not to report opinion polls. Available online at http://ukpollingreport.co.uk/blog/archives/5717

Note on the contributor

Joseph O'Leary is senior researcher at *Full Fact*, with a research focus on crime and immigration. He leads *Full Fact*'s work on data, including producing a house standard on graphs which has contributed to Government Statistical Service guidance. He regularly delivers talks and workshops on fact-checking and statistical communication and has provided training and guidance to statisticians and civil servants.

Data journalism and diversity

Not only should data journalism consider and reflect the diversity of the society it is writing about, it also needs to consider the diversity of the journalists who are hunting, gathering and processing that data, argues Aasma Day, investigative reporter and Lifestyle Editor at the *Lancashire Post*

Like all forms of journalism, data journalism and the processing and analysing of information aims to bring important information to light and to be a voice for the voiceless. Data journalism is often deployed in the coverage of issues such as health, crime and education. As such, data journalists need to utilise information that reflects the ethnic diversity of the country. But data journalism still has story-telling at its heart and talking to the people behind the data is imperative. Editors also need to consider the diversity of data journalists: indeed, we need to shatter the stereotypical image many hold of data journalists being white males.

There are many examples of great work in data journalism. For instance, data collected by the *Guardian* in its 'Counted' project was used by a US government pilot programme to count killings by police. They revealed the numbers were much higher than previously thought with the new method of counting 'arrest related deaths'. The controversy over the government's dearth of official data on killings by police followed the fatal shooting of Michael Brown, an unarmed black 18-year-old, which led to riots across the US in August 2014.

Significantly, the *Guardian*'s data revealed that black males aged 15-34 were nine times more likely than other Americans to be killed by law enforcement officers in 2016. They were also killed at four times the rate of young white men.[1]

Data gathered from police forces in the UK has also revealed that hate crimes involving racial and religious discrimination have risen at an unprecedented rate since the Brexit referendum. According to a report in the *Independent*, the number of hate crimes recorded by regional police forces rose by up to 100 per cent in the months following the Brexit vote in June 2016.[2]

The Grenfell Tower blaze on 14 June 2017 shocked the nation and controversy still surrounds the actual death toll. Many of the tenants killed and affected by the inferno were from black and ethnic minority groups and it is feared unaccounted-for migrants may also be among the dead. According to Labour MP David Lammy, the true figure of the numbers killed in the inferno may have been covered-up due to fears of riots.[3] Data journalists will certainly be at the heart of media operations documenting and displaying the true figures – once they come to light.

There are many other areas where data journalism plays its part in focusing on injustice, unfairness and discrimination against people from minorities. For instance, recently statistics emerged showing how massively under-represented ethnic minorities are in television commercials with black, Asian and other minority group actors appearing in only 5 per cent of almost 35,000 advertisements in a year. Actors from black and minority ethnic backgrounds were mostly likely to feature in government campaigns. Jabeer Butt, deputy chief executive of the Race Equality Foundation, commented: 'No one would want to stifle creativity by suggesting that we have to have a certain percentage of black and minority ethnic people portrayed in ads. However, these statistics suggest that advertisers are missing an opportunity to reach a growing segment of consumers.'[4]

Moreover, data from the Organ Donation and Transplantation Activity Report, published by NHS Blood and Transplant, revealed that three out of ten patients on the UK's active kidney transplant waiting list were from Black, Asian or Minority Ethnic (BAME) communities. However, only 23 per cent of patients who received a kidney transplant were from these communities (due to a shortage of donors from these ethnicities) and, on average, they had to wait a year longer for a transplant than a white patient.[5]

While issues relating to race and discrimination are important and must be reported on, data journalists of all races, ethnicities, religions and backgrounds should be able to report on them and shed a light on them. The whole ethos of being a journalist means being able to dig into any topic, research it and then report on it in a balanced and accurate way regardless of your own personal viewpoint or background or whether these issues have personally affected you.

The gaps and what we're losing out on

Homogeneity is a huge issue in an industry which aims to inform an increasingly diverse society. Having different viewpoints and voices is valuable for newsroom diversity and reflects the world we live in better. Simultaneously, the more diverse an organisation, the more creative it is and, in my view, newsrooms are definitely losing out by strangling all those different voices.

I firmly believe there is a need for greater diversity in journalism, but it shouldn't just be restricted to ethnicity or faith beliefs. Diversity is more than skin colour or religion and should emulate society by incorporating gender, age, social background, sexual orientation and disability. Newsrooms should aim to reflect the world they report about and the audiences they serve – while still retaining the values of hiring the best person for the job.

It may be this means those hiring need to change their mind-set and, instead of looking for journalists identical to those they already employ, take a risk by hiring someone talented yet different. The mainstream media at present fail to reflect accurately the diversity of the community and if the role of journalists is to hold the powerful to account, expose corruption and give a voice to the voiceless, how can they do that with only a limited viewpoint?

Lack of diversity in newsrooms: The data

When I first entered the journalism profession at the age of 21, not only was I a fresh-faced graduate, I was the only brown-faced journalist in the newsroom with one black reporter who left about a year after I joined. Fast forward almost 19 years and while I have seen many journalists come and go, not one has been from a black or ethnic minority background and I remain the sole Asian journalist at my newspaper.

Does this make me feel singled out or bereft in any way? Does it affect my day-to-day work or am I ingrained with an overwhelming desire to be surrounded by colleagues with the same colour face as me? Absolutely not as I judge people on their personalities and the way they treat me, not by the colour of their skin. Nor do I believe there is any conspiracy at play as I know very few numbers of people from these communities, if any, have applied for vacancies over this passage of time.

On a daily basis, it isn't even something that enters my thoughts. It is only when you stop and consider the statistics relating to the levels of diversity that you realise how troubling the figures are. My personal experience is not an anomaly. Nationwide, there is a real lack of diversity in newsrooms and journalists are less ethnically diverse than the workforce as a whole.

The 'Journalists at Work' 2012 report by the National Council for the Training of Journalists (NCTJ) revealed 94 per cent of journalists are white compared to 91 per cent of the UK workforce as a whole.[6] However, the figures are even more disturbing when considering the large concentration of journalists based in London and the South East, some of the most diverse areas of the country. Compared to the 2002 'Journalists at Work' report, there had only been a drop of 2 per cent of journalists from a white ethnic background. The report states:

> Journalists are less ethnically diverse than the workforce as a whole – 94 per cent are white compared to 91 per cent overall. This is particularly surprising given that we might expect journalists to have a higher proportion of non-whites because they are predominantly located either in London or other urban centres where the proportion of people from ethnic minorities is much higher. For example, the 2011 census data suggests that 59.8 per cent of London's population is white, with 18.5 per cent being Asian/Asian British and 13.3 per cent Black/African.

Social class also has a bearing on people becoming journalists. The 'Journalists at Work' report states: 'There remains concern that journalism is an occupation where social class impacts on the likelihood of entering the profession. As in 2002, young people entering journalism are likely to need financial support from their families.' Ian Hargreaves, Professor of Digital Economy at Cardiff University and former editor of the *Independent* and *New Statesman*, who wrote the foreword for the report, stated:

> Ethnic diversity remains troublingly low, especially for an industry where more than half of those employed work in London and the south-east. The parents of journalists tend themselves to work in higher status jobs. Unpaid internships are common and levels of student debt are much higher than 10 years ago.

The NCTJ report is not the only one highlighting a dearth in diversity in the profession. 'Journalists in the UK' published in 2016 by Reuters Institute for the Study of Journalism found that 'UK journalism has a significant diversity problem in terms of ethnicity with Black Britons for example under-represented by a factor of more than ten'.[7]

The researchers compared their data with the 2011 census and discovered that, apart from Jews and Buddhists, people from all religious groups are under-represented amongst UK journalists. Muslims are the most under-represented with just 0.4 per cent of British journalists of this religion even though almost 5 per cent of the UK population is Muslim. Hindus and Christians are the next most under-represented with 0.4 per cent of Hindu journalists compared to a 1.4 per cent Hindu population and 31.6 per cent Christian journalists in comparison to a 64.4 per cent Christian population in the UK. However, the research also stated 74 per cent of UK journalists felt religion was of little or no importance.

The same study, when looking at ethnicity, found black Britons made up just 0.2 per cent of UK journalists but represent around 3 per cent of the British population. In a similar vein, Asian Britons represent around 7 per cent of the UK population but just 2.5 per cent of the report's sample. All these statistics make shocking reading and even for those journalists like me who have not experienced discrimination in the workplace, it begs the question: why aren't more ethnically diverse journalists entering the profession?

Not just a box-ticking exercise

In 'Journalists in the UK' published in 2016 by Reuters Institute for the Study of Journalism, journalists from ethnic minority backgrounds completing a survey revealed how they felt that cultural expectations and social connections were part of what prevented more Asians going into journalism. The report states:

> Traditional familial ambitions for children to go into 'respected professions' like 'medicine, engineering and dentistry' make journalism a second-tier career and because journalism is highly competitive it requires 'either a lot of luck or someone you know' and 'Asian parents often don't know anyone in the media'.

Let's say you somehow manage to overcome all these mountains and accomplish your dream of becoming a journalist. Well done! But for some, the battle is far from over. No one wants to be the 'token Asian or black journalist' or part of a box-ticking exercise. Professional pride means we all want to be hired and promoted on merit. Nor should being black or from an ethnic minority background dictate the kind of stories you are expected to cover. I personally feel very strongly that I don't want to be seen as an Asian journalist but a journalist who happens to be Asian.

It is about wanting your work, skills and talents to speak louder than the colour of your skin and not wanting what's on the outside as being seen as your sole identity. It is certainly a fine balancing act between not wanting to be overlooked but not asking for any special treatment or favours either.

Data journalism: Fixing on the positives

Thus, while it is right and critically important that data journalists draw attention to disparities, wrongdoings and prejudices, however uncomfortable, there is a danger that they focus on the differences rather than promoting inclusion: in other words, there is a risk of perpetually painting people from minorities as the victims or further segregating them from society.

Instead of fixating on the negatives when it comes to diversity, data journalism needs to shine a spotlight on the positives too and be all-embracing. Future data projects, then, could look at the beneficial impact diversity and different voices make to society and communities and the human tales behind the numbers. The ultimate goal needs to be data journalism created by diverse journalists which is engaging and compelling enough to be consumed by diverse readerships from all walks of life. If data journalists are to lead the industry in innovation, they should be leading the trade to be inclusive and diverse.

Notes

[1] https://www.theguardian.com/us-news/2017/jan/08/the-counted-police-killings-2016-young-black-men.

[2] http://www.independent.co.uk/news/uk/home-news/brexit-vote-hate-crime-rise-100-per-cent-england-wales-police-figures-new-racism-eu-a7580516.html.

[3] http://www.mirror.co.uk/news/uk-news/mp-david-lammy-fears-grenfell-10694309.

[4] http://www.raceequalityfoundation.org.uk/news/black-and-minority-ethnic-groups-underrepresented-tv-advertising.

[5] http://www.kidney.org.uk/home/news-2/black-asian-and-minority-ethnic-communities-wait-longer-for-kidney-transplants/.

[6] http://www.nctj.com/downloadlibrary/jaw_final_higher_2.pdf.

[7] http://reutersinstitute.politics.ox.ac.uk/publication/journalists-uk.

Note on the contributor

Aasma Day is a multi-award winning journalist and investigative reporter and Lifestyle Editor at the *Lancashire Post* based in Preston. She is also a member of the Journalists' Advisory Panel for the Independent Press Standards Organisation (IPSO).

Putting the heart and humanity into DJ's hard numbers

According to Simon Rogers, empathy is at the heart of some of the most innovative data journalism. Too often, data work can be impersonal and anonymous: instead, it should connect more with the 'human'

It's easy to think of data journalism as a cold-hearted exercise in relaying facts and figures. But increasingly it's becoming more than that. There is a new field of data journalism which is about making those hard numbers more human.

Traditionally, a lot of data journalism and data visualisation has not been big on emphasising humanity. Former *New York Times* developer Jacob Harris wrote a prescient piece in 2015 calling for more empathy in data journalism.[1] He cited *ProPublica*'s Scott Klein in talking about the importance of the 'near' view, in addition to the 'far' view that data journalism often takes. Klein was talking about producing apps but it applies to all data journalism. He wrote:

> Your near view is the page at lowest level of abstraction, where your reader is looking at her own school, his own town, etc. The near view conveys association and identity. It is the means through which readers will understand the whole by relating it to the example they understand best.

In other words, data journalism can often seem abstract and removed from your personal life. Bringing it closer, the 'near' view, is what makes it real and concrete. It's the difference between flying over a place and remarking how the cars look like toys and being there on the road in the back seat of a taxi. One is remote and removed, the other is happening to you.

Typically, data journalism is often paired with traditional narrative reporting which can focus on teasing out the empathy part of the equation. That leaves the data work feeling anonymous and impersonal. But in a world where visuals have to stand alone, that is no longer adequate. Wrote Harris:

> The main question is this: should we even try with our graphics to make readers care? The Devil's Advocate would argue that it's not the responsibility of our interactives to make people feel something about a topic – that is usually handled by a narrative piece paired with them – but I feel that in these days where charts may be tweeted, re-blogged and aggregated out of context, you must assume your graphic will stand alone. Neither of these

40

arguments consider what the reader actually expects. What does the reader expect to feel from journalism and how can we learn from their experiences?

Two years is a long time in data. Now, empathy is at the heart of some of the most innovative data journalism and visualisation around. Take the work of Mona Chalabi, for instance, in which she brings her hand-drawn analysis to bear on issues ranging from politics to sex without ever dumbing-down or patronising.[2]

In 2017, data artist Giorgia Lupi gave a TED talk showing how data can bring us closer to ourselves, how we can find ourselves in that data. It has hit a nerve, with more than half a million views.[3] She has a background in this kind of work. Giorgia was one half of Dear Data, a year-long, analog data-drawing project with Stefanie Posavec – the two designers living on different sides of the Atlantic. By collecting and hand-drawing their personal data and sending it to each other in the form of postcards, they became friends. The visuals were simple, clear and rather beautiful, dealing with their everyday lives in innovative ways.

In WorldPotus, which Giorgia and her partners produced as part of our data visualisation project, they used Google Search data to explore how the rest of the world searched for the 2016 US Presidential election. It was playful, fun and smart, reflecting the uncertainty and nuance of the data itself.[4]

This is where art and data visualisation blur, and maybe it has always been so. Minard's famous visual exploration of the French army's retreat from Moscow in 1812 is both data visual and artwork, a piece from 1861 that tells us as much about ourselves and our reaction to it as it does about the subject at hand.[5] To some, it's the best dataviz ever produced. Personally, I love how it tells a story – but for me it's simply beautiful, and that's enough.

It's easy to say that this is about entertainment, but I disagree. At its heart, this is about accessibility. Just because a subject is difficult or sensitive, who's to say it can't be handled in a human way that makes it easier for more people to understand. After all, isn't that what journalism is essentially about?

One of the projects I have been involved in as Data Editor at Google is to work with designers around the world to develop new ways of visual storytelling, produced with artistic direction from Alberto Cairo. Cairo has taken on the issue of empathy as part of the epilogue of *The Functional Art*. In it, he cites the example of how to visualise the deaths of the 14 million people killed by the Nazi and Soviet regimes during the middle of the twentieth century. He wrote:

> *Fourteen million.* That's *fourteen million* non-combatants vanishing in a bit more than a decade. How can we envision *fourteen million* faces? We can't. The best we can do to honor them by explaining their fates is to devise models that represent them as accurately as possible, the same way we depict geographical reality on a map by first reducing it. The map can never be the same as the territory.[6]

The phrase 'the map is not the territory' is attributed often to the Polish-American philosopher Alfred Korzybski (1879-1950). The full quotation is relevant, too: 'A map is not the territory it represents, but, if correct, it has a similar structure to the territory, which accounts for its usefulness.' Essentially, this is about the difference between a representation and the object itself, and it's as old as art itself (see René Magritte's exploration of this conundrum in *Ceci n'est pas une pipe*, This is not a pipe, of 1929[7]). Data journalism and visualisation is about managing that representation. And in managing that representation, thinking about the data in the same old way is no longer enough.

One of the projects we worked on saw designers Shirley Wu and Nadieh Bremer apply their unique take on life to Google data. The pair together make up *Datasketch.es*. Shirley is based in San Francisco, Nadieh in Amsterdam, and the two regularly produce complementary work that tells beautiful stories. As part of our visual series, the team created not one but two visuals, as they looked at Google data we haven't explored before: translations and culture searches.

In *Beautiful in English*, Nadieh reveals the top searched words in Google Translate from different languages.[8] She explores how the words vary from the mundane to the sublime, and notes a common current of optimism through a number of the languages:

> 6 out of the 10 languages have a positive vibe going on, with 3 of them wanting to know the translation for good while the most often translated word across all languages is beautiful, or, as they say in Italian, *bella*.

And in the complementary visual, *explore-adventure.com*, Shirley looks at the top-searched cultural locations in different countries. She examined the thousands of cultural and tourism searches that take place on Google and illustrates how

different countries search in unique ways. For instance, cities are the most searched cultural destinations. But the searches also vary season by season.

Nadieh and Shirley have different styles but one thing radiates from their work: humanity. It showcases data we have never visualised before and does it in a way which is human, beautiful, and above all, fun. And that is something we need more of in data journalism.

Notes

[1] See https://source.opennews.org/articles/connecting-dots/.

[2] See http://monachalabi.com/.

[3] See www.ted.com/talks/giorgia_lupi_how_we_can_find_ourselves_in_data.

[4] https://simonrogers.net/2016/10/18/how-is-the-world-searching-for-the-us-presidential-election-a-data-visualisation-from-the-google-news-lab/.

[5] See https://datavizblog.com/2013/05/26/dataviz-history-charles-minards-flow-map-of-napoleons-russian-campaign-of-1812-part-5/.

[6] See http://ptgmedia.pearsoncmg.com/images/9780321834737/samplepages/0321834739.pdf.

[7] See http://enculturation.net/3_2/introduction3.html.

[8] See https://nbremer.github.io/inenglish/.

Note on the contributor

Simon Rogers is Data Editor at the Google News Lab and Director of the Data Journalism Awards.

Section 2:
At local and national levels diversity is the key

Martin Moore

The writers in this section show how important data has become to national and local journalism in the UK – and the diversity of its application. Data journalism, they write, is being used for everything from exposing executive perks at international corporations, to revealing deficiencies in NHS performance, to explaining political disengagement in individual wards around Bristol. The authors describe how they use digital tools to organise and navigate data. This includes those developed in-house by news organisations themselves, such as the 'Real Schools Guide' from the Trinity Mirror Data Unit, to those developed by civic entrepreneurs such as William Perrin's Local News Engine, as well as those freely available on the web, like Google Fusion tables.

Yet these chapters also emphasise the significant challenges facing data journalism. From the difficulty of accessing and gathering the data – whether from sports governing bodies, private companies, magistrates' courts or local authorities, to the exhausting process of cleaning and sorting the data, and making sure it is interpreted accurately, to the perils of inadvertently cherry-picking unrepresentative numbers to confirm a story. Data journalism is still relatively young in the UK but, as this section shows, it is growing up fast.

Lack of understanding about the value of data

Sport, Rob Minto writes in the first chapter, is a subject ripe for data journalism. Yet the field is mainly populated by ex-players, opinionated columnists and TV pundits. This is partly due to a lack of understanding about the value of data in sports journalism. Data is not the route to picking a winning team, as Michael Lewis describes in his celebrated book *Moneyball* (of 2003). Data allows journalists to better understand how a sport works, to explain the success or failure of a team or player and to expose misconduct and corruption. Yet, even when the value of data has been understood, Minto shows, its explanatory power can be overextended or misused. The most prominent recent use of data in sports journalism – an investigation into tennis match-fixing by *Buzzfeed* and the BBC in 2016 – was both an illustration of the potential of data sports journalism and a warning about the dangers of drawing too broad conclusions from a narrow set of data.

Leila Haddou, who worked in the *Financial Times*'s data team before moving to *The Times* and *Sunday Times*, vividly describes four ways in which data can be used to expose and explain stories that would otherwise escape scrutiny or remain hidden. The *FT* looked, for example, at what factors help to explain the rise in the popularity of right-wing populist parties across Europe, discovering that education level is more likely to distinguish a populist voter than exposure to immigrants. In the process, it also revealed the role that Twitter bots are starting to play in informing voters and directing them away from mainstream media. To investigate the cost of executive perks, the *FT* gathered two years of corporate filings to the Securities and Exchange Commission and systematically combed through them for disclosures of personal use of private jets. The consequent Corporate Jet Files revealed that some corporations were spending up to $40m.-a-year flying their executives on private jets. Haddou carefully sets out the complexity of doing these types of data-led investigations, the long process of data cleaning and sorting, and the critical role of journalistic insight in identifying the human stories.

In her chapter, Claire Miller shows how a dedicated data unit at Trinity Mirror has, since 2013, been able to provide breaking stories for the newsroom, lead and support long-running investigations and provide interactive tools to allow the public to dig deep into open-data sets. The key, for Trinity Mirror's Data Unit, has been making data local. By developing the 'Real Schools Guide', for example, they have been able to allow parents to compare schools in their area across a range of criteria beyond exam results. Their work with the World War I Graves Commission enabled them to help local residents search for relatives by first name, surname, town or street. Correlating FOI requests made it possible for the unit to expose the spiralling cost of NHS hospital parking. Much of this was done with tools that are open and freely available, such as Google Fusion tables.

Huge opportunity – and significant dilemma

For Adam Cantwell-Corn and Lucas Batt, of the *Bristol Cable*, data presents both a huge opportunity and a significant dilemma for local journalism. Data is central to uncovering trends across public services, to understanding democratic engagement and to revealing financial scandals. Yet it is also very time-consuming, frequently frustrating and requires an ongoing openness to learning new skills. Before Bristol's 2016 Mayoral election, the *Cable* set out to discover why there had been such a strikingly low turnout at the previous election in 2012. This led them to layer the indices of social deprivation on to Bristol's wards and to reveal a close correlation between levels of deprivation and low voter turnout. A separate investigation, into social housing properties sold at auction, led to the discovery that properties were selling for significantly more than the council's anticipated repair costs – and a consequent local outcry. As with the Trinity Mirror Data Unit, the *Cable* has benefited from the availability of free tools – like Carto for mapping and Import. io. Data journalism is, Cantwell-Corn and Batt believe, both central to the future of local journalism, and one of its biggest challenges.

In his chapter, Peter Geoghagan, one of the founders of the *Ferret*, describes how digital outlets can address some of the challenges. The investigative news site was established in Scotland, in 2015, in response to some of the economic and ethical challenges facing journalism. It has a mixed funding model and a strongly co-operative approach with its readers. Its first investigations – into fracking in Scotland – were voted on and crowd-funded. It survives by focusing all its attention and resources on the journalism itself (monthly overheads are less than £150), by being as transparent as possible with its readers (including with its finances) and by taking advantage of available tools on the web. Critical to its success has been the collaborative approach taken by its journalists in conjunction with the site's readers. By spring 2017, the *Ferret* had published more than 250 original stories, helped trigger an inquiry into fracking, exposed the rise of the far right on Facebook and informed debates in the Scottish parliament on the treatment of asylum seekers and workers' rights in Amazon warehouses.

Responding to the decline of court reporting

As the number of professional journalists able to report live from local councils and magistrates' courts has fallen, and the time they have to trawl through civic records has shrunk, so concerns have risen about the accountability of public authorities. To address this, William Perrin worked with a number of developers to create a prototype, Local News Engine, as he outlines in his chapter. The engine scraped data from three sources – the London Borough of Camden, the London Borough of Islington and Her Majesty's Court Service at Highbury Corner Magistrates' Court – and made it available on a weekly basis to local journalists and bloggers. In the process of developing the engine, the team discovered frequent problems with the data available (broken sites, dead links), numerous obstacles to gathering and organising it (the court records, for example, were listed within an emailed pdf of 300-400 pages) and deficiencies in its licensing. Yet, despite this, the tool was able to scrape and sort local authority data in just over half-an-hour (a process that would previously have taken days) and reduce the journalist's time to scan it to minutes.

Teresa Jolley writes about the urgent need for more data journalists to analyse transport and infrastructure developments in the West Midlands over the next decade. The major transport investments – in the HS2 rail link, two new rails stations, tram extensions and major changes to local motorways – have significant implications for the local population. Understanding what these implications are, and making people aware of them, will require sustained, detailed, local journalism

– reporting informed by the reams of data that will be, and are already, being produced. The West Midlands Combined Authority is using open source products and services built on Open Street Map in order to enable innovative uses of the data. Equally, there are various transport trials based around Birmingham whose success or failure will have much wider repercussions for the future of transport – such as the future car design project and testing of autonomous vehicles. Both the success of these projects and their broader acceptance will rely heavily on good journalism informed by data.

What does the price of Marcel Duchamp's best-known art work – a urinal – have to do with data journalism? Like data journalism, Isabelle Marchand writes in this section's final chapter, it is almost impossible to make sense of the price of Duchamp's work without context and background. We now live in a world awash with data, where a good data journalist not only has to discover a story within the data but communicate it in a way that is compelling, comprehensible and relevant. Marchand sets out ways in which to do this, and the questions journalists can ask themselves to make sure they are succeeding. The cost of not doing this is to produce a story that, even if it has vital importance, is ignored.

Sports: What needs to be done to improve the DJ game?

Sports DJ suffers from patchy access to data, resistance among traditional media and not enough serious practitioners. But the landscape is improving – and the possibility for impact is high, as Rob Minto explains

The paradox

Sport has a complicated relationship with data. The paradox is that, in sport, (almost) everything is measured: times, passes, goals, points. There is far less room for statistical uncertainty than there is in, say, GDP figures (Liesman 2016) or population statistics (Melamed 2014). We know who won and by what measure. And we can know a lot more than that with complete certainty.

Yet sport relies on data-blind narratives: the underdog, the carefree young challenger, the last-hurrah veteran. The eye is trusted by pundits more than the data.

Publishers: A veneer of statistics

Sports reporting, in the main, ignores data. Rivalries, controversies and personalities are the stock-in-trade. Pundits and commentators are mostly ex-players who have little or no grounding in journalism let alone statistics, and so call the game as they see it.

In broadcast journalism, statistics are wheeled out to inform the viewer and make the coverage seem clever, but are rarely given context. For example, possession statistics in football during the game are usually shown a few times. Yet are those numbers worth showing? Does one team typically play a low-possession game anyway?

Most national print newspapers publish charts and graphics to highlight pre- and post-match statistics. Again, most lack context or deeper meaning. A typical example: the historical head-to-head record between two teams is not an intrinsically bad statistic, but it doesn't reveal much either.

All too often, the charts present the data in a poor way. Small differences are blown up, numbers are shown in pie charts that make it hard to show any pattern to the data and cartoonish images are frequently used. This is not statistical analysis but the classic use of numbers to fill space and pad out a story.

Some publications aim for something a bit more meaningful and have almost inadvertently stumbled into sports data journalism. The *Guardian* doesn't proclaim itself in this area, but several of its journalists – Andy Bull and Sean Ingle, for example – often use data and statistics in analysis pieces to form a sophisticated argument. The *Guardian* also reports on sports statistical research done elsewhere, often by specialist academics or economists, the types of story that are not touched by the personality-driven tabloids and online publishers.

There are also sports journalists who stand out: for example Miguel Delaney, who has written for several publications. Jonathan Liew, at the *Daily Telegraph*, is another journalist who writes well about statistics as part of his wider job.

Which leaves us with the publications that advocate sports data journalism. There are only a few: the *Financial Times*, which ran the 'Baseline' column for a few years[1] (from 2014 to 2017), the *Economist*, which runs the 'Game Theory' blog[2] and Nate Silver's *FiveThirtyEight*, which is now owned by ESPN.[3] At those publications are some of the best sports data journalists: John Burn-Murdoch, at the *FT*, James Tozer and Dan Rosenheck, at the *Economist*, and Carl Bialik (and others) at *FiveThirtyEight*.

Sports data journalism is doing well in book form. For instance, in football there is *Soccernomics*, by Simon Kuper and Stefan Szymanski (2009), *The Numbers Game*, by Chris Anderson and David Sally (2014), and several others still worth reading. My book, *Sports Geek* (2016), was an attempt to draw together data journalism on lots of different sports into one place; most sports data books focus on one sport only.

Data in sport vs data journalism: The *Moneyball* problem

This is a big area of confusion. Mention sport and data to most people and the likely response is: 'Oh, like *Moneyball*, right?'[4] Michael Lewis's *Moneyball* (of 2003) is a great book – and a decent film, too. It is the story of how US baseball team the Oakland Athletics, under the guidance of General Manager Billy Beane, defied the odds. They did this by using data as a recruitment tool, to find players who did not look the part but could statistically contribute to the team. This meant that the As made the play-offs despite having a far lower wage bill than other top teams – and wages are usually the best predictor of results in baseball (and other sports too).

Moneyball, however, is not sports data journalism. It's a true story, and an underdog story in which data and statisticians play a key role. That's a different thing. And it encapsulates much of the confusion about sports data and sports data journalism.

There are excellent pieces of journalism about using data in sport. For example, *Wired* magazine in 2014 ran a feature about sports statistics (Medeiros 2014). It's a great read. But it isn't sports data journalism. The journalist, João Medeiros, hasn't gone through a dataset or used statistics for the reporting. Rather, it is a well-reported piece about the inner-workings of football clubs and their use of technology to find an edge. I could highlight many other examples, but the point would be the same: sports data as a topic is distinct from sports data journalism. Which brings us to the next question: the availability of data.

Finding the numbers

The challenge for sports data journalists is getting hold of the right data. There are two dynamics going on: one is the associations and sports governing bodies who are generally open (within limits) to making data available and the companies, such as Opta and Prozone, which create sophisticated proprietary data to sell to teams and broadcasters. The companies do not want it to be freely or openly available since that would undermine their business model.[5]

When researching *Sports Geek*, I continually had a love-hate relationship with some sports over the numbers. Typically, the sport authorities have the data, but they make it tough for journalists to use. Let's take tennis as an example.

There are two governing bodies in tennis, the Association of Tennis Professionals (ATP) and the Women's Tennis Association (WTA), which cover the men and women's tours respectively. Tennis lends itself to lots of types of statistical analysis: prize money, scorelines, the effectiveness of different shots and many others that you may be able to think of. How about prize money? Both the ATP and WTA only give out year-end prize money data in PDFs, which don't export easily to CSV (Simple File Format) or text – the rows are jumbled and messy and the data requires cleaning. The PDFs are also hard to find – the information is tucked away in a larger media PDF that isn't listed on the homepage and requires specific searching to root out.

There are also other annoying differences: the ATP gives out player data going back to 1991, but the WTA data only goes back to 2008. Neither body has download-friendly interfaces or an API (Application Program Interface) that coders or journalists can tap into. Which means data-savvy journalists need to look elsewhere. Perhaps the most comprehensive tennis dataset available is not from either body but, instead, from Tennis Abstract, run by Jeff Sackmann. Sackmann says he started Tennis Abstract because he wanted...

> ... a better way to access tennis stats. I wanted the dataset for my own research, but I also figured I wasn't the only one who wanted a more powerful way to view and filter results. I'm disappointed that in the six years I've been around, the ATP and WTA sites have done little besides making their sites slower and allegedly more mobile-friendly.

He describes the overall data situation in tennis as 'pretty bleak – there's virtually no tradition of analytics'. That makes proper data journalism hard, meaning that you either have to build datasets from scratch, as Sackmann has, or buy it from the same sources that bookmakers and broadcasters use.

Sackmann adds: 'What's most frustrating is that the tours possess scorecard data going back decades – point-by-point records of matches, as scored by the chair umpires – but don't make it available in any form.' He has previously made a public appeal for access to the data (Sackmann 2014), but so far in vain. Other sports have similar problems.

There is also a move to create new metrics, which may be more illuminating but also harder to understand. Alternatively, they may be a rather blunt tool. Football players, for instance, now have their pass completion rates mentioned and used to evaluate their performance. Pass completion, though, is a raw number without much context. It does not account for the quality of a pass – a safe, easy pass to a teammate counts the same as a brilliant, cross-field pass that stretches the opponent's defence.

There are more nuanced statistics being used in football – expected goals and time-to-shot are two, but they require a level of explanation that most football fans and writers do not want to get into and often instinctively distrust. In effect, analysis of football has, for the time being, become split into two statistical camps: one that uses simplistic metrics (e.g. goals, passes) and is used by broadcast and print/online media; and the other camp that uses more complicated metrics (e.g. expected goals, time-to-shot, expected points added) but is currently only discussed in more niche publications amongst sports statisticians and data enthusiasts.

The crossover into mainstream football reporting has yet to happen (though since the start of the 2017-18 football season, BBC's *Match of the Day* has shown Expected Goals in the post-match statistics, but so far this has not been discussed widely). This is partly a question of familiarity. As Simon Gleave, Head of Analysis at Gracenote Sports, a sports analytics company, notes: 'Some sports such as cricket are awash with numbers. Football has come to it relatively late.'

It doesn't help that one popular new metric, expected goals, has no universally accepted definition: several different statisticians are creating their own model (Chappas 2013) and usually keep their methodology private (MacInnes 2017). The likelihood of such new statistics being used in mainstream reporting seems a long way off. As Gleave puts it: 'A lot of the information that's now gathered on football – I'm skeptical about the value to the average fan. ... I'd rather it was used to tell a proper story.'

The best sports for data and understanding of statistics are in the US. Baseball is the pinnacle of sports stats – it even has a specially named discipline, Sabermetrics. But all the major US sports are served well with data. Interestingly, they are covered mainly by independent professional websites, such as the pro-reference sites and others.

There is a long tradition of using stats in US sports partly because the nature of the sports is more stop-start: baseball and American Football are both structured play-by-play, which helps hugely. Basketball is more fluid, but can still be broken down into possession-based statistics and individual contributions (points, rebounds, interceptions) relatively easily. As a result, statistics are used far more frequently in the mainstream media and new metrics – such as wins above replacement (WAR) in baseball, player efficiency rating (PER) in basketball – are adopted more readily.

This tradition of statistical analysis does not stop vigorous debate on the merits of certain statistics, but it does mean that there is less resistance to statistics *per se*.

Case study: *BuzzFeed's* tennis investigation

Perhaps the highest-impact data-driven sports story of the last few years was the investigation into match-fixing by *BuzzFeed* (Blake and Templon 2016) and co-published by the BBC (Cox 2016). The story appeared in January 2016, just before the start of the first major tennis tournament of the year, the Australian Open. In the main article, it was alleged that 15 unnamed players on the men's tour 'regularly lost matches in which heavily lopsided betting appeared to substantially shift the odds – a red flag for possible match-fixing'.

The investigation was conducted by *BuzzFeed's* John Templon (2016a) who analysed 26,000 professional matches from 2009 to 2015 using data from *OddsPortal.com*. He identified matches where the odds of the outcome moved from the opening price significantly – over 10 percentage points. Once these matches were selected, he then ran a series of simulations: 1 million times per player. This was to estimate the chance that a player would have lost as many (or more) high-movement matches as they did if the chances implied by the opening odds were correct. To give *BuzzFeed* credit, the story was published simultaneously with a full methodology and the code used on *GitHub* (Templon 2016b). This should be standard practice, and *BuzzFeed* was explicit about both the methodology and the limitations of the investigation. As Templon put it:

> Betting patterns alone aren't proof of fixing. Players can underperform for all sorts of reasons – injury, fatigue, bad luck – and sometimes that underperformance will just happen to coincide with heavy betting against them. But it's extremely unlikely for a player to underperform repeatedly in matches on which people just happen to be betting massive sums against him (ibid).

While the story delved into the previously-known story of a suspect match between the Russian Nikolay Davydenko and the Argentinian Martin Vassallo Arguello, back in 2007, *BuzzFeed* did not name the 15 players, stating:

> The analysis was undertaken with only the betting information that is publicly available. Tennis authorities and betting houses have access to much finer-grained data such as the accounts placing bets, as well as forensic evidence such as phone data and bank records. Without access to such information, it is impossible to know with a sufficient degree of certainty whether these suspicious patterns are, indeed, the result of match fixing. For this reason, *BuzzFeed News* has decided not to name the players.

The impact of the story was immediate. There was criticism of tennis authorities and, in particular, of the Tennis Integrity Unit (TIU) which appeared to have not got to grips with the problem. Chris Kermode, the chief executive of the Association of Tennis Professionals, was forced into denying any cover-up and defending the TIU's record.

There was another aspect: having failed to name the players, *BuzzFeed* also started an instant flurry of 'guess-who' speculations and legally-contentious posts online.[6] This was naturally intensified by the *BuzzFeed* teaser that stated:

> Winners of singles and doubles titles at Grand Slam tournaments are among the core group of players who have repeatedly been reported for losing games when highly suspicious bets have been placed against them.

That implicated at least one very high-profile player, which became the main angle of the story, rather than the question of widespread corruption.

Quite quickly the names came out – not surprising given that *BuzzFeed* published not just the published methodology but the code used for the analysis. This prompted various player denials and a flurry of statements, which prompted more speculation. Three journalists replicated the *BuzzFeed* analysis and published the names on the website *Medium* (Kaplan et al. 2016) four days later, a list that was corroborated by others.

One name stood out: the Australian Lleyton Hewitt, a two-time major winner and one of the great players of the last 20 years. His name above all others prompted a deeper analysis of *BuzzFeed's* investigation, given his status. Ian Dorward, who specialises in sports statistics, also published the previously anonymous names on his blog (Dorward 2016), and did a deeper analysis of Hewitt. He found reasonable explanations for Hewitt's suspicious matches – he had been returning from injury, played infrequently and saved his best for big tournaments. Dorward concluded:

> From the matches that I have looked at there is absolutely no suggestion whatsoever that Lleyton Hewitt has been involved in fixing matches and to simply post his name among a list of players suspected of fixing without performing any further analysis or providing context is simply irresponsible.

Carl Bialik, for *FiveThirtyEight* (Bialik 2016), pointed out three ways in which players might lose matches with big movements in betting odds without it being a fix: 'A player could tank a match – deliberately lose it – without fixing. ... Bettors could have inside information on a match outcome without the player's involvement... Betting markets could simply get the opening odds wrong.' He continued: 'None of this means that the *BuzzFeed* 15 haven't fixed matches – just that, as *BuzzFeed* and the BBC themselves have made abundantly clear, the data analysis by itself isn't conclusive.'

Following up, Sean Ingle commented in the *Guardian* (Ingle 2016): '*BuzzFeed's* algorithm is a reasonable first filter, generating a list of players and matches to investigate in further detail, but to suggest that it should equate to a red-flag against someone's name is hugely simplistic.' Furthermore, as Brian Blickenstaff noted on *Vice Sports* (Blickenstaff 2016):

> The other problem with Templon's approach is more about how match-fixing works in today's world. In short, the pre-match betting market isn't where most match-fixers operate. They prefer the live betting market. … Not only is the live betting market more lucrative for gamblers – and fixers – but in this scenario it's easy to fix a tennis match in a way where the favorite still wins.

As a result of *BuzzFeed*'s investigation, the main tennis authorities announced that an independent review panel would be appointed to look at 'integrity in the sport'. At the time of writing (June 2017) the IRP had yet to publish its interim report.[7]

Where next?

Overall, as sports clubs become more data-savvy, the reporters who cover them also need to understand how data is used. From reporting on data-use to using data in your reporting can be a bit of a leap, but it is happening. At the same time, statistically-minded journalists are moving into sport as it is an area ripe for data-driven features. This should create and intensify the demand for data, whether open or proprietary with a reasonable price. The question is, then, whether the audience is ready for more statistically-challenging content and ideas. I think it is.

Notes

[1] See https://www.ft.com/baseline, accessed on 22 June 2017.

[2] See http://www.economist.com/blogs/gametheory, accessed on 22 June 2017.

[3] See http://fivethirtyeight.com/sports, accessed on 22 June 2017.

[4] I have had this experience many times. It's not annoying though – worse is just blank stares. For the film, *Moneyball*, see http://www.imdb.com/title/tt1210166/, accessed on 22 June 2017.

[5] I appreciate the need for data companies to make a profit. However, I would welcome any moves to make more data free.

[6] I am not suggesting this was *BuzzFeed*'s intention, as the legal advice may have been to keep the players unnamed. However, it was predictable and gave the story an extra boost.

[7] See http://www.tennisirp.com/, accessed on 22 June 2017.

References

Anderson, Chris and Sally, David (2014) *The Numbers Game*, London: Penguin

Bialik, Carl (2016) Why betting data alone can't identify match fixers in tennis, *FiveThirtyEight*, 21 January. Available online at http://fivethirtyeight.com/features/why-betting-data-alone-cant-identify-match-fixers-in-tennis, accessed on 22 June 2017

Blake, Heidi and Templon, John (2016) The tennis racket, *BuzzFeed*, 17 January. Available online at https://www.buzzfeed.com/heidiblake/the-tennis-racket, accessed on 22 June 2017

Blickenstaff, Brian (2016) Did Lleyton Hewitt fix matches, or does betting data require more context?, *Vice Sports*, 22 January. Available online at https://sports.vice.com/en_uk/article/did-lleyton-hewitt-fix-matches-or-does-betting-data-require-more-context, accessed on 22 June 2017

Chappas, Constantinos (2013) Goal expectation and efficiency, *StatsBomb*, 6 August. Available online at http://statsbomb.com/2013/08/goal-expectation-and-efficiency/, accessed on 22 June 2017

Cox, Simon (2016) Tennis match fixing: Evidence of suspected match-fixing revealed, BBC, 18 January. Available online at http://www.bbc.co.uk/sport/tennis/35319202, accessed on 22 June 2017

Dorward, Ian (2016) No evidence of Lleyton Hewitt fixing matches, *DW on Sport*, 20 January. Available online at http://www.sportdw.com/2016/01/tennis-fixing-buzzfeed-hewitt-innocent.html, accessed on 22 June 2017

Ingle, Sean (2016) Tennis match-fixing allegations leave questions to be answered, *Guardian*, 27 January. Available online at https://www.theguardian.com/sport/2016/jan/27/buzzfeed-bbc-tennis-match-fixing-allegations, accessed on 22 June 2017

Kaplan, Russell, Teplitz, Jason and Wadsworth, Christina (2016) Finding the tennis suspects: Deanonymizing *BuzzFeed*'s tennis exposé, *Medium*, 20 January. Available online at https://medium.com/@rkaplan/finding-the-tennis-suspects-c2d9f198c33d, accessed on 22 June 2017

Kuper, Simon and Szymanski, Stefan (2009) *Soccernomics*, New York: Nation Books

Liesman, Steve (2016) Don't trust those GDP numbers, *CNBC*, 24 March. Available online at http://www.cnbc.com/2016/03/24/cnbc-analysis-dont-trust-those-gdp-numbers.html, accessed on 22 June 2017

MacInnes, Paul (2017) Expected goals and big football data: The statistics revolution that is here to stay, *Guardian*, 30 March. Available online at https://www.theguardian.com/football/2017/mar/30/expected-goals-big-football-data-leicester-city-norwich, accessed on 22 June 2017

Medeiros, João (2014) The winning formula: How data analytics is keeping football teams one step ahead, *Wired*, 23 January. Available online at http://www.wired.co.uk/article/the-winning-formula, accessed on 22 June 2017

Melamed, Claire (2014) Development data: How accurate are the figures?, *Guardian*, 31 January. Available online at https://www.theguardian.com/global-development/poverty-matters/2014/jan/31/data-development-reliable-figures-numbers, accessed on 22 June 2017

Minto, Rob (2016) *Sports Geek*, London, Oxford, New York: Bloomsbury

Sackmann, Jeff (2014) The untapped potential of umpire scorecard data, *Tennis Abstract*, 12 August. Available online at http://www.tennisabstract.com/blog/2014/08/12/the-untapped-potential-of-umpire-scorecard-data, accessed on 22 June 2017

Templon, John (2016a) How *BuzzFeed News* used betting data to investigate match-fixing in tennis, *BuzzFeed*, 17 January. Available online at https://www.buzzfeed.com/johntemplon/how-we-used-data-to-investigate-match-fixing-in-tennis, accessed on 22 June 2017

Templon, John (2016b) *BuzzFeed News*/2016-01-tennis-betting-analysis, *GitHub*, 17 January. Available online at https://github.com/BuzzFeedNews/2016-01-tennis-betting-analysis, accessed on 22 June 2017

Note on the contributor

Rob Minto is the author of *Sports Geek*: a visual tour of sporting myths, debate and data, published in 2016 by Bloomsbury. He also worked at the *Financial Times* for 12 years, including as the newspaper's first Interactive Editor.

Data journalism as a crucial investigative tool at the *Financial Times*

Leila Haddou, former investigative reporter at the *FT*, shows how the pink paper used data to probe populism, executive perks, pensions dumping and Chinese investment in Cambodia

A newsroom like that at the *Financial Times* runs on data. How are the markets moving? How is a currency performing or responding to current affairs? What are the polls saying and how do we explain election results? But using data for deep and original reporting is also a key part of its premium offering to readers. The *FT*'s focus on stories of global importance and its expertise in financial reporting informs its approach to data-driven investigations. It also presents the *FT*'s investigations team with unique challenges.

In this chapter, I will use four examples to show how the newspaper tackles these challenges. First, it will cover how it used data analysis to assess the rise of populism in Europe and to guide its reporters on the ground accordingly. Second, it will show the difficulties of trying to monitor the chronic use of executive perks at the expense of company shareholders by using open and public records that can be deeply impenetrable – even to investigative reporters. Third, explaining technical financial concepts to a reader when covering complex topics such as abuse of insolvency rules to pension dump. And finally, even in a newsroom best known for covering financial stories, bringing in the human story and consequences of business decisions, as shown via China's unprecedented investment and development in Cambodia. Each example will cover the story concept, the methodology used and the lessons learned from each.

Using DJ to investigate the rise of populism in Europe

In January 2017, the *FT* embarked on a major data-rich project examining the rise of populism in Europe ahead of national elections in the Netherlands, France and Germany.[1] The data unit examined more than 60 variables and demographic indicators such as age, employment rates and educational attainment obtained from national statistics organisations. This, in addition to analysing previous election results and immigration to specific areas with a leaning towards parties to the right of the political spectrum. The analysis yielded some stark results. In the Netherlands, for instance, education, rather than exposure to immigrant populations, was the clearest indicator for voters more likely to support the nationalist Party for Freedom.[2] Voters who had left the academic system without a degree or higher vocational qualification were more likely to support the populist leader, Geert Wilders.

Another previously unexplored factor was the rise of 'fake news' – or 'alternative facts', as it is known in some circles – and how social media is used to spread such misinformation. In a landmark study, the *FT* set out to review the role that social media, particularly automated Twitter accounts, played during a national election campaign.[3]

The immediate challenge when examining social media trends and networks is the sheer volume of data involved. How can a reporter find stories and maintain accuracy without getting lost in endless analysis? The approach taken by interactive journalist David Blood was to combine sample Twitter data obtained from third-party social media analytics firm Crimson Hexagon with supplementary data from Twitter's own API to examine the behaviour of Wilders' followers on the social network. Guided by research originally published by the Oxford Internet Institute at Oxford University, the study included an examination of accounts exhibiting 'bot-like' attributes, i.e. those posting improbably high volumes of tweets per day.

These were found to have significant influence among a segment of Wilders' 750,000 followers, directing his Twitter audience away from professional news sources. Overall, Wilders' followers were found to be more likely to share stories of Russian origin, such as articles published on Russia Today (RT) and Sputnik than content from the Dutch national broadcaster, NOS. Both RT and Sputnik had previously been named by the Office of the Director of National Intelligence in the US as being part of Russia's 'state-run propaganda machine'.

Revealing executive corruption – through DJ techniques
The second example highlights how public data can be difficult to interrogate systematically for stories because of the format it is presented in. Executives' personal use of the corporate jet has become one of the most prominent symbols of excessive CEO pay going back to the 1980s. Since the financial crisis, companies have scaled back on overspending and the regulator – the Securities and Exchange Commission (SEC) – has required more detailed disclosure on so-called executive perks. But while publicly-listed companies are now forced to disclose this information, no public database exists to reveal the overall scale of spending on personal perks for executives.

The *FT* looked into this with the Corporate Jet Files, a project using data reported to SEC to uncover how much companies were spending to provide private planes to its executives for personal use.[4] Companies are required to declare such perks valued at more than $25,000 per named executive in their annual proxy filings, which are then published in the public domain on their website.

The investigation looked at two full years of data available since SEC disclosure rules came in, with a focus on companies in the Standard & Poor's 500 index. A lack of rules dictating the exact format in which companies need to disclose this data posed a problem from the outset. It meant that it was not presented in a standardised or structured way that would be easy to collate and query using automation and code. Some companies included it as part of their summary compensation table whilst others gave the number in a footnote, for instance.

A big challenge, then, for reporters Robin Kwong and David Crow was how to compile the database from 1,000 annual proxy filings (also known as DEF 14A filings) when the usual ways of automatically scraping the records is not an option. A variety of approaches were considered, from outsourcing the data entry work to scraping a portion of the filings and manually inspecting the rest of it. In the end, a decision was made to inspect manually all 1,000 filings and conduct random spot-checks on the entered data.

To improve efficiency and ease the process of finding all the filings, the team used the SEC's file transfer protocol server to download an index of all the relevant documents for the time period. Then they used R, the statistical programming language, to filter that index and compile a list of URLs for the filings of interests. The review ignored all those disclosures of personal use of corporate jets valued at less than the $25,000 SEC threshold to ensure consistency within our dataset. That left 322 executives across 184 companies.

From there, a Google spreadsheet and an R script was used to analyse the top spenders in 2013 and 2014. This revealed that the distribution of jet spending was skewed, with a handful of companies accounting for a large proportion of total spending. The script also allowed compared spending more widely for the same years, breaking the data down by industry, gender of the executive and geographic location of companies' headquarters.

An examination of the spending history of the top 10 companies going back a decade to 2006 revealed that the biggest publicly-listed US companies spent $40m. in 2014 giving free flights on corporate jets to some of their highest-paid executives.

There was an unexpected advantage to inspecting the documents manually. A number of interesting anecdotes and facts from the filings which we might otherwise have missed emerged. In one case, a global telecommunications company called Comcast allowed its executives to use the corporate jet for personal travel at a cost of $1.2m. However, further inspection of the documents also showed that a $3.75m. tax deduction had been denied to the firm as a result of this, making the true cost much higher. Rather than merely offering a figure for the financial cost of a perk, the *FT* was able to show a more complete picture, which included wider implications for the company.

A key lesson from this type of investigation is that even when parts of the process can only be done manually, it is worth thinking about what aspects can be automated to improve efficiency and avoid human error. Before committing the time and resources to compile a manual dataset, try a small sample first to test the hypothesis you are working towards before diving into the full project. In so doing, you can assess what the minimum and maximum story you can derive from the exercise would be and, thus, whether the investment is worth making.

It is also worth noting that just because information is publicly available does not mean that anyone has actually looked at it in a systematic way, or that it is accessible to the public. There are potentially really good agenda-setting scoops hiding in plain sight. For the third example, we used documents filed at Companies House to investigate an increasing problem of pension dumping by companies using a British insolvency law.[5]

The increasing problem of pension dumping

When a company is struggling financially it often goes into administration – whereby an outside party is appointed to take over the company and bring about the best outcome for creditors who are owed outstanding monies. This is achieved either by restructuring the company, selling it or liquidating the assets to raise much needed funds.

But, in 2002, the government created the Enterprise Act in an effort to foster an entrepreneurial spirit to stop companies going to the wall unnecessarily and offer 'honest bankrupts' a second chance at business. The law created the conditions for 'pre-packaged administrations' where a struggling company is sold in a secret deal before creditors or even employees realise the company is in financial difficulties. Yet these 'pre-packs' have proved controversial, not least because the effect has been to absolve the company of financial obligations to creditors, the taxman and pensioners.

Moreover, the Enterprise Act was somewhat discredited two years after its creation when the government created an industry-backed 'lifeboat' fund to protect the pensions of those employed by failed companies. The two laws produced a toxic combination that offered the potential for abuse and pension dumping. The Pension Protection Fund (PPF) was supposed to be a destination of last resort, but after a succession of high-profile companies restructured to exploit the rules and dump their liabilities, politicians started to raise concerns.

Companies such as Bernard Matthews, a well-known British turkey producer, was sold by its private equity owners in such a deal, netting the company a £14m. profit, whilst small business creditors could recoup only 1p in the pound, and the pension fund got nothing to plug the shortfall in funding.

When the PPF admitted, during a parliamentary committee hearing, that it had not monitored the number of schemes it had absorbed following a 'pre-pack', the *FT* proceeded to answer the questions the PPF couldn't. How widespread was the use of pre-packs? What role did they have in pension dumping? And at what cost to the lifeboat fund?

The main obstacle from the outset was to agree a formal definition where there was none in the industry. The *FT* turned to the authors of a recently concluded government review into pre-packaged insolvencies and adopted the same, narrow definition – businesses sold in whole or part to a new owner on or before the date they formally became insolvent.

The investigation involved three separate phases – the data collation, the identification of pre-packs and the cost to the lifeboat fund. It began with a thorough review of the insolvency documents filed at Companies House of all 868 schemes to have entered the PPF since its creation a decade previously. The first step was to match a list of pension schemes from those published on the PPF website to their respective companies and obtain a list of company numbers. As with the Corporate Jet Files, the filings were not organised in such a way as to automate the process of data retrieval. But a script was written using the company registration number to navigate to the page and download any document entitled 'Statement of Administrator's Proposal'.

Again, the company filings were inconsistent. Many terms were used in place of 'pre-pack', such as 'accelerated sales process' or 'accelerated M. & A.'. Some even failed to provide that. As a result, we were forced to look closely at the date the company was sold in relation to the date an administrator was appointed. Those sold on or before this date were counted as 'pre-pack' insolvencies. The study found that 148 schemes entered the fund using a pre-pack, with more than £3.8bn in pensions liabilities being offloaded into the PPF as a result. The outcome was 53,000 workers facing severe cuts to their retirement incomes. A further 20 schemes with liabilities of hundreds of millions of pounds were in the assessment period for entry.

The members of failed workplace pension schemes receive a capped 'compensation payment', usually significantly lower than their original retirement benefit entitlement. The *FT* also found that two in three pre-packs involved the sale to the existing owners and directors, prompting accusations that 'phoenix companies' can exploit the process to dump their liabilities and then continue trading.

Successive governments have tried to deal with the problems created by pre-packs. Former business secretary Vince Cable commented in response to the *FT*'s research that there were unintended consequences from good motives – where the PPF is the go-to fund instead of the rescue body. The investigation led to calls for an urgent review of insolvency procedures, with politicians accusing firms such as the owners of Bernard Matthews of lining their own pockets at the expense of pensioners.

Data-driven, human-interest stories: Cambodia case study

Finally, financial stories heavily driven by data are still about the human stories behind them. In 2016, the *FT* examined the Cambodian corporate registry to reveal how China had bought its way into Cambodia.[6]

Its Prime Minister Hun Sen once derided China as 'the root of everything that is evil' for its role in supporting the Khmer Rouge, which killed an estimated 1.7 million people during the genocide of the 1970s. He is now its most reliable supporter in Southeast Asia. The data and supporting documents showed how big money, secret dealings and high-level backing from the ruling party had brought Cambodia into China's sphere of influence.

Pitched as a way to reduce the red tape faced by investors in the country and to improve its consistently low ranking on global surveys for ease of starting a business locally, Cambodia launched an online business registry. Fearing that existing company data would be lost as a result, Global Witness, a UK-based campaign group, created a bespoke database, opening up the data in an easily searchable format. The *FT* was given early access to the database and focused specifically on Chinese companies which had been investing in Cambodia at an unprecedented rate. Billions of dollars had been pouring into the country, but analysis of the data showed a dark side to China's corporate embrace.

The investigation utilised common data journalism methods with both relational and graph databases to look for patterns indicative of well-documented abuses including corruption and land-grabs. Pivot tables summarised and counted the most common names and companies in our database, and we employed techniques to find matching names that appeared in lists of prominent Chinese government officials and businessmen and land concession recipients to find potential stories.

We centred on characters such as 'Big Brother Fu', a former officer in China's People's Liberation Army who had won a rare land concession to develop one of the most beautiful stretches of Cambodia's coastline into a $5.7bn tourist resort. So close to the country's Prime Minister was Mr Fu that he enjoyed the protection of Hun Sen's personal bodyguard unit, the leader of which was captured on video proclaiming: 'Mr Fu's business is our business' as he pledged to create safe passage for all of Fu's endeavours in Cambodia.

Exploring the data using graph software such as Neo4j enabled us to spot curious behaviours such as supposedly separate companies, all with different-named directors but with the same email addresses and telephone numbers. It appeared to be a lazy attempt to conceal a circumvention of land laws in the country.

Following the data led our reporter James Kynge to the Preah Vihear province of Cambodia where a large Chinese sugar company was establishing a new $1bn sugarcane crushing facility. After being granted concessions, they seized the land of thousands of farmers who often had sacred and ancestral ties to the land and who were given no compensation.

Cambodia's land laws prohibit a single company from obtaining land concessions greater than 100sq. km. A representative of Heng Fu Sugar told our reporter openly that the company had skirted this law by setting up five separate companies – Heng Rui, Heng Yue, Heng Non, Rui Feng and Lan Feng – each one receiving a contiguous land concession slightly under the legal limit, according to the concession documents.

Thuang Sot, a 53-year-old farmer with six children, told the *FT* that Heng Fu Sugar had seized his land without offering him or thousands of other farmers any compensation. The company bulldozed large areas of jungle sacred to his ethnic group. The firm even burned the cemetery where his ancestors had been laid to rest, he added in an emotional interview.

These stories are just two of the many examples of cronyism and corruption found in the database compiled by Global Witness. But the human impact of these activities goes far beyond mere deception by firms to bypass the rules. The United Nations has long criticised land-grabs and the disregarding of human rights by Chinese companies in Cambodia. The government complains that Western investments come with conditions to improve democracy and human rights which goes some way to explain why Chinese interests own an area larger than the Netherlands and have been granted 60 per cent of all concessions given to foreign companies in the country since 1994.

Conclusions

The four examples used here are an attempt to show how open source software combined with manual inputs can overcome common challenges when pursuing investigative data stories: using web scraping and the APIs of websites such as Twitter to create datasets to examine bot-like accounts, semi-automating tasks for projects requiring manual collation as seen in the corporate jet and pension dumping case studies and, finally, utilising graphs alongside relational databases to examine China's corporate embrace of Cambodia.

Much of the information of interest to financial reporters is provided through third-party proprietary software which limits how investigative and data journalists can use it. But even the finite corporate data available publicly can be unlocked using technology alongside more traditional research methods to tell impactful human stories.

Notes

[1] See https://www.ft.com/europopulists?mhq5j=e1.

[2] https://www.ft.com/dutchvoting.

[3] https://www.ft.com/content/b1830ac2-07f4-11e7-97d1-5e720a26771b.

[4] http://ig.ft.com/sites/business-jets/.

[5] https://www.ft.com/content/f3f574fa-0f2c-11e7-a88c-50ba212dce4d?mhq5j=e1.

[6] https://www.ft.com/content/23968248-43a0-11e6-b22f-79eb4891c97d.

Note on the contributor

Leila Haddou is a data journalist for *The Times* and *The Sunday Times*. She formerly worked for the *Financial Times* investigations team exposing corporate fiddles to dump pensions, the dark side of China's corporate embrace in Cambodia and in-depth business profiles of political heavyweights including Philip Hammond. She previously worked for the *Guardian* covering offshore tax leaks, corporate land banking and issues surrounding social justice. She has an avid interest in the use of technology for data-led investigations and co-organises the monthly Journocoders meet-up event.

How journos are turning the data avalanche into the regional's daily splash

While data journalism has often been defined by eye-catching, ground-breaking projects, local journalism has been the place to bring stats stories to the masses. Claire Miller reports

Local journalists have always written data stories – on crime figures, GCSE results, unemployment rates and so on. But the amount of data available has increased, the tools for analysing it have become more accessible and the move to online news has opened up opportunities for presenting these stories in more interesting ways (Miller 2013: 4).

Local journalists were just as quick and keen to embrace data journalism as national and international news brands. However, since local newspapers draw from a broad demographic (politically as well as economically), with readers united chiefly by where they live or work, there is a particular need for data journalism to be not just locally relevant but clear and accessible. It should be important, or useful to people's daily lives. Data journalists on local titles typically have less time and resources, so innovation is key.

The UK's data journalism revolution

A number of factors emerged from around 2009 that both inspired the growth of local data journalism and laid the groundwork for the Trinity Mirror Data Unit. These included more data becoming available, the growing visibility of data journalism and the development of online content management systems that could do more than just host text versions of print stories. Simon Rogers, at the *Guardian* Datablog, once described data journalism as the new punk (Rogers 2012) – take a dataset, and maybe another, add some free analysis and visualisation tools and you've got data journalism.

The unit shares a lot of this attitude in terms of how we work and the content we produce – be ambitious, come up with as many ideas as possible, experiment with content and visualisations and interactives, go back and improve the things that work. The unit grew out of the idea that vast quantities of story-laden data were being routinely published or could be accessed through other means, such as scraping or the Freedom of Information Act, but that these stories were being missed due to lack of resources or skills.

A starting point

The Trinity Mirror Data Unit, set up in April 2013, divides its work into various streams, including long-term investigative projects, building tools to explore and visualise data – and news. In terms of news, the unit divides its output into two types – reactive and proactive, depending on how the data was obtained. Reactive stories are those which can be mined from datasets which are published by the Office for National Statistics, government departments, etc, and where the raw data is available and broken down into local units.

The unit can take this data, find lines of local importance and write bespoke copy for titles across the group which can be used 'as is' or built upon by local teams using local contacts and knowledge. Proactive stories are those where the data which underpins them is not published, at least in the form in which it is presented in the story. This category includes investigative stories where datasets are obtained using FOI; stories which involve scraping websites and stories in which different datasets are synthesised or correlated.

Either type of story may be suitable for some form of visualisation or an accompanying interactive gadget to allow people to explore the data. Either may form the basis of a longer-term data investigation or exploration of a particular issue. In any case, data stories need to pass a quality threshold, just like other news. Is this important? Is this interesting? And how can we tell this story to make it as engaging as possible for the widest possible audience?

You're in a newsroom: Find the news, set the agenda

The news element of the unit's work is run much like a normal newsroom. There is a diary based on potentially newsworthy upcoming statistical releases, daily conferences and news lists. While some data teams are set apart from other reporters and only work on long-term projects, we have always felt that we could maximise our value by also providing newsrooms with a stream of data-led exclusives.

Simply cleaning and analysing data released by the Office for National Statistics and government departments have allowed our journalists to break hard-hitting local stories, often months or years before the issues began to be felt at a national level. Data unit monitoring of regularly-published data on NHS performance meant we could reveal that the numbers delayed leaving hospital had reached a five-year high (*WalesOnline* 2015) two years before the winter crisis of 2016/17 when pressures on social care became more widespread headline news.

This approach can also prove a springboard for campaigns and further investigation into issues by newspapers across the group. For example, a data unit story about the fact the number of homelessness acceptances in two areas of Greater Manchester had jumped by 40 per cent led to a further exclusive about hidden homeless who were found living in caves in Stockport (*Manchester Evening News* 2013).

Most big stories don't just appear. Often, the roots of the issue can be seen in the data months or even years before crisis hits. Obtaining, analysing and writing about this data can expose vital stories that would otherwise get missed. It was precisely this sort of data which allowed the unit to produce a socially-shareable map showing how cuts hit councils across the country unevenly after the Conservatives' 2015 election victory (*Manchester Evening News* 2014a) or to dig out the soaring cost of hospital parking in an often-overlooked NHS report (*Birmingham Mail* 2016).

As well as building interactives for long-term projects, the unit has also developed quick turnaround interactives that make it easier for readers to explore the data behind stories. For example, templates can mean it's possible to produce a searchable round-up of changes to funding at school level, hours after the data has been published (*Coventry Telegraph* 2017).

Another hugely popular templated interactive allows people to look up how their MP voted on key issues. One version detailing how MPs voted on the bombing of Syria after the marathon 2 December 2015 debate was viewed 150,000 times on the *Mirror* website (*Mirror* 2015a). The set-up makes it simple for journalists across the group to re-use this gadget for different votes. It runs from a Google sheet, meaning reporters can simply update the information for each MP, choose a relevant title and sub-text, then copy the generated code into their CMS.

Finding stories proactively

While potentially interesting data is published on a regular basis, great stories are also to be found through FOI requests, scraping or bringing together datasets to get a new perspective on an issue, or find new correlations. The unit has used FOI extensively to produce scores of front-page exclusives such as the rising numbers of stress-related sick days among police officers (*GazetteLive* 2014), families waiting years for NHS negligence pay-outs (*Liverpool Echo* 2016), reported crimes by Uber drivers (*Mirror* 2016a) and the postcode lottery for police enforcement of middle-lane hogging (*Manchester Evening News* 2016a).

Bringing together several sources of data helps give deeper insight into an issue, such as highlighting the general unhealthiness of people's lifestyles across Britain (*Leicester Mercury* 2016) or digging into the impact of drugs and alcohol in different areas (*Mirror* 2016b).

Innovate and evolve

While employing people with coding, design and video skills has massively increased what the unit can do, a number of our big projects date back to when the unit started, when there were just two people in the team showing it is possible to take on ambitious projects and find workarounds to make those projects a reality.

The 'Real Schools Guide' was an attempt to go a step beyond the normal exam-based league tables that have long been a staple of newspapers. The idea was to take advantage of the vast quantity of school-level data that is published to give a more comprehensive overview of how schools are performing (*Manchester Evening News* 2016b). The guide has two main elements: the first is a nationwide scoring system that takes into account not just examination performance but also progress, attendance and outcomes for different groups of pupils. The second is a database with a detailed page of data for each school, showing performance over time.

The original versions of these pages were written in simple Javascript using an ID code for each school to look up the data, stored in a Google Fusion table, needed to populate graphs and tables on a page. The HTML for each page was created in bulk – but the individual pages needed to be created by hand. Over the past five years the pages that make up the schools guide have racked up millions of views and both the pages and process for creating them have evolved and expanded. Employing a graphic designer means the pages look better, while employing coders means the system for uploading the pages has become better automated.

Another popular perennial that has evolved over time are the tools used to gather fan player ratings for football, rugby and other sports. These began life as Google Surveys (*WalesOnline* 2013a) that were turned into gauges and charts to show results in real time. While these, too, have changed with the addition of specialised design and coding staff (*GetWestLondon* 2015), they show it is entirely possible to create useful interactives that engage readers with even simple, freely-available tools.

One of the unit's best-read early interactives was one that allowed readers to compare the popularity of different baby names over time. That was built in Tableau, which provided all the functionality required (*WalesOnline* 2013b). The basic shape of the interactive stayed the same over the years even as it moved to a version that was specifically coded for the Trinity Mirror sites (and, more importantly, looked and worked better on mobile devices) (*Examiner* 2016).

Making complex data readable

While technology and coding skills open up new ways of presenting complex datasets to readers, an interactive is only as good as the idea behind it. The growing availability of data broken down to often tiny geographies offers huge opportunities but also brings huge challenges in terms of design.

Consider the *English Index of Multiple Deprivation*, a publication that takes data on a number of factors and uses them to quantify the relative deprivation of small areas across the country. It is produced by Oxford Consultants for Social Inclusion on behalf of the government. It is easy to boil this down to a list of the most deprived areas in the country or to make a map with many colours but not much meaning, but is this the most interesting and engaging solution? The unit felt the best way to give people an insight into this data was to build an interactive that allowed them to type their postcode and see where the neighbourhood they lived fell on the scale of relative deprivation, both overall and for each individual domain (*Mirror* 2015b). Doing this turned a potentially dry story into one that readers really related to, with 92,000 views on the *Mirror* alone. It allowed us to share much more detailed information in an interesting way that worked on every device.

The key element in local journalism is location. Every story written turns on that factor. Building postcode-search interactives allows us to personalise data and let the reader explore what matters to them. It opens up opportunities to tell as many stories as there are postcodes in a way that simply would not be possible with a 300-word story.

The Data Unit's World War I interactive is based on exclusive access given by the Commonwealth War Graves Commission to their incredibly-detailed records of more than one million casualties of the war. The unit was able to turn this not only into bespoke graphics and stories for each town in the country but also into an interactive used by millions of people which allowed them to search for casualties by first name, surname, town or street – or a combination of these (*Manchester Evening News* 2014b).

Tools for the newsroom

While much of the unit's work is focused on storytelling, we also put our resources to work building tools for newsrooms that can be reused and repurposed. Many of these come from suggestions of what would be useful – such as an interactive allowing people to check their finishing position and time in local runs (*Manchester Evening News* 2015) or a league predictor tool letting fans work out where their team might end up (*Chronicle Live* 2015).

Adding value is often key in designing newsroom tools. The unit's 'Find My Seat' interactive, used in the run-up to the general election, aimed to give readers not only a list of candidates and past results but a real insight into issues in their area, using a range of local indicators – on topics like health, the economy and demography – and how these compared with other areas and how they had changed since the last election.

The unit also builds a range of interactives to display election results live on the night. These have included a fully-automated interactive combining the live PA xml feed with a rolling tally of seats, a map and an option to search for constituencies, which was the single most-read piece of election content on *MirrorOnline* in 2017 (*Mirror* 2017). For council and devolved parliaments, the unit has also created an interactive that takes results entered by reporters into a pre-prepared Google sheet and turns it instantaneously into a live results service on our websites (*WalesOnline* 2016).

Functionality, originality and innovation are as much as part of the unit's work now as they were in the days when it began. You don't need to have a data unit to turn the huge amount of data available to local and regional journalists into great content – just a willingness to learn some data journalism skills, an ability to think your way around problems, and a good old-fashioned news sense.

References

Birmingham Mail (2016) Birmingham Children's Hospital DOUBLES patient parking charges, 21 October. Available online at http://www.birminghammail.co.uk/news/midlands-news/birmingham-childrens-hospital-doubles-patient-12051480

Chronicle Live (2015) Newcastle United survival battle: Use our predictor to work out whether the Magpies are going to stay up, 8 May. Available online at http://www.chroniclelive.co.uk/sport/football/football-news/newcastle-united-survival-battle-use-9220758

Coventry Telegraph (2017) New schools funding formula: Cuts will affect your school and this is how, 22 March. Available online at http://www.coventrytelegraph.net/news/coventry-news/new-schools-funding-formula-cuts-12779681

GazetteLive (2014) Cleveland Police: Number of sick days taken by officers for mental health reasons up 267%, 11 February. Available online at http://www.gazettelive.co.uk/news/teesside-news/cleveland-police-number-sick-days-6695054

GetWestLondon (2015) Who did you vote for as Chelsea's player of the season?, 28 May. Available online at http://www.getwestlondon.co.uk/sport/football/football-news/who-you-vote-chelseas-player-9346108

Huddersfield Examiner (2016) Interactive: Which are the most popular baby names? Enter yours to see where you rank, 7 September. Available online at http://www.examiner.co.uk/news/west-yorkshire-news/interactive-most-popular-baby-names-11851247

Leicester Mercury (2016) How healthy is Leicester and Leicestershire? Use your postcode to find out how your area ranks, 17 August. Available online at http://www.leicestermercury.co.uk/how-healthy-is-leicester-and-leicestershire-use-your-postcode-to-find-our-how-your-area-ranks/story-29630476-detail/story.html

Liverpool Echo (2016) Family's £7.3m. payout for negligence case against Liverpool Women's Hospital, 26 November. Available online at http://www.liverpoolecho.co.uk/news/liverpool-news/familys-73m-payout-negligence-case-12232534

Manchester Evening News (2013) Scandal of Greater Manchester's hidden homeless forced to seek shelter in caves, 12 June. Available online at http://www.manchestereveningnews.co.uk/news/greater-manchester-news/scandal-greater-manchesters-hidden-homeless-4303590

Manchester Evening News (2014a) Cameron slashes Manchester's 'spending power' by £28m. (but Surrey's goes up by £27m.), 22 December. Available online at http://www.manchestereveningnews.co.uk/news/greater-manchester-news/cameron-slashes-manchesters-spending-power-8313554

Manchester Evening News (2014b) World War One: Use our widget to search for anyone in your family or your street who died in the Great War, 5 November. Available online at http://www.manchestereveningnews.co.uk/news/nostalgia/world-war-one-search-soldiers-7519123

Manchester Evening News (2015) Great Manchester Run 2015: Check your finishing time and position here, 11 August. Available online at http://www.manchestereveningnews.co.uk/news/greater-manchester-news/great-manchester-run-2015-check-9219781

Manchester Evening News (2016a) How GMP have tackled middle-lane hogging and other daft driving over last three years, 4 September. Available online at http://www.manchestereveningnews.co.uk/news/greater-manchester-news/police-careless-inconsiderate-driving-fines-11839881

Manchester Evening News (2016b) Abraham Guest Academy, 1 July. Available online at http://www.manchestereveningnews.co.uk/news/local-news/abraham-guest-academy-7540212

Miller, Claire (2013) Getting started with data journalism: Writing data stories in any size newsroom, *Leanpub.com*. Available online at https://leanpub.com/datajournalism

Mirror (2015a) How did my MP vote on bombing Syria? Search full results after marathon Commons debate, 3 December. Available online at http://www.mirror.co.uk/news/uk-news/how-mp-vote-bombing-syria-6942117

Mirror (2015b) The 20 most deprived places in England revealed - how does your area compare?, 30 September. Available online at http://www.mirror.co.uk/news/uk-news/10-worst-deprived-places-england-6548105

Mirror (2016a) Woman claims she was raped by Uber driver on back seat after night out, 3 September. Available online at http://www.mirror.co.uk/news/uk-news/woman-claims-raped-uber-driver-8759773

Mirror (2016b) Top 10 worst places for drink and drugs revealed – tap in your postcode to see how your area compares, 9 December. Available online at http://www.mirror.co.uk/news/uk-news/top-10-worst-places-drink-9421076

Mirror (2017) Who won the 2017 general election? Full results and map with every constituency as Tories endure shocking night, 10 June. Available online at http://www.mirror.co.uk/news/politics/who-won-2017-general-election-10588118

Rogers, Simon (2012) Anyone can do it. Data journalism is the new punk, *Guardian*, 24 May. Available online at https://www.theguardian.com/news/datablog/2012/may/24/data-journalism-punk

WalesOnline (2013a) British and Irish Lions tour 2013: Live fans' stat pad from Lions v Western Force, 5 June. Available online at http://www.walesonline.co.uk/sport/rugby/rugby-news/british-irish-lions-tour-2013-4051925

WalesOnline (2013b) Royal baby name: How the contenders for the name of the new royal baby have fared over the years, 23 July. Available online at http://www.walesonline.co.uk/news/wales-news/royal-baby-name-how-contenders-5262616#.Ue5Ldd_cWwM.twitter

WalesOnline (2015) Bed-blocking levels on acute wards hit almost five-year high, new figures reveal, 26 March. Available online at http://www.walesonline.co.uk/news/health/bed-blocking-levels-acute-wards-hit-8923335

WalesOnline (2016) Assembly election 2016 full results as they happen, 6 May. Available online at http://www.walesonline.co.uk/news/politics/assembly-election-2016-full-results-11292057

Note on the contributor

Claire Miller is the Deputy Head of Data Journalism at the Trinity Mirror Data Unit and the winner of two Regional Press Awards, one for the *WalesOnline* Datastore and one as part of the Data Unit, and a Data Journalism Award for investigative reporting.

Using data journalism in local media

The seemingly chronic decline of local journalism comes alongside the vast increase in data available to journalists. According to Adam Cantwell-Corn and Lucas Batt, of *The Bristol Cable*, this development presents an opportunity to address some of the key weaknesses affecting both local journalism and data journalism in a mutually beneficial way

One of the central and valid critiques of data journalism is that a fundamental element of successful journalism is often missing (or hidden) among the numbers and visualisations: The human angle that brings trends, charts and statistics down from the abstract and into people's living rooms and conversations. Not all data stories need a clichéd human case study, though the inclusion often provides the necessary hook into a story that otherwise may be dense. While this is hardly an original observation and many data journalists are keenly aware of this, the challenges and difficulties of humanising and making public interest data interesting to the public remains.

In the meantime, local publications, whether they be corporate titles or new models such as *The Bristol Cable* (*thebristocable.org*), are grappling with the challenges of trying to recover or reinvent what has been lost for many years by most local media: namely, a strong sense of individual and communal affiliation with a local news source (that ideally leads to revenue either through sales, clicks or membership subscriptions in the case of the *Cable*).[1] Part of the problem-solving for local publications is to avoid myopic localism by engaging with national and international issues, providing context and insight into our interconnected world, while at the same time tapping into local identities, histories and idiosyncrasies that make journalism pertinent and relevant to people's families and communities.

In sum, much of data journalism needs engaging human stories to lift it off the page and local journalism sorely needs stories that meet the dual standards of engaging local communities as well as providing the wider context and trends that surround it.

Indeed, while there are clearly issues with resources, capacity and skills, it seems there is ample opportunity for data journalism to flourish particularly in a geographically-defined area: the impact of data journalism can be amplified where people know first-hand the implications of data concerning neighbourhoods, the latest big housing development, hospitals, schools and local authorities.

The recent history of austerity in local government has presented problems for local journalists. Redundancies and cutbacks have hit council departmental teams, meaning that compliance with the FOI Act is routinely delayed and the publishing of open data is slow or non-existent. Another major factor is the restructuring and reshuffling of council departments and areas of responsibilities, sometimes on an annual basis. For the data journalist, using comparator data sets over a period of years to search for trends and anomalies becomes very difficult with the regular changes in database structuring, maintenance, language and content.

With an emphasis on issues specific to local journalism, here are some thoughts and several examples where *The Bristol Cable* has produced data journalism on a local level.

Interactive: The real reason thousands of Bristolians don't vote? 15 April 2016

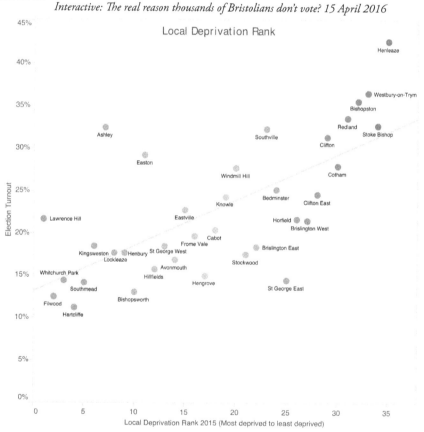

Deprived of the vote: The real reason Bristolians don't vote?

Much is often made of the reasons for low turnout at elections. Anecdotes abound, but one strength of data journalism is to highlight trends using evidence. In the run-up to the 2016 election for the Mayor of Bristol we sought to provide a backdrop and add explanatory power to a startlingly low 27 per cent turnout in the first election in 2012.

We layered 2012 ward level voter turnout with data taken from a subset of the *Indices of Multiple Deprivation*, the UK government's qualitative study of deprived areas in English local councils. The data demonstrated a definitive trend. The five least deprived wards in the city recorded the highest turnout and four of the five most deprived wards showed extremely low levels of voting. While the main figure used in the press was the average turnout of 27 per cent, the data showed a range of 11 to 42 per cent, providing a much richer context for voter disengagement. To display the data, we used a choropleth map ranked by level of deprivation, with the electoral turnout labelled on each ward, making geographic navigation and disparities easily navigable. An additional scatter plot showing deprivation versus turnout clearly demonstrated the trend.

The data was complemented by interviews with residents in the area to add a 'human' and qualitative element to the bigger picture. Such analysis could feed into debates around voter apathy, in particular challenging individual-centred explanations for voter disengagement versus measurable social and economic factors.

Investigating working conditions in the catering sector

Operating in a relatively small area presents particular opportunities for the modern desk-bound journalist to peel themselves away from the keyboard and collect data from the surrounding areas. In the following example, this was particularly important when encountering absences in data.

The first investigation the *Cable* undertook was such a case: a survey of employment and working conditions in the city's hospitality sector. Finding there was no data produced on a national or local level, either by government, trade unions or others, *Cable* journalists designed a methodology and survey that could capture an indicative cross-section of the city's hospitality workforce. In order to have 95 per cent confidence that our results were representative with a 10 per cent margin of error in a total population of 14,500, the required sample size needed to be at least 96. The final survey compiled results from

Laurence Ware

102 people in different job roles across 35 establishments, large, small, independent and chain.

While there is a general understanding that working conditions in the catering sector are not good, the results gave qualitative and quantitative indications of a sector where 50 per cent of those surveyed had a zero hours contract or no contract at all, or where 70 per cent worked more than set hours yet 40 per cent of these respondents reported they were not fully paid for these extra hours. As the data was the first of its kind in the sector, the research was subsequently featured on a prominent BBC Radio 4 programme on the topic.

Crowdsourcing and external partners

Data journalism is best when done collaboratively, both in and between newsrooms. This is something the Bureau Local, a project of the Bureau of Investigative Journalism, is seeking to emphasise. The project employs a small team of data journalists to uncover or create important national datasets which can be made useful and unique across local newsrooms. Their initial approach is to partner with trusted news organisations on specific projects and encourage collaboration on a closed online forum.

The Bristol Cable worked on the two of these first projects with the Bureau Local. The first of these related to how specific groups of voters could affect the outcome of the 2017 General Election. The project centred on relevant datasets collated by the Bureau Local, including modelling by statisticians. This data was released on a day when five locations around the UK hosted events with participants who shared ideas and findings in a closed online chat room. With the statisticians on hand, they were able to update the modelling as local feedback informed how the model might need to be improved.

The data demonstrated the potential power of electoral coalitions between parties or within constituencies regarding tactical voting. This drove the impetus to publish an online article on tactical voting in Bristol, exploring how alliances between various parties might have changed the 2015 General Election results. The research was compiled by a custom-built bar chart gadget where various filters could be explored. Primarily, though, we provided a short analysis for each constituency. This breakdown simplified a complex array of information into relevant sections, while also providing readers with the opportunity to explore the data themselves in a more interactive way. But the gadget was not relied upon as the primary storytelling device so as to not risk losing important information inside a restrictive interactive element.

The second project we worked on with the Bureau Local related to Facebook advertisements during the General Election campaign. Partnering with the Bureau Local, a group called Who Targets Me? built a browser extension which could record the Facebook adverts served to the user who installed it. We published an article encouraging people in Bristol to install the extension, explaining we would be working on an investigation using the data.

The Bureau Local provided *The Bristol Cable* with the local results which we were able to analyse and use in an article. News organisations across the UK were also provided with local versions of the dataset and dozens of unique stories were published using the crowdsourced data. In Bristol, 268 people installed the extension. Although our data collection is far less sophisticated than Facebook's and our sample size and scope disproportionately populated by younger males in the constituency of Bristol West, we did see interesting trends.

With only our users' age, constituency and gender, it was hard to see whether people were being targeted by parties for these characteristics or because of Facebook's other algorithmic 'under-the-hood' data. However, we did see that 'dementia tax' adverts attacking the Conservative Party's controversial social care policy was served by Labour and the Lib Dems only to Facebook users over 50 years old. A Conservative advertisement warning Labour leader Jeremy Corbyn would reduce defence spending was only spotted in Bristol North West, closest to the major aerospace manufacturing and Ministry of Defence hubs in Filton.

The significance of such a story, as with much of the journalism we do at the *Cable*, is to bring stories of national and international importance, in this case the power of big data in elections, to a level of relevance and proximity for our local readers.

Where to find data and what to do with it

Bristol City Council holds a lot of important data which is only accessible through Freedom of Information requests. This is, unfortunately, a slow process as often requests are delayed for months. The requests are necessary, however, as the council's approach to open data is apathetic, neatly expressed by a Freedom of Information officer's surprise when we informed him the council had an open data portal: 'No one told me!'

We have, however, acquired important datasets from the council. One instance is a list of social housing properties sold by auction in recent years. This helped add context to the local debate and protest surrounding the open auctioning of council houses. We did two things with this dataset. Firstly, we batch geo-located the addresses using a free online tool and then mapped it using another free online tool, Carto. Using the 'torque' temporal mapping feature on the column containing data about when properties had been auctioned and tweaking the CSS to force the dots to remain after they appeared, the map showed where and when council houses in Bristol had been sold.

There was plenty more we could find out; however, it would require a lot of additional time. Following the basic question: 'Did the council achieve a decent deal at auction?' we used Import.Io to build a scraper using available price paid data from the Land Registry. With this, we found the sale price as well as the subsequent resale prices.

The results were surprising and the data was immediately compelling: most of the properties had been resold for substantially larger sums. As we were dealing with hundreds of properties over a large date range, we decided to focus on a defined subset: 23 properties resold by the initial private buyer within one year of their original council auction, since 2009. This would limit the amount of variables at play and place all of the sold dates beyond the financial crash of 2007/8.

Still, we were aware that there were a lot of variables to consider. One way in which we accounted for this was by finding the average property market changes for the MLSOA (Middle Layer Super Output Area) of each property between each sale. By using the expected percentage change, we found to what extent the property conformed to general market trends. And we conducted a planning history search for all properties to determine if any significant changes had been made in the relevant period.

The council's policy for auctioning properties was to do so only when the cost to repair would be more than £20,000. However, the *Cable's* research showed that, of the 23 properties auctioned since 2009 and then resold within a year, 10 were sold with a mark-up double that of the council's repairs limit. Three properties were sold for a huge increase of 60 per cent less than 230 days after the council auction and a further eight sold for more than 40 per cent their auction price within a matter of months. The vast majority of properties were sold for significantly more than the council's anticipated repair costs of more than £20,000. Some properties saw huge daily increases in value up to the point of sale, such as £544-a-day for 172 days and £413-a-day for 226 days.

Although the Mayor at the time made robust arguments in favour of the sales, the investigation again highlighted the need for scrutiny on the wisdom and manner of selling public assets. Moreover, following our investigation and parallel public outcry, the newly-elected mayoral administration initiated an immediate moratorium on private auctions of council properties.

Going once, twice, sold ... then sold again. 18 July 2016

BOOMING ... BUT WELL BEYOND THE MARKET

This graph shows the increase from auction price to sale price corrected for rising property prices. Within just one year properties were sold for a lot more than they were bought from the council. This means that 3 properties were sold for a huge increase of 60% less than 230 days at er the council auction, and a further 8 sold for over 40% their auction price within a matter of months. The vast majority of properties were sold for significantly more than the council's anticipated repair costs of more than £20,000. Some properties saw huge daily increases such as £544 for 172 days and £413 for 226 days.

% 20 – 30 (2 houses)

% 40 – 50 (5 houses)

% 0 – 10 (3 houses)

% 50 – 64 (6 houses)

% 10 – 20 (5 houses)

% -17 (1 house)

INCREASE IN % FROM AUCTION TO RESALE (MARKET ADJUSTED)

Toast of Bristol

Conclusion

Data presents a great opportunity to bring local media firmly into the digital age, particularly with the increasing data literacy of both journalists and the general public. Yet with emerging trends and technology much of the challenges remain the same: telling compelling stories and obtaining the resources to do so!

Note

[1] *The Bristol Cable* describes itself as 'a pioneering media co-operative – so far owned by over 1,800 members as of September 2017 who can all have a say in how we are run. We produce a free quarterly magazine, regularly publishing website, and run media training and local events which are free or cheap for members. Our aim is to redefine media ownership, bringing it back from corporate control into the hands of ordinary people. We want local news to be investigative, inclusive and relevant; holding our representatives to account is important'. See https://thebristolcable.org/about/

Note on the contributors

Lucas Batt is a coordinator at *The Bristol Cable*, overseeing distribution, web, and analytics. Lucas also produces the occasional data-driven story in collaboration with other journalists in the *Cable*.

Adam Cantwell-Corn is a co-founder of *The Bristol Cable*. Adam currently works on multiple aspects of the co-operative including project development, editorial and admin.

Catering investigation: Laurence Ware

Council house sales: Toast of Bristol

Data journalism in a cold climate: The case of the *Ferret*

Recent years have seen a marked increase in the number of digital journalism start-ups, with many new outlets establishing as co-operatives (Hunter et al. 2013). But there is a relative lack of detailed, empirical research about such outfits and their approach to data journalism. This chapter seeks to address this gap by examining the work of the *Ferret*, an investigative journalism co-operative launched in Scotland in 2015 that the author co-founded and co-directs. By Peter Geoghegan

Introduction

The last decade and a half has seen the emergence of a plethora of digital journalism start-ups (Jarvis 2011; Price 2017). Some of the biggest players in this nascent media market – *Vice, Buzzfeed, Huffington Post* – are funded predominantly by the traditional advertisement-led model augmented by advertorial and other curated content. At the same time, there has also been a growth in alternative approaches to building sustainable journalism start-ups, particularly among outfits dedicated to investigative and public service journalism. In the United States, for example, the 'not for profit newsroom' *ProPublica* has won Pulitzer prizes. *ProPublica* is one of a number of independent publishers funded mainly through philanthropic donations (Uskali and Kuutti 2015). There has been a similar emergence of new digital outlets in Europe and Australia (Carvajal, García-Avilés and González 2012; McChesney 2016) with a number establishing themselves as co-operatives (Hunter et al. 2013).

I was among the small team that launched the *Ferret* as a digital investigative platform in Scotland in the summer of 2015. It was established by professional journalists, mainly freelance, partly in response to the retrenchment of local media in Scotland and the withdrawal of limited resources from investigative journalism over the previous decade (Geoghegan 2016). The *Ferret* aims to provide independent investigative journalism that 'noses up the trousers of power' (Price 2017). There is also a conscious appeal to community and educative values: the *Ferret* is registered as a co-operative and administered by a mix of journalists and readers while it is funded from a variety of sources including subscriptions, crowd-funding, grants, training and events.

As Price (2017: 3) points out, in its origins, the *Ferret* bears some interesting similarities to the larger and more established French online investigative journal, *Mediapart*, which was founded in 2008. As with the French start-up, the *Ferret* consciously sought to respond to a series of democratic, economic and ethical crises facing journalism in its home country. Over the past decade, Scotland's devolved parliament has become more powerful and the focus on Scottish issues more pronounced. At the same time, the financial clout of the Scottish press decreased sharply (Geoghegan 2014). Scotland used to boast one of the highest concentrations of newspaper readers in the world. In 2005, the *Scotsman* had more than 500 journalists and production staff. By 2016, that figure had fallen to just 130. Sales of the Glasgow *Daily Record* fell by 63.5 per cent between 1992 and 2011 (Geoghegan 2016). Scottish journalism has gone through these democratic and economic challenges at the same time as the wider industry has faced serious ethical questions in the wake of phone-hacking and other revelations of press malfeasance (Franklin 2014).

The *Ferret* deliberately sought to address the perceived legitimacy gap between journalists and audiences by affording would-be readers a say in its journalism from its inception. At its launch, readers were asked to vote on their favourite of three potential investigations: NHS cuts, asylum seekers or fracking. Almost 800 people took part, with fracking topping the vote. A crowdfunding campaign was launched in July 2015, with a target of £3,800, to fund the fracking investigation. The campaign raised almost three times its target. The money funded a lengthy investigation involving FOI requests, document searches and interviews which produced a lengthy series on fracking. The crowdfunding campaign also 'boot strapped' the *Ferret* financially to do more work and to begin attracting subscribers. By April 2017, the *Ferret* had more than 500 subscribers paying between £3-a-month and £100-a-year for full content access. The *Ferret* has won a number of journalism awards and, in the spring of 2017, launched a fact service (FFS) backed by a one-year, €50,000 Google Digital News Initiative grant.

The *Ferret*'s model reflects a long-standing entrepreneurial approach to journalism (Rafter 2016). Pioneering English journalist Daniel Defoe (1660-1731) and Edinburgh's 18th century pamphleteers were supported by subscriptions and patrons. The *Economist* and the *New Yorker* today rely predominantly on subscriptions, too. But the *Ferret* has attempted to expand the range of reader engagement beyond the bare cash transaction by actively asking readers what subjects they would like to see investigated. The *Ferret* also seeks to build trust between audience and journalists through its institutional structures. Every subscriber is automatically a member of the co-operative with full voting rights and readers are represented on the project's board. In this way, the *Ferret* fits neatly into what Hunter and Van Wassenhove (2010) call 'stakeholder media': i. e. media that serves communities who believe that they cannot obtain comparable quality of information or coverage of their issues of concern in mainstream media outlets.

Somewhat unwittingly, the *Ferret* has broadly followed Porlezza and Splendore's (2016) guidance for best ethical practice for journalism start-ups by publishing mission statements and reports of finances. The *Ferret* also runs regular public events that frequently mix workshops and skills transfer and live debates and discussion. It has built sustainable revenue streams but does not yet support a full-time staff beyond a fact-checker funded through the Google grant – while the five journalist directors on the nine-strong board are paid a small monthly retainer. The organisation manages to keep its overheads down to less than £150 per month. The vast majority of the *Ferret*'s revenue is spent on journalism, with much of this being 'data journalism'. I will now outline the contours of the *Ferret*'s contribution to data journalism and put this work in the context of its wider attempts to encourage active, reciprocal engagement within and between its user community.

The *Ferret*'s data journalism

That data journalism has transformed newsrooms in the digital age has become something of a truism (Bradshaw 2014). On the one hand, journalism has always relied on 'data' in some form, but technological advances and a proliferation of new sources of information has radically changed the scale and scope for storytelling, particularly online. Data journalism techniques and approaches have become mainstream. The *Washington Post*, *The New York Times*, *CNN*, the *Guardian* and others have all invested heavily in data journalists and graphics teams. Stories based on huge FOI trawls or massive information leaks have become ever more frequent. But among local and regional press, shrinking staff and resources mean many journalists have limited capacity to create and visualise data stories and have struggled to integrate new digital advancements into their online story offering (Gray, Chambers and Bounegru 2012).

Many of the *Ferret*'s journalist directors came to the project with significant experience of data journalism and a degree of frustration at the limited use of these approaches in Scottish newsrooms. As well as looking to create a sustainable platform for investigative journalism, the *Ferret* hoped to innovate in terms of storytelling, using the capabilities and possibilities afforded by digital production to present stories in new ways. In June 2016, the *Ferret* published 'A second Syria' by London-based freelance journalist Brindusa Ioana Nastasa. This story charted the journey of Syrian refugees to a new life in Turkey through interlaced text, video, photography and interactive audio. Such an approach has rarely been taken by other Scottish media outlets and the story formed part of an award-nominated entry by the *Ferret* on the plight of refugees.

Such ambitious storytelling remains more the exception than the norm for the *Ferret*, in large part due to the financial outlay required. In general, the *Ferret*'s engagement with data journalism has largely pivoted around three key areas: creating and visualising data sets, data scraping and mapping data sets to allow readers to explore material independently. Let's look at each of these three in turn.

Creating data sets

The *Ferret* is – quite literally – a product of freedom of information. The small collective that became the founders of the project began as a closed email group for Scottish journalists to discuss FOI requests and to advise one another on strategies for overcoming official intransigence. Consequently, freedom of information has formed a backbone of the *Ferret's* work, often using information released by FOI to build larger data sets that lead to original stories. As part of the *Ferret's* first fracking investigation, a series of FOI requests were used to identify and map areas of Scotland where companies had bid for onshore oil and gas licences. At the time, the Scottish government had introduced a moratorium on fracking. The *Ferret* investigation revealed a series of new stories including that a pro-fracking consultant had been contracted by the Scottish government to examine the environmental impact of onshore oil and gas. In early 2017, the Scottish government launched a public consultation on fracking, in part as a result of civil society pressure. Privately, a government official said that the *Ferret's* work played a significant role in this decision.

For its journalist directors, part of the appeal of creating – and joining – the *Ferret* was the opportunity to work collaboratively. Even in the halcyon days of the Scottish press, investigative journalists were few in number, often left to work in very small teams or, more commonly, alone. The *All the President's Men* image of clandestine meetings belies the reality that much of the most successful investigative journalism is a product of group endeavour (Houston 2010). For the *Ferret's* journalists forming a co-operative was a way to work more closely together.

One example was a major probe into investments held by Scottish universities. The investigation, in the summer of 2016, was based on FOI requests submitted to every Scottish university. As a task for a single journalist, the story would have taken a significant – and almost certainly prohibitive – length of time. Instead, each of the *Ferret's* journalist directors took responsibility for sending two-to-three FOI requests – all worded identically – and contributed to building a database of all university investments from the resultant responses. Once the database was complete, one journalist took responsibility for analysing the investments against the various universities' stated corporate social responsibility aims. The result was a front page story in the *Sunday Mail* and a longer piece on the *Ferret* that included an Excel spreadsheet of all university investments that the public could search and analyse. The *Ferret* has also run numerous workshops on freedom of information and access to information. The aim of these events is both to create a stronger relationship between the *Ferret* community and its journalists and to empower and educate active citizens who can go on to access information themselves and understand in more depth their wider civic rights and responsibilities.

Data scraping

Coding is an increasingly important part of journalism, particularly investigative work (Gray, Chambers and Bounegru 2012). While coding remains a minority concern, the number of journalists who can code is rising, and computer programmers have come to play an ever larger role in newsrooms. As noted, Scottish journalism has been slow to take up technological developments, making the presence of a 'coder-director' on the *Ferret* board particularly novel. Data scraping – using a computer program to extract data from another program – has become a common journalistic technique (Fink and Anderson 2015). The *Ferret* has built scraping tools to allow it to build data sets from publicly accessible information that has journalistic value. One example of this was in February 2017 when journalist- and coder-directors worked together to scrape data from the Facebook pages of all the major UK and Scottish political parties. This data led to an extensive investigation that charted the success of the far-right on social media. It also produced 16 spreadsheet files recording every Facebook post made by the major UK and Scottish political parties. These files were made publicly available via the *Ferret* site with readers invited to examine the data themselves and alert journalists to any interesting information they came across.

Mapping open data

As of April 2017, the *Ferret* had published more than 250 original stories with a notable increase in subscription rates on the back of strong content. Some of these stories were published in tandem with major outlets and received widespread attention. Many were the product of extensive investigations involving multiple sources over lengthy periods of time. But the most popular story the *Ferret* published was one of its briefest.

In May 2016, the International Consortium of Investigative Journalists (ICIJ) published edited extracts from the Panama Papers, a leak of 11.5 million documents from Panamanian law firm Mossack Fonseca. The *Ferret* mapped all 4,835 UK addresses in the ICIJ database using Google fusion tables. The resulting map was published on the *Ferret* community forum alongside a short blog post inviting subscribers to investigate the data (with the added proviso that publication of the addresses did not amount to any accusation of wrong-doing). The Tumblr post was shared more than 1,500 times on social media. Elsewhere, the *Ferret* has mapped open data such as complaints against private sector care home providers upheld by the Care Inspectorate in Scotland. The *Ferret* website contains a database of the source documents used in its stories, which allows subscribers to search data for themselves and examine what is most relevant to their lives.

Conclusion

Stakeholder media has been identified by some as a possible solution to the crisis of funding journalism (Hunter et al. 2013). In an increasingly atomised public sphere, where established media players have struggled to regain trust and legitimacy, co-operatives have been held up as a model for a more democratic form of media that speaks directly to specific interest groups (Rootwilm 2014). Concerns about echo chambers aside (see Flaxman, Goel and Rao 2016), the *Ferret's* experience suggests co-operative approaches could potentially offer a sustainable model for its investigative journalism. In less than two years, the *Ferret* website garnered almost three-quarters of a million page views, despite operating a porous paywall that allows three free page views a month. In the second year, turnover and subscriptions were set to double and the project secured significant grant-funding from a major media player.

The *Ferret's* stories have been frequently cited in debates in the Scottish parliament on everything from workers' rights in Amazon warehouses to the treatment of asylum seekers in the Scottish system. It has also brought issues of data journalism on to the political agenda in Scotland. *Ferret* journalists have been at the forefront of an on-going campaign to highlight concerns about how Freedom of Information legislation has been interpreted by the Scottish government. This has prompted two debates at the Scottish parliament in Edinburgh.

But challenges remain for the *Ferret* and its co-operative model. It has achieved slow and steady growth but it is heavily dependent on a largely unpaid core team of journalists and a relatively small active community. In an effort to retain as much resources as possible for journalism, the *Ferret* operates a disaggregated newsroom with journalists spread across Scotland. Slack allows the *Ferret* to communicate online with separate channels open for different investigations and projects. Monthly board meetings guide overarching strategy and more regular informal meetings between board members and contributors help coordinate specific stories and investigations. But, as *Ferret* journalists are not in the same physical space, the capacity for co-working can be constrained, particularly on intensive investigative work that often relies on 'Eureka' moments. At the time same time, turning a largely passive online readership into an active community requires intensive engagement, particularly through events which can be time-consuming and often force journalists beyond their newsroom comfort zone.

The challenges for the *Ferret* mirror those facing other stakeholder media. The internet has lowered the barrier to entry for new outlets and given comparatively niche publications the opportunity to connect up with segmented communities that possess the social and financial capital to form viable businesses (Naldi and Picard 2012). But many journalists struggle to think – and act – like businesspeople. As Price (2017) notes, the growth of digital start-ups in the US has shown that new media outlets need to move beyond concentrating only on producing 'good journalism' and towards cultivating larger and more diversified revenue streams. The *Ferret* remains overwhelmingly reliant on subscriber funding for its core business but risks burnout of key members without the injection of fresh capital in the medium-term. Yet the evidence from the *Ferret* strongly suggests that quality still remains the *sine qua non* of any successful journalism start-up and that co-operative models could play a useful part in a wider sustainable journalistic eco-system.

References

Bradshaw, Paul (2014) What is data journalism?, Zion, Lawrie and Craig, David (eds) *Ethics for Digital Journalists: Emerging Best Practices,* Abington, Oxon: Routledge pp 202-219

Carvajal, Miguel, García-Avilés, José A. and González, José L. (2012) Crowdfunding and non-profit media: The emergence of new models for public interest journalism, *Journalism Practice,* Vol. 6, Nos 5-6 pp 638-647

Fink, Katherine and Anderson, Christopher W. (2015) Data journalism in the United States: Beyond the 'usual suspects', *Journalism Studies,* Vol. 16, No. 4 pp 467-481

Flaxman, Seth, Goel, Sharad and Rao, Justin M. (2016) Filter bubbles, echo chambers and online news consumption, *Public Opinion Quarterly,* Vol. 80, Special Issue pp 298-320

Franklin, Bob (2014) The future of journalism: In an age of digital media and economic uncertainty, Journalism Studies, Vol. 15, No. 5 pp 481-499

Geoghegan, Peter (2014) *The People's Referendum: Why Scotland Will Never Be the Same Again,* Edinburgh: Luath Press

Geoghegan, Peter (2016) The end of the Scottish press?, *London Review of Books,* Vol. 38, No. 8 pp 201-221

Gray, Jonathan, Chambers, Lucy and Bounegru, Liliana (2012) *The Data Journalism Handbook,* Sebastopol, CA: O'Reilly Media

Houston, Brant (2010) The future of investigative journalism, *Daedalus,* Vol. 139, No. 2 pp 45-56

Hunter, Mark Lee and Van Wassenhove, Luk N. (2010) *Disruptive News Technologies: Stakeholder Media and the Future of Watchdog Journalism Business Models,* Fontainebleau, France: INSEAD Business School

Hunter, Mark Lee, Van Wassenhove, Luk N., Besiou, Maria and Van Halderen, Mignon (2013) The agenda-setting power of stakeholder media, *California Management Review,* Vol. 56, No. 1 pp 24-49

Jarvis, Jeff (2011) *Public Parts: How Sharing in the Digital Age Improves the Way We Work and Live,* London: Simon and Schuster

McChesney, Robert W. (2016) Journalism is dead! Long live journalism?: Why democratic societies will need to subsidise future news production, *Journal of Media Business Studies,* Vol. 13, No. 3 pp 128-135

Naldi, Lucia and Picard, Robert, G. (2012) Let's start an online news site: Opportunities, resources, strategy and formational myopia in start-ups, *Journal of Media Business Studies*, Vol. 9, No. 4 pp 47–59

Porlezza, Colin and Splendore, Sergio (2016) Accountability and transparency of entrepreneurial journalism: Unresolved ethical issues in crowdfunded journalism projects, *Journalism Practice*, Vol. 10, No. 2 pp 196-216

Price, John (2017) Can the *Ferret* be a watchdog? Understanding the launch, growth and prospects of a digital, investigative journalism start-up, *Digital Journalism* pp 1-15. Available online at http://www.tandfonline.com/doi/abs/10.1080/21670811.2017.1288 582

Rafter, Kevin (2016) Introduction: Understanding where entrepreneurial journalism fits in, *Journalism Practice*, Vol. 10, No. 2 pp 140-142

Rottwilm, Philipp (2014) *The Future of Journalistic Work: Its Changing Nature and Implications*, Oxford: Reuters Institute for the Study of Journalism

 Uskali, Turo I. and Kuutti, Heikki (2015) Models and streams of data journalism, *The Journal of Media Innovations*, Vol. 2, No. 1 pp 77-88

Note on the contributor

Peter Geoghegan is a lecturer in journalism at the University of the West of Scotland and a co-founder and director of the *Ferret*.

Local News Engine: Can the machine help spot diamonds in the dust?

Local News Engine was a prototype – running from autumn 2016 to spring 2017 – to examine whether computers can help journalists and bloggers spot story leads in the complex and messy world of local public data in the UK without having to read hundreds of pages of lists every week. In this detailed assessment, William Perrin concludes that relatively simple sorting by computers did make it easier to spot leads, shedding many hours of reading time and adding new possibilities such as viewing across local government boundaries

The lead mine

Weekly lists of local civic information (magistrates' courts, housing development, business licensing etc) have been a major source of story leads for local journalists for decades. These lists can total more than 500 pages a week, requiring patience, detailed local knowledge and much time to read. Traditionally, journalists have scoured these lists for story leads – such as local people (politicians, criminals, celebrities etc) doing newsworthy things (appearing in court, changing their house etc).

Some of these lists are published online or at least shared electronically as pdfs. But the local lists are often not visible to search engines, are awkward to use and require coding skills to extract data to scan them by machine. Declining numbers in newsrooms and the scant resources available to new hyperlocals mean that the time available to check these lists is diminishing. This gives rise to concerns about declining local accountability (Ramsay and Moore 2016).

Local News Engine[1] (LNE) prototyped an efficiency tool to automate the searching of these lists by computer. The project team comprised journalism practitioners, data scientists, user researchers and academic advisors.[2] We searched the lists for appearances by newsworthy people, places or companies. We defined those as any that had appeared in a local newspaper or appeared multiple times in the local lists we were analysing. We called this approach 'interesting people, doing interesting things'.

Local News Engine turned planning and licensing lists[3] from two neighbouring London boroughs and the local magistrates' court's scheduling list into structured data[4] that could be queried for newsworthy people, places and companies. The output of the searches was not published but made available securely to local bloggers and journalists.

Creating a database

We used data from three sources, the London Borough of Camden, the London Borough of Islington and Her Majesty's Court Service at Highbury Corner Magistrates' Court. Camden is one of England's larger and better-resourced boroughs, Islington one of the smallest and least-well resourced. Highbury Corner is one of the busiest magistrates' courts in the country serving much of North London, with first hearings of criminal cases. Like most magistrates' courts, Highbury Corner's external digital services are poor.[5]

The London Borough of Camden: It has a modern 'data store' from which we used the planning data, updated daily. The licensing information covering everything from bars and clubs to London Zoo's licence had to be scraped out of the website. Parliament requires this information to be published to enable the public to see what is being done and to comment on it.

The London Borough of Islington: All data had to be scraped from its weak website. For instance, a member of the public could not look at the list of licensed properties and landlords on the site: a particular problem in a borough with very high rental levels and notorious landlord problems. We raised this with the council who could not fix it. We found a way to get the aggregate data from the website very slowly.

Highbury Corner Magistrates' Court: A court clerk usually sends out to a local email list on a Friday a 300 to 400-page un-encrypted pdf of the following week's scheduled cases. The pdf is computer-generated and fairly standardised. We parsed this into data and have made that parsing code (but not the data) available in the public interest.[6] The court's data is sensitive, containing unproven charges as well as dates of birth and addresses. The list has historically been made available to journalists so they can decide which cases to attend. We used a simple calculation on declared date of birth to remove juvenile offenders at the point of conversion from pdf to data.

Some of the councils' databases went back many years. The council data was generally poorly licensed for reuse – generally with no visible licence.

The information gathered above was turned into JSON format[7] and stored in a secure database. As all the entries have some form of address attached, it was possible to geocode the data and then in later processing use standard geographical units to filter it by local authority ward, borough etc.[8] We took care that the data contained a principal name – for instance, the person applying to build a house (and not the council officer processing the form nor, say, the consultees).

We aimed for a weekly output cycle as this was most useful for publishing schedules. The scrapers would run for several days and then their output would be harvested on a Friday after the weekly court list had arrived in email. Camden planning data is downloadable in seconds as structured data; other public data took days to acquire each week.

Interesting people and places: Who and where is newsworthy?

By default, LNE intends to reduce the number of lines the journalist has to read or skim. It must discard the majority. Which names should we select for further scrutiny? Early on in the design process, we discussed the concept that all the people who had featured in the local newspapers were by definition 'newsworthy' and we then applied a computational approach to list these people. We were able to download a copy of the *Camden New Journal* and *Islington Gazette* websites which at that point covered up to six years of stories.

Academics and data processing companies have for some time been using software to extract, find or index items of information from huge bodies of text.[9] Known as 'named entity extraction', the technique looks for proper nouns (names of people, companies etc and places). We performed a 'named entity extraction' on the local newspaper websites – apparently for the first time in the UK. The entity extraction yielded a list of names of people, places and companies that had appeared on the papers' sites that could be ranked by frequency of occurrence, with the date, URL etc for each story. This was the 'newsworthy names' JSON data. The crude list of proper nouns and numbers of mentions (right) extracted from the *Camden New Journal* serves as an illustration.[10]

The developers reported that this was a relatively straightforward task. The retrospective construction of this list caused some interest amongst the *Camden New Journal* journalists who had not seen this sort of ranking of their stories before. We understand that only a few

31	165	Lauderdale House
32	162	Wigmore Hall
33	162	David Cameron
34	156	Whittington Hospital
35	156	Kings Place
36	156	City Hall
37	150	Sarah Hayward
38	149	Jeremy Corbyn
39	148	Royal Opera House
40	145	Union Chapel
41	140	Electric Ballroom
42	139	HMV Forum
43	137	Trafalgar Square
44	137	Frank Dobson
45	136	Burgh House
46	131	Parish Church
47	131	Finsbury Park
48	131	Finchley Road
49	129	Tufnell Park
50	129	Parliament Hill
51	126	Upper Street
52	126	Highgate Hill
53	121	York Way
54	119	Tulip Siddiq

publications keep such databases and, in my experience, I had not come across blogs doing this (although some may have used tags to annotate posts).

In addition to the names from the papers, we also decided that anyone who featured regularly in one of the data sets could also be considered newsworthy. We wrote a small piece of code that brought those who occurred frequently towards the top of the list.

Matching names

Matching names from disparate databases is a well-known problem. The developers employed fuzzy matching techniques[11] and annotated the code on GitHub:

> The data for leads.html is generated by grouping the names by fuzzy matching, such that each group represents a single person with a certain degree of confidence. This generally works well for typos and different forms of the same name, but can give false positives in case of similar names. The output of this should always be treated with caution![12]

Where LNE matched several names from different databases, good design by the developers ensured it would display them together. We could quickly see where it had made mistakes and move on.

Newsworthy people engaged in newsworthy activities

We worked through a number of prototypes showing interesting people doing interesting things through a user-led design process run by a contractor Neontribe. Such a process helps order user priorities and express them in such a way that the developers can implement them. The process led to adding in filters and breaking the data up to improve readability. We delivered versions featuring only that week's

PRET A MANGER MATCHED NAMES: PRET A MANGER LTD		
Total Appearances 52	Camden Planning 20	Camden License 16
Islington Planning 16		

Latest Appearance: Camden Planning 2016-09-05

:@computed_region_6i9...	112
:@computed_region_hx...	16
applicant_name	Pret A Manger
application_number	2016/4685/A
application_type	Advertisement Consent
case_officer	Charles Thuaire
case_officer_team	Planning Solutions Team
comment	http://planningrecords.camden.gov.uk/Northgate/PlanningExplorer17/PLComments.aspx?pk=443656
development_address	Kiosk in 'egg' ventilation shaft to front of King's Cross Station Kings Cross Square Euston Road London N1C 4TB
development_description	Display of internally illuminated lettering to fascia and to 4 shopfront panels.
earliest_decision_date	2016-08-31T00:00:00.000
easting	530318
full_application	http://planningrecords.camden.gov.uk/Northgate/LandProperty/Web/Redirection/redirect.aspx?linkId=EXDC&PARAM0=443656
last_uploaded	2016-09-15T03:01:49.000
latitude	51.532371
location	[object Object]
longitude	-0.122617
northing	183165

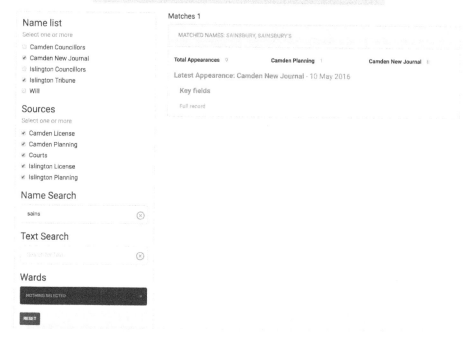

These results indicate a name in your search terms appears in the lists searched. You must verify it is the person you are searching for. An appearance on a court list DOES NOT mean the person actually appeared in court on the date indicated, or on the charges listed, or entered the plea indicated - that must be checked by you before publication

data, called 'leads', and another with the all historic data to date (many years in some cases) except courts lists, called 'explorer'.

The first prototype generated a simple planning story about a chain shop replacing an independent which I would normally have missed as I don't read the Camden planning lists for my Islington blog (Perrin 2016a). It also lodged with me for future reference the scale of this popular sandwich chain's activities.

LNE vastly simplified the huge reading task of digesting the weekly lists. By the end of the project it took a developer only 35 minutes to load the data from the scrapers, data store and parsed court lists and then run. And for the blogger, scanning the list took a matter of minutes.

We did not work the prototype intensively for stories, we were more focused on making the system work, but LNE played a role in the following:

- LNE managed to scrape important accountability data on houses licensed for multiple occupation from Islington borough's broken website. This enabled me to write an investigative piece about a notorious Islington landlord (Perrin 2017).

- LNE generated a lead to a staple local story about a forthcoming franchise change for a closed local restaurant (Perrin 2016b).

- By grouping names together LNE revealed several applications for tree surgery by Islington resident and former Labour Party Leader Lord Kinnock, which the *Islington Gazette* turned into a story (Couvée 2016).

What did we learn?

It is possible to reduce the effort needed to generate story leads from local lists using a data tool such as LNE. Reading times are cut dramatically as the chaff is blown away. Nothing is perfect, though: our approach was to look for already-known names and so has a bias against the novel. Whilst one cannot be certain that there weren't stories in the chaff, in my judgment making the task of reading the lists easier will, for

Islington Tribune Friday 21 October 2016

Ex-Labour leader's 'postage stamp' garden in shadows

Lord Kinnock wants to give neighbours' tall trees the chop!

by KOOS COUVÉE

Neil Kinnock, pictured here in a mock-up image, has asked the Town Hall for permission to cut back trees belonging to four of his neighbours

AFTER months of unsuccessfully trying to stop his own MP Jeremy Corbyn winning the Labour leadership contest, former party leader Neil Kinnock is finally seeing the light.

In his own back garden that is, because Baron Kinnock PC, of Huddleston Road, Tufnell Park, has applied for planning permission to chop back some of the trees in four of his neighbours' backyards.

The applications, made under his full name with his title – Lord – last month, had the *Tribune* for a moment thinking the former MP for Bedwellty, later Islwyn, had built up a small property empire not declared under the House of Lords register of interests.

However, it transpires Lord Kinnock and wife Glenys's garden gets very dark when the trees in neighbouring gardens get too high.

The applications are for cutting back an ash in one neighbour's garden, followed by a lime tree in another, the removal of a climber vine, and two sycamores and an ash in another.

In a fourth neighbour's garden, Lord Kinnock is expected to commission a group of tree surgeons to cut back seven lime trees, a sycamore, a mulberry and an acacia.

When contacted by the *Tribune*, Lord Kinnock said the applications were made "in full and ready" agreement with neighbours – and he revealed his "postage stamp" garden is so small it does not contain a single tree.

Residents in the area need to apply for planning permission to be able to cut back the trees because they are protected and can only do so up to a certain point.

many, make the difference between looking at them at all and not in hard-pressed modern news production.

There is huge potential to discover new information by turning local public lists and news stories into structured data: we have barely scratched the surface in this project. As resources diminish in newsrooms, this could become a vital productivity tool and open up new frontiers for investigative work.

The modern data techniques in LNE turned some almost unusable data into something useful. We found the sorting of courts data especially dramatic: a court has a huge catchment area and the courts list is very unwieldy – a 300-odd page pdf of sequential court cases. The ability to sort this geographically (by address of defendant and location of offence where given) cut the reading task from several hours to a few minutes. Islington's landlord data was unusable and we were able to produce a useful story when the data had been processed using modern techniques.

We were struck by how easy it was to skim the information when it was all presented in one place in a homogenised format, rather than spread across several screens, tabs and formats as when reading at source. It demonstrated that it was possible to group together people's and companies' activities across data sources and time. We also saw for the first time activity grouped across local authority boundaries. For me, having spent some years scanning the lists, it was a revelation. I could just sit there eating a sandwich and keep tapping the screen down until something interesting came up. What used to take hours suddenly took minutes.

People can often find this sort of data processing unsettling. Several people in public life whom we talked with felt that LNE sounded a little 'spooky', removing any leeway for public figures as they go about normal life and the relentless computer tracks them down. Or that the computer, by making it easier to do, would lead to an increase in press intrusion – for instance, partners of 'interesting people'. We felt that this was a form of 'technophobia' – after all, the decisions about publishing the results of processing data are taken by humans within a legal and cultural framework.

In conversation with the local papers in the LNE prototype, we judged that they had an ethical framework that would stop such behaviour progressing to a 'spooky' level. This may not be the case for other papers, of course. The Data Protection Act exemptions for journalism give a broad scope for action when the journalist believes it to be in the public interest and we demonstrated here that this work is firmly in the public interest.

The LNE approach requires customising for each area in which it operates. The team had broad experience of working with local data from across the UK. Our view was that, while the principles can be applied anywhere, each area in the UK has a data landscape sufficiently different that LNE would need code tailoring for each deployment. This increases cost and time of implementation. Nonetheless, my judgment is that the LNE approach would work for many urban publications where there is rich local data or rural areas where the breadth of coverage is such that the journalists are swamped.

Where next for LNE?

LNE was developed with grant-funding from the Google Digital News Initiative as a prototype. We have open-sourced the code on GitHub for anyone free to use. More than the code, we have demonstrated a technique for mining local lists for story leads and would welcome anyone taking this up in the wider public interest. I am talking to several organisations about evolving the technique further.

Notes
[1] Project website: https://talkaboutlocal.org.uk/local-news-engine-prototype/.
[2] William Perrin co-ordinated the team at Talk About Local. Open Data Services developed the software, Neontribe ran the user research. Richard Osley, at *Camden New Journal*, and Koos Couvée, at *Islington Tribune*, were also closely involved.
[3] In the UK, people wanting to make substantial alterations to a property, change its use to say a business or build a new structure, have to ask local government for 'planning permission'. The list of such applications is displayed for public comment. A similar process is followed when companies want to do things that might cause a nuisance or

have public health or safety implications such as bars, clubs, restaurants and pet shops known as 'commercial licensing'.

[4] 'For the most part, structured data refers to information with a high degree of organisation, such that inclusion in a relational database is seamless and readily searchable by simple, straightforward search engine algorithms or other search operations, whereas unstructured data is essentially the opposite. The lack of structure makes compilation a time and energy-consuming task. It would be beneficial to companies across all business strata to find a mechanism of data analysis to reduce the costs unstructured data adds to the organisation.' See https://brightplanet.com/2012/06/structured-vs-unstructured-data/.

[5] Local News Engine conformed to the News Media Association/Society of Editors' 'Protocol for sharing court registers and court lists with local newspapers'. Available online at http://www.newsmediauk.org/write/MediaUploads/PDF%20Docs/Protocol_for_Sharing_Court_Documents.pdf.

[6] LNE courts parser code: https://github.com/TalkAboutLocal/local-news-engine/blob/master/courts_parse.py.

[7] JSON is system for structuring data so that a computer can read it and it makes sense to a human. It allows one item of data to be linked to many others in a structured way.

[8] Wards are the smallest sub-unit in British politics – in the urban areas of the LNE pilot about 1 kilometre long and 500 metres wide.

[9] See Paul Bradshaw's work on the Chilcott Inquiry. Available online at https://onlinejournalismblog.com/2016/07/07/all-the-chilcot-iraq-inquiry-report-documents-structured-by-entities-and-dates/.

[10] Full list from *Camden New Journal* data. Available online at https://gist.github.com/Bjwebb/d8000e1aa0acccd3cf4665bb0fcc221c/b0d0b2081613372039a6e6f6b4e73c253fdb03bc.

[11] The developers employed trigram string similarity using the dice coefficient. 'Dice's coefficient measures how similar a set and another set are. It can be used to measure how similar two strings are in terms of the number of common bigrams (a bigram is a pair of adjacent letters in the string).' See https://en.wikibooks.org/wiki/Algorithm_Implementation/Strings/Dice%27s_coefficient.

[12] For all code for the project, see: https://github.com/TalkAboutLocal/local-news-engine.

References

Couvée, Koos (2016) Lord Kinnock wants to give neighbours tall trees the chop, Islington Tribune, 21 October. Available online at http://archive.islingtontribune.com/kinnock-trees-chop

Perrin, William (2016a) Sausages out, Sandwiches in, *Kings Cross Environment*, 5 October. Available online at https://kingscrossenvironment.com/2016/10/05/kings-cross-square-sausages-out-sandwiches-in/

Perrin, William (2016b) Flatiron steak replacing TED on Cally Road, *Kings Cross Environment*, 1 December. Available online at https://kingscrossenvironment.com/2016/12/01/flatiron-steak-replacing-ted-on-cally-road/

Perrin, William (2017) On the Panayi property trail, *Kings Cross Environment*, 14 March. Available online at https://kingscrossenvironment.com/2017/03/14/on-the-panayi-property-trail/

Ramsay, Gordon and Moore, Martin (2016) *Monopolising Local News: Is There an Emerging Local Democratic Deficit in the UK Due to the Decline of Local Newspapers?* Available online at https://www.kcl.ac.uk/sspp/policy-institute/CMCP/local-news.pdf

Note on the contributor

William Perrin is a local activist, blogger, campaigner and philanthropist. William was a civil servant in the UK government for 15 years where he helped create Ofcom and was a policy advisor to Prime Minister Tony Blair. He is also a trustee of *360giving.com*, Good Things Foundation, the Indigo Trust and founder of Talk About Local. William was one of the early movers in the UK's open data movement.

How data journalism can revolutionise local transport:
A West Midlands case study

Never has there been a greater need for the transport sector to welcome the skills of data journalists, argues Teresa Jolley

DJ and the future of transport: A collaborative approach

Transport is a challenging area for data journalists to cover. Data is siloed, inconsistent and inaccessible while access to industry and technical resources is difficult. But never has there been a greater need for the transport sector to welcome the capabilities and skills of data journalists. This traditional, engineering-focused sector knows it must prioritise user needs and inspire new young talent to join its ranks, but needs help doing so.

Transport is a vital service that profoundly affects our health, quality of life, choice of employment, how we spend our leisure time and where we live. Rather than journalists becoming transport experts, or transport engineers becoming journalists, why not bring the skills of both together in a facilitated collaborative environment to enable the much-needed changes to happen?

By providing the opportunity for data analysts, scientists and statisticians to share knowledge and experience of data related to transport, we can facilitate a more rapid and deeper understanding of what we need to do to solve the key transport challenges.

In collaboration with Transport for West Midlands and the Innovation Birmingham campus, a Data Discovery Centre has been set up. It intends to:

- provide access to all the key datasets as a common resource for all to work with and improve (Birmingham in Real Time, and Demo Data Discovery Centre with OpenDataSoft);

- provide multiple visualisation, analysis and exploration tools to explore and understand the data;

- be a resource for a variety of public and private sector organisations with expertise and interests in data analytics, statistics, visualisation, machine learning, traffic and transport, open data, journalism, accessibility and more;

- be home to SME's building and demonstrating the next generation transport and travel solutions;

- be open for registered members to come and research/explore innovative solutions in a collaborative environment with relevance to the region, which are not possible inside existing organisations or contracts;

- act as a resource for schools, universities, colleges, companies, professional institutions, other local authorities and transport organisations, Department for Transport and others to visit, learn and collaborate.

The West Midlands challenge

Between 2017 and 2026, the West Midlands will be home to significant transport investment that will support the region for years to come. Projects include the construction of the High Speed Two (HS2) line and two new stations (Curzon Street and Solihull) (HS2 Interactive Map), major improvements to the region's motorway, trunk road, rail and utilities/telecoms networks, an extension of Birmingham's tram network and a variety of transport improvements by local authorities.

Alongside these significant transport changes and improvements, there is a declared ambition to build 100,000 new homes to meet the region's growing population. Where should the new homes be built? How should transport connect to these new homes, and existing ones, to help people live more happily and healthily and be able to work and travel more easily? How can we ease congestion, improve air quality and reduce dependency on the car as the only viable form of transport for many?

The construction and improvement activities during this nine-year period will impact on all the transport networks across the region, many of which are already close to capacity. It is, therefore, critical that the impact of any disruptions is minimised, with a clear view of the effect of closures and re-routing across the various modes of transport (car, train, tram, bike, walking etc). It is also essential that accessible and accurate information about delays/best alternative routes is made widely available to all users, including:

- commuters,

- freight and business delivery organisations,

- business travellers,

- tourists,

- blue light services (ambulance, police, fire and other incident responders),

- public service fleet operators of buses, refuse trucks and work vans,

- community transport services,
- those living close to main routes who can be expected to have concerns about air quality, noise and property values.

Transport for West Midlands, the transport arm of the West Midlands Combined Authority, is clear that disruption and congestion can only be managed by modal shift. In other words, helping people choose different transport modes in place of their habitual choice of the motor car (bus, tram, cycle, walk, taxi/Uber/rideshare, train) and being able to switch between different modes when needed for a smoother, easier journey.

Recognising this challenge, West Midlands Combined Authority is leading a Network Resilience Strategy with three key themes (West Midlands Combined Authority Regional Resilience Plans 2017):

- investing in the foundation of data sharing principles and standards, and evidencing benefits of opening up datasets to encourage innovation and collaboration;
- co-ordinating activities between all transport organisations and stakeholders to minimise the chance of unforeseen clashes of works;
- engaging with the community through local groups, communication and PR teams, and local and national media so that relevant and accurate information on travel options, reliability and best routes is available to all.

Access to datasets from a wide variety of sources is critical to success in all three areas. Understanding what data is available, its purpose and how it can be used in new ways to better inform user needs is key: recognising where there are gaps in data, such as local air quality data and campaigning for better data to be available locally in communities.

The opportunity for data journalists

Whilst this is a daunting challenge, the expertise and level of enthusiasm for change already present in the region makes this an exciting opportunity. For data journalists, the West Midlands provides a useful combination of story angles, access to datasets and technical resources to fuel immersive, engaging storytelling.

Coverage of transport by the media tends to focus either on local crashes and closures or large-scale problems with large organisations. This means there is a latent opportunity for grassroots, community-driven local journalists to collaborate with the active open data and tech communities and social value groups across the region to help reconnect the transport system with its users.

By pioneering a data-enabled, technically informed yet accessible form of storytelling, this will, in turn, help people in a busy, congested region take an active part in defining future transport technologies.

How transport missed out in £3.4 billion funding

An example of an important, data-driven exclusive focused on the £3.4 billion funding under the New Homes Bonus programme made available from the Department for Communities and Local Government (DCLG) to local authorities between 2011 and 2016 (Chatterjee 2015). The funding was not ring-fenced, meaning it was up to each of the receiving local authorities to decide how they spent the money.

Transport Network, a leading industry media channel, decided to investigate how much of this cash local authorities actually chose to allocate for transport or road improvements. No central and accessible sources of data were available on how the fund was spent, so the required data was requested from local authorities under the Freedom of Information Act. Responses from 261 English councils revealed only 17 of those 261 local authorities allocated a specific portion of the funds to transport or highway infrastructure.

The investigation – published on the *transport-network.co.uk* website – revealed the projects that were part- or fully-funded using the New Homes Bonus funds, and offered some shared perspectives on how that was achieved and delivered in different local authorities. Some examples included local authorities supporting the reopening of old railway lines, with new housing developments close to refurbished or new stations.

When data journalists delve deeper

Several new services and solutions are being trialled in the region, like Mobility as a Service (MaaS) (the first UK trial of the MaaS Global Whim app), future car design (by Jaguar Land Rover) and the testing of autonomous and connected vehicles on 40 miles of roads around Coventry (the UK CITE project).

Data journalists can play a major role in promoting the debate over these initiatives. How are these advances potentially impacting people's lives? How will these technological developments change the way we live and move around? Who benefits or who loses out? These are the kind of crucial questions data journalists can explore.

Access to datasets

Until now, users have had to rely on services from global providers such as Google, Apple and TomTom to navigate their way around local and national transport networks. This reliance is not going to be good enough for the demands of the West Midlands in the coming years, or strong enough to support improvements to local open source alternatives.

West Midlands Combined Authority is one of three global city regions, alongside Melbourne (Australia), and Bloomington, Indiana (US), to work with Mapbox to solve smart cities congestion challenges with open source products and services built on OpenStreetMap (Franken 2017). OpenStreetMap, the collaborative, global editable map, has a vibrant local community in the West Midlands, called Mappa Mercia. They have done a lot of work with Birmingham City Council to make highways and transport data available on OpenStreetMap (Prangle 2017). *Wikidata* also has a strong local community in the region and is exploring open, editable resources for defining and linking data.

The Open Data Institute has a Birmingham node, based at the Innovation Birmingham campus (ODI Birmingham), which is also home to a large number of technical, digital and data start-ups. In addition, the campus hosts the Transport Systems Catapult and Transport for West Midlands Intelligent Mobility Incubator, supporting SMEs to develop future transport solutions (Transport Systems Catapult 2015). SMEs need access to reliable and open data sources to build their products and services.

Open source is a way to assist future transport solutions that are more collaborative and valuable to wider society needs. But there are perceived and real security risks around choosing which data to open up (Gleave 2017).

As well as benefiting from improved access to data to inform stories, journalists are better placed to answer a range of important questions. For instance, how is personal data protected? What are the risks and opportunities to individuals and businesses? And how can individuals and communities contribute to and police this?

Technical resources to boost DJ in the region

The region's universities have internationally recognised expertise in related fields which are useful research resources for more in-depth stories by data journalists. Birmingham City University (located adjacent to the new HS2 Curzon Street station) has specialisms in digital media and technology, including two MAs run by Paul Bradshaw: Multiplatform and Mobile Journalism, and Data Journalism (Bradshaw 2017).

Aston University specialises in transport and engineering. The University of Birmingham has strengths in energy sources, sensor technology and city-focused data analytics and research through its CitiREDI programme at the Birmingham Business School (CitiREDI). The recently opened National College for High Speed Rail is located in Birmingham whilst the National Transport Design Centre is based in Coventry.

Schools and academies are keen to support Science, Technology, Engineering and Mathematics (STEM) and STE(Arts)M activities, and welcome engagement and involvement with 'real-life' industry challenges such as through the UK Engineering's Tomorrow's Engineers programme (Tomorrow's Engineers). Academies include the seven Royal Society of Arts (RSA) academies across the West Midlands (RSA Academies) and Aston University Engineering Academy.

Conclusion

The collaborative approach highlighted here provides a high quality, fast-paced, industry-led innovation centre that enables research, prototyping and development of solutions to help solve the West Midlands transport challenges in a user-centred way. By welcoming data journalists as key participants, they will be able to access data and knowledge to inform their stories. This will provide the greater depth and quality to transport-related stories that have previously been so hard to attain.

In turn, the closer involvement of journalists with the transport sector will raise awareness of the way our transport network operates and how readers can shape and influence it to deliver a future transport system that meets society's real needs.

References

Bradshaw, Paul (2017) Here's the thinking behind my new MA in Data Journalism, *Online Journalism Blog*, June. Available online at https://onlinejournalismblog. com/2017/07/01/data-journalism-course-teaching/

Chatterjee, Pupul (2015) New homes prove no bonus for transport, *transport-network. co.uk*, 28 May. Available online at https://www.transport-network.co.uk/Exclusive-New-homes-prove-no-bonus-for-transport/11767

Franken, Christina (2017) West Midlands is getting smart about transport disruptions, Mapbox, February. Available online at https://blog.mapbox.com/west-midlands-is-getting-smart-about-transport-disruptions-d3567187210c

Gleave, James (2017) Cyber security in transport revolution, *Transport Future* blog, January. Available online at https://transportfutures.co/cyber-security-in-a-transport-revolution-4fa09c1ea5d9

Prangle, Brian (2017) Massive release of highways asset data in Birmingham, *Mappa Mercia* blog, March. Available online at http://www.mappa-mercia.org/2017/03/massive-release-of-highways-asset-data-in-birmingham.html

Transport Systems Catapult (2015) Centro and the Transport Systems Catapult to run Intelligent Mobility Incubator, July. Available online at https://ts.catapult.org.uk/news-events-gallery/news/centro-and-the-transport-systems-catapult-to-run-intelligent-mobility-incubator/

West Midlands Combined Authority (2017) Regional resilience plans. Available online at https://www.wmca.org.uk/news/regional-resilience-plans-approved/

Website resources

Association of Community Rail Partnerships: https://acorp.uk.com/

Aston University Engineering Academy: http://www.auea.co.uk/

Birmingham in Real Time: http://dmtlab.bcu.ac.uk/alandolhasz/birt/data.html

CitiREDI: http://www.birmingham.ac.uk/schools/business/research/city-redi/about.aspx

Demo Data Discovery Centre with Open Data Soft: https://datadiscoverycenter. opendatasoft.com/pages/homepage/

HS2 Interactive Map: http://interactive-map.hs2.org.uk/

ODIBirmingham: https://theodi.org/nodes/birmingham

National College of High Speed Rail: https://nchsr.ac.uk/
National Transport Design Centre: http://www.coventry.ac.uk/business/ntdc/
OurNewUnion.org: http://ournewunion.org/
Royal Society of Arts (RSA) Academies: http://www.rsaacademies.org.uk/
Tomorrow's Engineers: http://www.tomorrowsengineers.org.uk/
UKCITE project: UK Connected Intelligent Transport Environment: https://www.ukcite.co.uk/

Note on the contributor
Teresa Jolley is Creative Director of DEFT153 Ltd – delivering efficiency for transport for the 153 local authorities in England.

Storytelling: The key to unlocking the meaning of data

Populism Sedan

IBM estimates that around 2.5 quintillion bytes of data are created every day. Corporations are literally drowning in information. With big data has emerged the struggle to communicate insights to an untrained audience. Data journalist Isabelle Marchand goes through a series of steps to ease general understanding by building a convincing storytelling technique

Originally just focused on the accuracy of the analysis, the challenge has now broadened to encompass the ability to share it in an engaging and digestible format. Effective storytelling simplifies complex analysis and helps organisations to reach a decisional consensus.

Insight + Storytelling = Effective decision making

None of the facts and figures matter until you have some sort of emotional connection

Recent political events reveal that the emotive appeal of a well-wrapped story has often more impact on people's decision-making than facts and figures alone. An analysis of the 2016 US Presidential Election revealed that the then-Republican candidate and now 45th US President, Donald Trump, made around 560 false claims during his campaign. In an era when fact-checking has never been so easy, this counter intuitive triumph of myth over reality begs the question: how did he get away with it?

As a reality TV star, Trump was well aware of the importance of storytelling over hard facts. His narrative pitted himself as the underdog; persecuted by the media at home and abroad, fighting his noble quest against Mexican immigrants, globalisation and the establishment elites in order to make America great again. Any individual working with numbers should take heed of the Trump saga: whilst not all people may be data literate, everyone can relate to a good story. Corporations, therefore, should seek to explore and exploit this opportunity to increase the power of their insights.

From story listener to story teller

As data visualisation expert Stephen Few said: 'Numbers have an important story to tell. They rely on you to give them a clear and convincing voice.' The good news is that we are all naturally geared up to produce stories. Not convinced? Let's try and see.

He went to the store.

Fred died.

Sharon went hungry and wept.

Can you answer the following questions: why did Sharon weep? Why did she go hungry? You may have deduced that Sharon wept because Fred died. Or even that Fred went to a grocery store and that's why Sharon went hungry. Read again. Couldn't 'He' be John or Arthur instead of Fred? Is Sharon really weeping because of Fred's death or could she be sad for another reason? If you have linked those facts it's because the brain, by default, creates a story from a series of events even if they are unrelated. Scientists are particularly familiar with the dangers of this cognitive bias and seek to negate its influence. By applying the mantra 'correlation does not imply causation', they avoid the temptation to assume that two events occurring together have established a cause-and-effect relationship.

Tracking down the unicorn

In the absence of a magic formula that guarantees a good story from data, there are a series of steps that anyone can take to help them build a convincing argument that should be understood by a wide audience. Consider this urinal (right) and give it a price.

Now that you have a figure in mind here is a bit of background information: Marcel Duchamp submitted the original artwork (for artwork it is) under the name 'The Fountain' to the 1917 Parisian Salon des Indépendants. The art fair committee

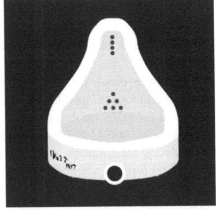

To see the original visit: http://www.tate.org.uk/art/artworks/duchamp-fountain-t07573

turned it down for display but the application launched what was to become an iconic art movement – conceptual art. As for comparison, LHOOQ, a cheap postcard reproduction of Mona Lisa on which Duchamp drew a moustache and a beard, was sold for $607,500 USD May 13 1999 at Christie's auction house

Given this context, how much do you think Duchamp's urinal is worth? Your original estimation may well have evolved now that you have been given more information. The answer is: Sotheby's sold one of the eight 1964 replicas of 'The Fountain' in 1999 for $1.7 million.

Raw data is much like the urinal analogy above, and far too often people just throw it at their audience's face. Unless further background and context is provided, then the gap between the data and the audiences' understanding is doomed to widen. By following a simple process such as the one below you can reduce this risk significantly.

The 3Cs

1. Choose a Message
In marketing you would come up with a message first and then find a dataset to back it up. In journalism you may want to analyse a dataset first and then define what the message is. In both cases, the first step is always to set your mind on a clear objective.

2. Contextualise
You may have spent hours on your data but remember that your audience hasn't. This is typically known as the 'curse of knowledge'; this cognitive bias occurs when someone who is very familiar with a topic assumes, therefore, that everyone is. Unfortunately, more often than not information that is not easily understood will automatically be discarded.

To avoid such a fate with your own analysis, you should give it some context. Depending on your content, you may need to explain the why, what and how. Why have you gathered the data? What conclusion have you extracted from your analysis? How do you think it will help the business?

3. Compare
Compare your data to the same dataset in the past, or even against another trend or brand. You can also compare the current situation to a potential improvement, a risk, or to what could happen if no action is taken. In other words, put your data into perspective. However, choose carefully as your choice of comparison will influence your audience towards your message. A positive comparison will make your results appear in a favourable light where as a negative one will underline an issue.

The eight questions

Once a message is chosen and the data is contextualised and compared to a relevant dataset, it's time to articulate it in an engaging format. To do so, variables need to be considered and questions answered.

1. Who is your audience?

Creating content without a clear understanding of the audience risks providing them information they don't understand, don't have time to process or simply don't need.

2. Is your audience knowledgeable about your topic?

The use of jargon and abbreviations may be commonplace in your area of specialisation. However, consider the fact that it may not be widely understood by your audience. One of the easiest ways to avoid this mistake is the pub test. When putting your content together, imagine that you are explaining your reasoning to a friend in a pub. This should significantly decrease the odds of being misunderstood.

3. Do you know how much time your audience will spend on your content?

Always remember that you are competing for your audiences' time and attention. You should consider them as time-poor by default. Make sure that what interests them most is both quickly and easily accessible. Sometimes it means putting the conclusion or key insights first and follow up with the explanation. Breaking your content down with informative subheadings and an index where possible is an option.

4. Can you link each element of your content to a central theme?

Elements that are not directly contributing towards your main theme may distract instead of inform your audience. A unified, coherent and clear message is easier to memorise and to share.

5. Do the elements have a logical flow?

Linking the different parts of your analysis together not only helps your audience to memorise it and it also provides strength and conviction to your argument thus increasing its persuasive power.

There are many possible scripts you can follow:

    a. Underline what the problem is.

    b. Come up with a solution.

    c. Define a call to action.

Or

a. Describe the main situation (e.g. global).

b. Focus on a specific area.

c. So what?

Or

a. Beginning.

b. Twist.

c. Conclusion.

These examples are not exhaustive. Feel free to build your own based on the message's requirements.

6. Can you find a twist in your data? Something unexpected?
A surprising element is always an excellent hook. It can also be the reason why the content is produced in the first place.

7. Can your audience relate to your work? Is there a way you can link it to their personal experience or environment?
   It is easier for people to understand and remember a story if they can relate it to something familiar to them. *The New York Times* is an excellent source of inspiration for inclusive titles, such as 'The voting habits of Americans like you' or 'Money, race and success: How your school district compares'. When using big numbers always keep it simple. Ideally try to find an appropriate practical comparison. Compare the difference between the two statements below:

Each day, every customer generates c.5,000 MB of data.

Or

Each day, every customer generates enough data to make two full-length feature films.

8. Do you want your audience to take action after reading your content?
The final objective should always be to action the insights you have presented. Make sure that what you are suggesting flows naturally from the content. Inform but be careful not to be patronising. Make it easy for your audience to check your references, hyperlink where you can.

The cherry on top
Once you have built a well-structured argument that answers any questions the audience may have and provides impactful recommendations then the last but by no means least difficult step is to give it an engaging headline. Remember that readers will scan it and make an instant decision: is it interesting, intriguing or can it be ignored? Too often this critical stage is neglected, leading to titles of reports where people end up bored before they have even read the first sentence.

Another difficult step is to tailor and trim the level of detail to the needs of the audience. This can be almost heart-breaking when considerable time and energy have been put into producing an analysis. The harsh truth is that even in the best of cases half of all information and understanding will be lost on the audience anyway.

When data alone is not enough

If you still aren't convinced by the potential of storytelling, then perhaps an anecdote on the dangers of letting data speak for itself may help change your mind. In the mid-19th century, a Hungarian physician, Ignaz Semmelweis (1818-1865), was appointed as an assistant at a Vienna hospital. The hospital contained two maternity clinics. Medical students were taught at one while the other was exclusively managed by midwives. In both clinics mothers were regularly dying of an illness called puerperal or childbed fever, which was not uncommon at the time. What was surprising, however, was the difference in mortality rates between the two centres. On average the medical students' mortality rate was more than two times higher than that of the midwives'.

When comparing the data, Semmelweis realised that the main difference between the two clinics was in the schedule they maintained. It was common practice for students to execute autopsies in the morning and to spend the afternoon in the maternity ward – without ever washing their hands. Midwives were never in contact with corpses. Concluding that a poison must be getting transferred from dead bodies to mothers through the students' hands, Semmelweis decided to impose chlorinated lime solution hand-washing in all clinics. The results were impressive as after few months the death rate was lowered to 0 per cent.

Whilst Semmelweis's conclusion became more widely known after the French scientist Louis Pasteur and his germ theory of diseases was developed, the general opinion at the time was that 'doctors are gentlemen and a gentleman's hands are clean'. Even if the data clearly proved he was right, Semmelweis failed to communicate his findings in an engaging way. He relied heavily on data to prove his point, neglecting to introduce storytelling. As a result his discovery was strongly opposed by the establishment. He was quickly dismissed and banned from finding any similar position in Vienna.

Adopting and embracing new practices and procedures is an essential requirement for success in any industry. Now that data is increasing at an exponential rate the need to create and explain insights that are easily understood and acted upon is a trend that has never been more relevant.

Note on the contributor

Isabelle Marchand is a Senior Data Journalist for the Customer Insights department of Lloyds Banking Group. She specialises in extracting actionable insights and creating visual storytelling. She is a regular speaker and has deep experience in producing dashboards, infographics and online tests for companies such as Dropbox, the Ford Motor Company and the World Bank.

Section 3:
Elections, referenda and data journalism: Coming of age?

John Mair

Nowhere is data more obvious than at elections: the big events where countries make up their individual and collective minds about the future. They provide the big television set-pieces – the Factual Cup Finals – in which the networks compete to be first and, usually, right with the results. Getting the facts on air has become quicker and, at the same time, more sophisticated. Data is king but presentation is the queen.

This section explores the use of data to predict and broadcast elections on a variety of platforms – TV, radio and online plus the use of social media to influence voter behaviour and how to measure that and its effects. Most interestingly at the end, two writers from *Sky News* and Channel Four explore how they mine their own in-house data using material gathered from subscribers to opinion polls and to micro target advertising. That is the future of data in television.

First off, two election data veterans John Walton and Bella Hurrell, of the BBC. They have reported elections in the UK and the US for the last two decades. Walton and Hurrell distil their experience into 'Ten top tips for data journalists about covering elections'. Some are self-evident truths like careful planning, even for the unplanned, using history as a learning point while others are less obvious: listening to geeks, planning coverage post-election to fighting off the bosses' continual demands for more and more explanatory graphics. Save the goodies for the end – the Big Election Night. As they say: 'It may sound odd but elections do resemble a special theatrical performance, for one night only, and as such it's wise to rehearse.' The hit rate for their team's work on *BBC News Online* shows that they are obviously finding audiences worldwide.

Beneath the radar of opinion polls

Modern elections are now fought as much on the internet as on the TV screens. Social media is coming to the fore as witnessed by the unexpected triumphs of Donald Trump and the Brexiteers in 2016. Both below the radar, and heavily dependent on the use of the services of companies like Cambridge Analytica (CA) to target social media messages to the right audiences and micro audiences. Robert Mercer – the man behind CA – may have had as much influence for Trump as Vladimir Putin is alleged to have done in the US Presidential Election. Martin Moore (one of the editors of this book) and his colleague at King's College London, Gordon Ramsay, have found ways to measure beneath the radar of straight opinion polls. They wrote about measuring online in a previous edition of this mini-series. They had developed software called Steno for that. Now, in their new chapter, they show how during the 2017 election they were able to go beyond that to gather and analyse tweets (2,000 parliamentary candidates and their offices, plus Central Party tweets) and, more importantly, break the privacy wall around Facebook using a specially recruited panel of forty volunteers.

It is a massive database which they are yet to analyse properly. But, by using the 'below the radar' data they may be able to examine in detail some of the big issues thrown up by the election – such as the drastic decline in support and trust for Theresa May and the surge of Jeremy Corbyn, the reasons why voters did not treat it as a 'Brexit election', why immigration was less a worry/theme than during the 2016 Referendum and the efficacy of the use of social media by both Labour supporters and candidates. Moore and Ramsay are mining underground; the opinion polls, mining overground, once again proved to be very unreliable.

George Gallup, the founding father of opinion polling, had a striking metaphor for what it involved. He talked about opinion polling being 'like tasting whether a pot of soup has enough salt. You don't need to eat the whole pot – if you've given it a good stir, a spoonful will do the job'. Mori et al. failed the taste test in 2015, 2016 and 2017. So, how do you poll to get more accurate results? How do you stop the soup being over-salted? Polling in person, by phone or on the internet costs money to achieve samples, especially ones which are quota accurate. The TV exit poll, for example, has a sample of 20,000 in more than 140 polling stations. It is paid for by four broadcasters. Some television companies, though, have a ready-made reservoir of people to poll their subscribers. Sky, one of the success stories of British broadcasting in the last three decades, now (in 2017) has more than eleven million subscribers – approaching 20 per cent of the British population. They know their demographics, they know their income, they know their viewing preferences. In his chapter, Harry Carr, who was brought from a legacy polling company, Ipsos Mori, to Sky, outlines how he created Sky Data which has then utilised that massive database to select and weigh a sample to poll.

Sometimes they do it quickly by text to feed the *Sky News* rolling news machine; at other times it is more leisurely and more like traditional opinion polling. It works, as he says: 'We were able to break new ground in using a large customer base to conduct traditional polls, introducing representative polling by SMS and in placing Sky Data front and centre of *Sky News'* political coverage.' Sky Data, in 2017, won a prestigious Royal Television Society award for this innovation.

However big the pool, the usual rules apply. As Carr's Sky colleague Hugh Westbrook puts it in his chapter: 'Telling election stories through data at *Sky News*, the data for an election is central to everything we do. The results programme on TV and our accompanying look-up service on our digital platforms is the core of our offering – and being fast and accurate is all that matters.' *Sky News* prides itself on innovation in gathering, presentation and delivery of news.

What do they do with the polling data once gathered and how do they marry this with more traditional data including election results and snap polls in the big election night results programme is explored by Westbrook. All elections involve choice but not all are the same. Hours have to be devoted to the 'what if' scenarios. Planning for the 2016 Referendum was complex for *Sky News* for many reasons: firstly, it was a binary election and constituency results only mattered as constituent of the final total. In the US Presidential Election later that year, there were complexities of the independent candidates, the timing of when to 'call' a state for one side or the other and the vagaries of the electoral college compared to the popular vote But all the fixes to mend these involved the danger of disturbing the equilibrium of the rest of the model.

Promises and pitfalls of the referendum coverage

All the British television networks said they had planned for the 'hung parliament' vote but still, when the close of the exit poll by Strathclyde University psephologist Professor John Curtice was broadcast on 8 June, it was a big surprise. Most were left running fast to catch up. Graphic or data presentation has become the Alsace Lorraine of the media battleground on election nights. The BBC with its Jeremy Vine/virtual reality set and projection of the 'result' on to Broadcasting House has been in the van for the three act drama of the 2015 General Election, the 2016 Brexit Referendum and the 2017 General Election. Jonathan Spencer has been the creative genius behind all of that. In his chapter, he examines the promises and pitfalls of the referendum coverage in 2016. They had a big problem: this was a straight binary election where constituency results really did not matter. The design they came up with had to be tweaked as they went along. The pressures of production took over from good design. There simply was not enough time to test ideas to drive out the bad. As Spencer, the guru of VR Graphics – he once put Jeremy Vine in virtual Wild West Saloon – puts it: 'Subsequent discussion of the nature of the coverage and the accurate visual representation of statistics has led me to conclude that the most legible solution could be seen as unacceptably minimal and that the balance between an acceptable level of artifice and clear communications is an ongoing challenge.'

Finally, back to using the viewer as data. In her chapter, Sarah Rose, Channel 4's Director of Consumer Insight, shows how that broadcaster is gathering audience, collating and analysing data but for another purpose. The incoming C4 Chief

Executive, David Abraham, told his staff in 2010 that 'data was oil'. They took him at this word and collected and collated all the data they could from viewers registering for their catch-up service All4. They were able to measure not just their demographics but also their taste in programmes and much more. That provided the nucleus of their first person data operation. According to Rose: 'We recruited an 8,000-strong viewer panel, named Core 4, from within our registered base and used them to better understand attitudes, motivations and lifestyle interests, as well as to test programme ideas and brand concepts.' That informed all programmes and advertising on the channel. You went one step further by inserting the first name of the registered viewer into the ad. 'Coca Cola was the first advertiser to use this, inserting the viewer's first name on a Coke bottle resulting in an astonishingly high 59 per cent of viewers who saw the advert to take some positive action as a result.' Burberry followed suit.

The oil rig is firmly in place. 'Now we have started mining the oil, we intend to flow it not just through our internal operations but also through our future strategy and vision for C4,' Rose concludes.

So from simple (and too often wrong) opinion polling to much more scientific sample selection from the subscriber base, from simple BARB head counting to sophisticated and targeted analyses of audiences, from simple newspaper content analysis to deep diving into the underworlds of Twitter and Facebook, data journalism has truly come of age in the electronic age.

Ten top tips for data journalists about covering elections

John Walton and Bella Hurrell offer some crucial guidance for data journalists new to covering elections – and for those whose memories are sometimes as poor as their own

Imagine you have a time capsule kept in a safe place. Inside it is a message from the past. The label on the outside of the capsule reads: 'In case of an election, break glass!' This chapter is that time capsule. Inside it you'll find some of the accumulated, forgotten and re-accumulated wisdom gathered in covering the results of close to 25 different elections and referendums over the past 20 years for the *BBC News* website.

Elections are an incredibly intense part of the working life of those journalists swept up in their wake. They are demanding, exciting and important. What they are not, however, is a full-time job; they are more of a temporary gig, a sojourn for a few weeks or months. In the UK, they only come around in some form or another once a year. This makes it so incredibly easy to forget the lessons you learned just 12 months ago. Once the ballot boxes have been emptied and their contents counted and pored over to the satisfaction of our audiences and editors, journalists return to old routines and old beats and their memories fade. So, sadly, knowledge and skills newly acquired in the campaign can be lost.

Politicians may claim there is no early election planned, and point with innocent faces towards the Fixed-term Parliaments Act. But with so much at stake, politicians may be tempted to rewrite the rulebook and seek out advantages where they can, leaving the unwary data journalist flat-footed should a snap decision to call an early election descend out of the blue. So, keep this time capsule close at hand. It is written for those data journalists new to covering elections and for those whose memories are sometimes as poor as our own.

1. Know your audiences

The right and proper place to start when covering democracy in action is with the voters themselves or, for our purposes, the audience. What do they want from election coverage?

'People expected an exciting presentation of numbers done in a way to deliberately engage a wider audience,' says research into audience expectations of BBC election coverage.[1] We know our readers expect a lot of us on all our platforms and we also know that they are very diverse in terms of their interest in and understanding of data. Some love complex visual analysis while others have trouble engaging with simple charts and graphs.

They also vary in terms of where they come across our visual content – differing by device and platform from TV to desktop, mobile web, mobile app or via one of our many social media accounts. So, one size does not fit all and this challenge is not unique to *BBC News*. When coming to plan your coverage it is likely that you will be thinking about what works best where and for whom.

When coming to election coverage after working on other stories it can be a surprise to be reminded that alongside the audience desire for 'exciting presentation' there is an equal demand for basic information on what an election is, how to vote, what the parties stand for and which constituency people live in – postcode searches are very popular. Like some journalists, large sections of your audience are also unlikely to follow politics all year round.

Find out all you can about the people coming to your website and social media accounts and use that knowledge to frame your thoughts when planning your stories. Even if you think you know about your audience, refresh that knowledge as people's habits change constantly. Also make the effort to dig out any documentation from previous elections, from old emails about audience figures to minutes of project retros – they'll help to get you started.

2. Gather your data – lots of it

Preparation is key – you can't turn up on the night of the election and know how to cover it as a data journalist without having put in plenty of preparation. It may sound odd but elections do resemble a special theatrical performance, for one night only, and as such it's wise to rehearse.

Consider carefully several results scenarios and how you might cover them. Absorb the conventional wisdom about the upcoming result and then work out in how many different ways it might be flawed and where that might take your story. Check you've got past data, that you've got the correct map boundaries (beware boundary changes since last time) and that you've gathered any data you may want to use in regressions. Try out new ideas with data from the last election. Run and re-run any scripts you might need.

If you have live graphics updating from a feed, will they still look as good as planned if the results take an unexpected turn? Are all the scales, axes and tick marks able to handle unexpected landslides or unexpected draws?

Flick through the electoral rulebook; make sure you know what's needed for a majority or, more crucially, a working majority. What happens to the Speaker's vote if things get tight? Who gets first go at forming a government if parliament is hung? And what is a hung parliament anyway? Does it matter if one side has more votes, but the other has more seats?

Rulebooks may be a little tedious so it can be fun, we think you'll agree, to spend a bit of time looking into the electoral record books. It's a certainty there will be a few 'first times', a few 'biggest evers' and a few 'largest sinces' at every election. So it's good to have a handle on which records are likely to tumble so you can speedily weave them into your reporting. The saying goes: 'Nobody likes a know it all,' but on election night we beg to differ.

3. The campaign: It's the journey and the destination

The election campaign can throw up a few dilemmas for data journalists. The trickiest decision early on is to work out how much time to spend on the day-to-day coverage of the campaign, versus the detailed and thorough preparation you will need to do in order to cover the results with speed, flair and accuracy. People may be forgiving if you make a misstep in your campaign coverage, but they will definitely remember if you make any mistakes when you are covering the results.

Also, expect that whatever commitments you have taken on at the start of campaign, it's a certainty that either you or your boss, or their boss, will frequently have more ideas for stories or graphics. This is all well and good, and to be embraced, but remember you can't do them all. Take on too much work during the campaign and your all-important results coverage will suffer. If pushed, remind your boss that the online audience, in particular, peaks in the few days immediately before and after an election and that this is the time and place on which to focus your best efforts.

4. The polls: Be clear about their uncertainty

For data journalists, numbers often speak louder than words. Hence, whatever their reputation for accuracy, we love the opinion polls. So too, it turns out, do the audience. During the 2016 US election campaign, the BBC's election poll tracker received more than 24 million page views and the UK poll tracker for the 2017 UK election – a much shorter campaign period – got more than four million page views, with similar figures during the 2015 General Election campaign.

Voting intention polling is a core stalwart of campaign coverage indicating the mood of the people and the national debate and so to omit it would be perverse, despite the problems it has thrown up in recent UK and US elections and referenda. That said, the polls are not the only prism through which the campaign should be framed and the question remains: how can we present polls in a way that makes clear the possibility of error but doesn't leave the reader overwhelmed with detail and less clear than they were before reading our coverage?

One possibility would be to move away from showing a single average or poll of polls as seen in the BBC's US poll tracker from 2016 (below), which implies a high level of certainty about the outcome and, instead, find a way to display the uncertainty.

From this...

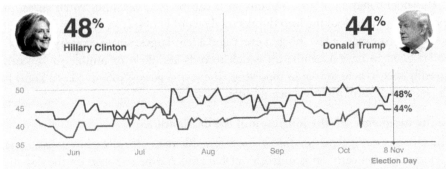

US Election poll tracker 2016, **BBC News**[2]

That could be by plotting all the polls on a chart showing the range of opinions from different polling companies, the solution reached by the *BBC News* website in 2017. This can present challenges for the user interface on a mobile phone, but sacrificing simplicity for accuracy is perhaps worthwhile in this instance.

... to this:

Voting intention

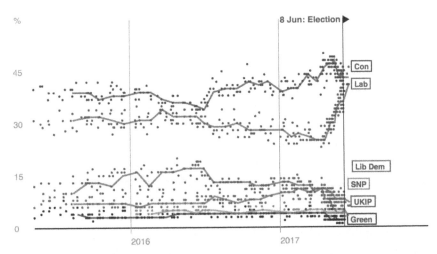

UK voting intention poll tracker 2017, **BBC News**[3]

Another approach might be to choose to indicate graphically the margin of error for each poll. Whatever you decide, don't forget to augment your coverage with insights from psephologists, pollsters and other experts to add context to the debate, rather than leaving your graphics marooned in visual isolation. Also, don't forget polls are tricky. The more eye-catching or interesting an individual opinion poll looks, the more likely it is to be an outlier, so beware.

5. Have a plan for social media

In 2015, we focused on creating playful 'one thought' data-led graphics for use on Twitter and Facebook during the General Election campaign. We found colourful illustrations and simple animations were often more successful than static charts or maps as they can be easier to understand at a glance and are more engaging. We know this type of bespoke social media content gets well shared and can boost referrals back to the main news site.

208 women have been elected
- up 12 from before the election

It's a record high but still only 32% of MPs

A BBC graphic published on social media the day after the UK general election[4]

Building on this approach in 2017, we decided to focus on appealing more to younger female audiences across all our accounts – chiming with a broader BBC online focus – targeting specific Facebook accounts and creating Instagram stories with the intention of getting our visual content in front of audiences that just weren't coming to the BBC website.

Whatever your approach, make sure you have a social media strategy during the campaign and for election night rather than simply recycling data visualisations you have already done for your main website. And once again, don't focus all on the campaign as election night will generate the biggest audiences by far.

6. Always try something new

Who doesn't want to pull something exciting out of a hat when standing centre stage? But elections are high pressure, and an important lesson to remember is to make sure that you have at least built a working prototype of your new product or process and tested it end-to-end before the big night.

For the EU Referendum, we experimented with publishing every result live to Twitter using the same graphics engine as our TV coverage. This was in addition to our normal results service on the *BBC News* website. Our TwitterBot automatically published results throughout the night as they came in and was a big success. We reprised this 'bot' for the US Presidential Election, this time generating both state results and an updating national scoreboard – and even extending the service to Spanish for our BBC Mundo service.

So, when the snap UK General Election was called, we knew we wanted to publish results on Twitter again, and having run it twice without much trouble we were well placed. But even with the experience of two previous elections, the night was not plain sailing. The way the vote count around the country unfolded created a bottleneck of results and the volume during peak hours was much heavier than during the previous two elections. Keeping up with the pace of results proved tricky. In the end, we had to carefully monitor a log of posts to make sure no constituencies were missed.

The lesson here is to be prepared for bumps along the way and if your innovation relates to your only results system then always have a fall back.

7. In praise of local elections

Local elections are great. When their results are counted we get fresh numbers and new data to dig around in. You may hear the occasional moan from colleagues that local election campaigns are not as exciting as general elections, that there's less at stake and that it feels as if no one is interested.

Don't listen. How many councils are up for grabs may vary each year in the UK, and with that the number of people voting, but whatever part of the electoral cycle you may find yourself in you can be certain that millions of people will have voted and that therefore, come the results, millions of people will want to know what has happened. Traffic to your site will be high – be sure you're able to make the most of it.

Local elections can also give you an opportunity to keep trying out new experiments with your coverage, making your general election reporting, when it comes round again, that much better.

8. Everyone loves maps

We've found over the years that election results stories with 'map' somewhere in the headline do well. Perhaps geography is more approachable and visually more familiar to most people than other more complex graphics. Also, we would guess that the reader can place themselves on a map in a way they can't a bar chart or a line chart. Whatever the reasons for it, results maps go down really well.

For the 2017 election, we produced 17 different interactive maps, showing who had won which seat, which seats had changed hands, share of the turnout, share of the vote by each main party and the change in the share of the vote by each main party. We also produced proportional maps for the main results and for change in turnout.

That's a lot of maps. But there's a reason for this apparently scattergun approach. By covering so many different bases in our preparation this meant we were ready with graphics that would help us tell the story of the election, whichever way it turned. Bearing in mind the unpredictable nature of recent results, this was a real asset.

To those familiar with them, maps can really sing. At a glance you can see a wealth of information: that the Conservatives are strong in the south and in rural areas, and Labour is strong in towns and in the north of England. That the four nations of the UK all have their own very different stories to tell. The key is making sure that you communicate that knowledge to your audience.

As with social media, maps work well when they contain a single thought. The map below is a case in point. It is simply attempting to show where Donald Trump boosted the success of the Republican Party, by showing those states and counties where he increased the Republican share of the vote. What happened to the Democrats is reserved for other maps.

Counties where Trump increased the Republican vote

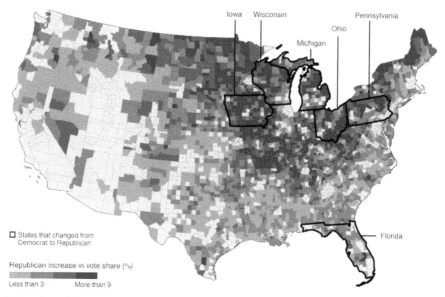

Where Donald Trump improved on the share of the vote achieved by Mitt Romney, the US Republican presidential candidate in 2012[5]

Proportional maps are another storytelling tool that the data journalist can bring out at election time. Their strength is to show how the nation looks when all its seats are the same size. For the UK, the most striking differences emerge as rural areas, especially in Scotland and Wales, shrink down in size when compared with the northern cities and especially when compared with London.

They offer a fresh perspective, but remember large chunks of the audience may not be familiar with them and as different news organisations use different-looking proportional maps it can be hard for that familiarity to build up. Animating transitions between proportional and traditional maps can help people see how the two things relate to each other.

9. Leave no geek behind

We've mentioned earlier that it is important to know your audience and be prepared to focus on the basics and while that's certainly true it is also a time when you can cater for those parts of your audience who really love politics, elections and numbers.

There are plenty of people who follow politics like others follow sport. They want to know all the details during the pre-match build-up and will happily devour any content that offers an early insight into the likely result, as well as detailed post-mortems once the whole thing is over. If you can't serve up a little content especially for the data nerds at election time, when can you?

10. Expect the unexpected

Last but not least, always expect the unexpected. It could be that your brand new cross-platform election results system spectacularly fails just a few hours before it is needed. The time for an earnest analysis about what went wrong is not on the night; instead, you'll need to boot-up your fall back option, however basic it might be.

When this happened to the *BBC News* website a number of years ago, we drafted in extra staff and manually published each result. Happily our 'Plan B' delivered a surprisingly fast service that turned out to be quicker than our rivals using more complex publishing systems.

And do remember history, it turns out, isn't one to spare the blushes of pollsters. So make sure you consider the 'what happens if' question during your careful planning for post-election coverage. And of course, don't forget to enjoy it all.

Notes

[1] *Impartiality Review – BBC Reporting of Statistics Report on Qualitative Research with the BBC Audience*, BBC Trust, 2016. Available online at http://www.bbc.co.uk/bbctrust/our_work/editorial_standards/impartiality/statistics.

[2] US election poll tracker: Who is ahead – Clinton or Trump? *BBC* News, 8 November 2016. Available online at http://www.bbc.co.uk/news/election-us-2016-37450661.

[3] Poll tracker: How the parties compare, BBC News, 3 July 2017. Available online at http://www.bbc.co.uk/news/election-2017-39856354.

[4] General election 2017 social media, *Storify* 2017. Available online at https://storify.com/CJeavans/general-election-2017-social-media.

[5] US election 2016: Trump victory in maps, *BBC News*, 1 December 2016. Available online at http://www.bbc.co.uk/news/election-us-2016-37889032.

Note on the contributors

John Walton is the data journalism editor for the *BBC News* website and Bella Hurrell is the assistant editor of the BBC's Visual Journalism team. Between them they have worked on digital coverage of every major UK and US election and referendum since 1997.

Using data to track mainstream and social media during the 2017 UK Election campaign

Martin Moore and Gordon Ramsay discuss how they tracked dozens of media outlets, thousands of candidates, hundreds of thousands of tweets and a few dozen Facebook newsfeeds using specially designed data software during the 2017 General Election campaign

The race to track GE2017

MPs and journalists were not the only ones scrambling to get organised after Theresa May's snap decision to hold a General Election in June 2017; those of us who research news and election campaigns were racing to get our act together too. At the Centre for the Study of Media, Communication and Power, at King's College London, we track digital news and social media during election and referendum campaigns. Normally, we have months if not years to develop our software, prepare our political dictionaries and work up hypotheses. For the 2017 General Election we had days. This chapter is about what we did and what we have – so far – discovered.

We started tracking media and social media in earnest during the 2015 General Election campaign (see Moore and Ramsay 2015a), using software we developed in-house called 'Steno'. Steno is able to collect online news articles – the text itself plus the byline, headline, date-time published and other metadata – or tweets, and store them in a structured database. We also built a simple Steno desktop app that allows us to do search queries, tag and export articles and tweets. Ask Steno for every news article published about George Osborne during the 2015 campaign, for example, and it spits out 1,069 articles. In total during the 2015 campaign, we captured more than 250,000 news articles and more than one million tweets.

We were, it is important to stress, far from the only research centre analysing news and political communication during the 2017 General Election campaign. Despite May's surprise election announcement, there were many other UK research projects studying different aspects of campaign communication. Loughborough University had a team reviewing press and broadcast coverage – as they have had since 1992 (Loughborough University 2017, Deacon et al. 2017). Cardiff University were analysing television coverage of the campaign (Cardiff University

2017, Cushion and Lewis 2017). The Centre for the Analysis of Social Media at DEMOS were using Method52 to collect and analyse GE2017 on Twitter (CASM 2017). Others were looking at 'fake news' during the campaign, at fact-checking, at specific political issues and at the news output of individual outlets. The initial findings of some of these analyses are published in the excellent Political Studies Association's *Election Analysis 2017* (Thorsen, Jackson and Lilleker 2017). Our approach was slightly different to these – thanks chiefly to Steno and, as will be explained in this chapter, new software we have developed called FaceLog. We used this software to collect as much online news content and data as possible and then use digital techniques to test hypotheses and study different political agendas.

Findings from GE2015 and the 2016 EU Referendum

During the 2015 election campaign, our main purpose was to explore the dynamics of agenda-setting between the political parties, mainstream media (not including broadcast bulletins), and influencers on Twitter. We discovered, amongst other things, that both main parties appeared to go out of their way to avoid discussing immigration. The Conservatives 'won' the battle to set the agenda, centring campaign debate on the economy and the deficit. It was also a very stage-managed campaign, with candidates rarely saying anything controversial to mainstream media or on Twitter (Moore and Ramsay 2015b).

For the 2016 EU Referendum campaign we wanted to focus in detail on the inter-relationship between the campaign and mainstream media agendas. We were keen to map the evolution of communication over the 10-week campaign – tracking the use of particular slogans like 'Take Back Control', and specific narratives – such as the association of the Remain campaign with 'the Establishment'. We found, for example, that coverage of immigration more than tripled over the course of the campaign, rising faster than any other political issue. British sovereignty, though widely covered as an issue, was discussed almost entirely in the context of the economy or immigration, and – in about half the articles in which it was referenced – in terms of 'taking back control'. Overall, we used both quantitative and qualitative analysis to review 351,166 articles published online by twenty news outlets during the campaign.

What GE2017 data to collect?

In 2017, we learnt there would be an election on Tuesday 18 April. By Thursday 20 April we were already tracking whatever we could. We knew from experience that you cannot analyse what you do not collect. So, despite the lack of warning we tried to gather as much digital news content as we could. This included all the articles published online in mainstream media, the candidates' tweets, and as much 'alt-media' as we could find – outlets like the *Canary*, *Skwawkbox* and *Breitbart London*. We had an inkling that alt-media would play a bigger part in 2017 than in any previous UK election. Just in case there were any concerns raised about Russian influence we collected articles from RT too.

We also tried something highly experimental: something that, to our knowledge, has never been attempted before by researchers in the UK. We tried to collect all the posts that a carefully selected group of volunteers were exposed to in their Facebook newsfeeds. Since the UK General Election of 2015 we – like many others – had been frustrated by the fact that increasing numbers of people were getting their news from Facebook, yet we had no way of knowing what people were shown (and not shown). The problem gained more urgency in 2016, after concerns were raised that people were becoming cocooned in information filter bubbles on social media and that Facebook users were being exposed to high quantities of 'fake news' in their newsfeeds (Viner 2016, Silverman 2016). It is virtually impossible to test either of these concerns since Facebook newsfeeds are closed to all but the user and to Facebook. This struck us as politically and democratically unacceptable, so in 2016 we started building software to do something about it.

To explore the filter bubble question and better understand exposure to news in the Facebook newsfeed we developed some software called 'FaceLog'. Facelog is made up of two parts. First, there is the FaceLog Chrome browser extension (written in Javascript), which you can install on Chrome just like any other extension (you can find it on the Chrome Store). Next, there is the FaceLog web server (written in Go), which captures and stores all the data collected. After a volunteer downloads the browser extension it sits dormant until s/he opens up Facebook. It then wakes up and, as the user looks through their Facebook posts, so the extension records all the relevant information – date/time posted, title, description, likes and shares etc. This includes any new content dynamically added to the page – for example, when the user scrolls downward and a new batch of posts appears. These collected posts are stored locally, then every seven minutes the extension sends them up to the server. The server provides a simple registration screen which assigns the user a random ID, under which their uploaded posts are filed. There is also an API endpoint which the extension uses to perform the actual upload. All communication between the extension and the server occurs via encrypted HTTPS connections to ensure privacy and prevent eavesdropping.

When the election was called, the FaceLog software was still in alpha development so we hurried to get it up and running before the campaign was over. There would have been no experiment, of course, without volunteers willing to participate. For this we have to thank Ipsos MORI, with whom we partnered to run the experiment. Ipsos MORI invited members of their panel to participate – fully explaining what this meant and providing assurances as regards privacy and data protection. Forty people kindly agreed to take part.

By 9 June, the day after the vote, we had collected a mountain of rich data. We had 236,452 news articles from twenty mainstream news and ten alt-media sources, more than 200,000 tweets from 2,041 Twitter accounts (from the final three weeks) and data from the Facebook newsfeeds of forty volunteers (jointly exposed to a total of 12,661 posts).

Wading through the GE2017 data

At this point we are just starting to wade our way through the data. Once we are happy that it is all clean (in other words free from duplicates, clear of non-news content), the next stage will be to separate out coverage of the election itself from general news. We will then create political dictionaries for all the main issues discussed in the campaign – from health to welfare to housing – and use these to tag all articles and tweets. This will allow us to see which issues dominated the news agenda and how this changed over the course of the campaign. Still, even from the initial data, there are some fascinating findings emerging (with the caveat that some of these numbers may change once the data is fully sorted and cleaned).

Initially, there was considerable coverage of Brexit in the mainstream media – as anticipated and encouraged by Theresa May who called the election to strengthen her hand in Brexit negotiations. Yet mainstream coverage of Brexit then dropped over the following four weeks – by 5 per cent in week two, 3 per cent in week three, 7 per cent in week four and another 23 per cent in week five. Only in the final fortnight of the campaign did Brexit coverage increase again (along with coverage of the election overall).

Rather than Brexit monopolising campaign attention, specific issues came to dominate short spells of the campaign. After Will Heaven, of the *Spectator*, used the term 'dementia tax' to describe the Conservative proposals for adult social care, 538 articles were published referring to it. By contrast only 42 articles were published on the so-called 'garden tax' (a tax on land value proposed by Labour). Some 631 articles talked about the pensions 'triple lock', most notably the decision of the Conservatives not to guarantee it. The Conservative plans to introduce means-testing of the winter fuel allowance generated 509 articles across mainstream media. And, 340 articles referred to 'police cuts', particularly after Labour emphasised these in the period following the Manchester Arena bombing on 22 May. Each of these debates about specific policy issues diverted attention away from Brexit as the central election theme in the media.

Theresa May's efforts to make the campaign presidential – with the media spotlight on the personality of the two main party leaders – was successful (at least in terms of quantity of coverage). More than 13,000 articles referred to Theresa May and over 9,000 to Jeremy Corbyn. Many of the articles about Corbyn linked him either with the IRA (595 articles), with political views and policies dating from the 1970s (323 articles) or with the potential of a 'coalition of chaos' (570 articles) – a phrase often used by the Conservatives to refer to the dangers of a Labour vote.

Alt-media and Twitter in GE2017

The alt-media sites we studied were more politically engaged, as a proportion of their output, than mainstream media. Over half the articles (55 per cent) published by the ten sites analysed explicitly referred to the election. Many more articles talked about issues directly related to the election without referring to it (for example, talking about specific senior politicians). By contrast, around 10 per cent of the articles published by mainstream news outlets referred explicitly to the election. Within alt-media coverage of the campaign, there was also a strong focus on the two leaders. Of 4,363 articles published on the ten sites between 20 April and 7 June, over a third (1,500) mentioned Theresa May and 30 per cent (1,346) mentioned Jeremy Corbyn.

On Twitter, we concentrated on tracking the candidates' tweets. Building from the list of twitter profiles compiled by Democracy Club, we captured the tweets of 569 incumbent candidates, 1,460 challengers and the party twitter accounts and associated press offices. One striking difference from 2015 was the behaviour of the main party press offices. In 2015, both Conservative and Labour press offices used Twitter as virtual spin-rooms, rapid response units reacting to emerging campaign news. In 2017, both were much less prolific and pugnacious and focused more on simply promoting campaign slogans and messages. @CCHQ press published an average of twenty tweets-per-day in 2017 as opposed to 92-per-day in 2015. @LabourPress published about 11 tweets-per-day in 2017 as compared to 57-per-day in 2015. The busiest of the party-political tweeters were the LibDems who, from the party and press accounts, tweeted over 2,100 times in the last three weeks (approximately 100-a-day).

Candidates are not the most frequent users of hashtags. However, when they were used, hashtags that favoured Labour significantly exceeded those favouring the Conservatives – even with regard to official party slogans. #forthemany was tweeted over a thousand times as against #strongandstable which was used less than 150 times in the final three weeks (having perhaps been over-used in previous weeks). Even #weakandwobbly outperformed #strongandstable, appearing in more than 200 candidate tweets during this period.

What next?

There is much more work to be done to analyse and interpret 2017 election media and campaign communication, not least because public support for the parties changed so significantly during the campaign itself. This, many agree, was an election campaign that significantly affected the outcome. Some of the questions we are looking to answer include:

- Were the economy and immigration less central to news coverage and campaign communication in this election than in 2015 or 2016?

- Did news coverage of Jeremy Corbyn change substantially during the campaign – both in quantity and tone?

- Was the success of Labour supporters and activists on social media reflected in the use of social media by Labour candidates?

- How central – or peripheral – was the election to people on Facebook?

As with every election or referendum that we analyse, we have learnt – and are learning – how to do things better next time. Next time, for example, we plan to expand our analysis of alt-media (itself a term rapidly feeling outdated), particularly given how widely non-mainstream news articles were shared. We will aim to extend our collection and analysis of social media, especially with a view to better understanding what news is shared – and why – on social platforms. And, we will try to recruit more Facebook volunteers to do a broader examination of news exposure and test the filter bubble thesis.

Of course, this rather depends on when the next election is, and on how much notice we receive. Elections and referendums are now following one another so quickly that we hardly have time to publish the results of our last analysis before starting a new one. Still, it makes for many and varied opportunities to do data journalism research.

References

CASM (Centre for the Analysis of Social Media) at Demos (2017). Available online at https://www.demos.co.uk/research-area/centre-for-analysis-of-social-media/

Cardiff University, JOMEC (2017-ongoing) Blogs available online at http://www.jomec.co.uk/blog/category/politics/general-election/

Cushion, Stephen and Lewis, Justin (2017) Were the broadcasters impartial? , Mair, John et al. (eds) *Brexit, Trump and the Media*, Bury St Edmunds: Abramis pp 378-385

Deacon, David, Downey, John, Smith, David and Stanyer, James (2017) Two parts policy, one part process: news media coverage of the 2017 election, Mair, John et al. (eds) *Brexit, Trump and the Media*, Bury St Edmunds: Abramis pp 367-371

Loughborough University, Centre for Research in Communication and Culture (2017) News Media Coverage of the 2017 General Election. Available online at http://www.lboro.ac.uk/news-events/general-election/

Moore, Martin and Ramsay, Gordon N. (2015a) Data journalism and the 2015 UK General Election: Media content analysis for a digital age, Mair, John (ed.) *Data Journalism*, Bury St Edmunds, Abramis pp 84-94

Moore, Martin and Ramsay, Gordon N. (2015b) *UK Election 2015 – Setting the Agenda*, October, Centre for the Study of Media, Communication and Power, Policy Institute, King's College London

Moore, Martin and Ramsay, Gordon N. (2017) *UK media coverage of the 2016 EU Referendum campaign*, May, Centre for the Study of Media, Communication and Power, Policy Institute, King's College London

Silverman, Craig (2016) This analysis shows how viral fake election news stories outperformed real news on Facebook, *Buzzfeed*, 16 November. Available online at https://www.buzzfeed.com/craigsilverman/viral-fake-election-news-outperformed-real-news-on-facebook

Thorsen, Einar, Jackson, Daniel and Lilleker, Darren (2017) *UK Election Analysis 2017: Media, Voters and the Campaign*, Political Studies Association

Viner, Katherine (2016) How technology disrupted the truth, *Guardian*, 12 July. Available online at https://www.theguardian.com/media/2016/jul/12/how-technology-disrupted-the-truth

Note on the contributors

Martin Moore is Director of the Centre for the Study of Media, Communication and Power, at King's College London, and a Senior Research Fellow in the Policy Institute at King's. Gordon N. Ramsay is Deputy Director of the Centre for the Study of Media, Communication and Power, at King's College London, and a Research Fellow in the Policy Institute at King's. The two are joint authors of a study of media coverage of the 2015 election and of media coverage of the 2016 EU Referendum.

Sky Data: Building a polling organisation in a media corporation

Sky TV has a distinctly imaginative – and award-winning – way of using opinion polls to generate news stories. Here, Harry Carr explains how they do it – using the 2017 General Election as a case study

Modern opinion polling essentially began in the 1930s and is today, perhaps, the most frequently used and easily recognisable source for stories in data journalism. Yet in the UK until recently news organisations have rarely dabbled in recruiting staff to run opinion polls directly.

In 2015, I was brought in by *Sky News* from the research company Ipsos MORI to head up an initiative devised by their new Political Editor, Faisal Islam, to use the data and resources available to Sky as a wider media organisation to inform their journalism.

The initiative became Sky Data, a unique capability to run nationally representative opinion polls which would go on to win a Royal Television Society award for its impact just two years later.

George Gallup and the *Literary Digest*: The birth of modern opinion polling

Given the prominence and preponderance of opinion polls in journalism, all journalists should have a basic understanding of what opinion pollsters do and how polling works. The founding story of modern opinion polling is set in the United States in 1936, ahead of the Presidential Election campaign between Republican Alf Landon and the Democratic incumbent, Franklin Delano Roosevelt.

The *Literary Digest*, a popular magazine, ran a gigantic poll of 2.4 million Americans at great expense. The magazine stressed that the responses were reported 'exactly as received… neither weighted nor adjusted'. They predicted a dramatic win for Landon.

George Gallup, on the other hand, conducted a poll of 40,000 Americans (still far more than the industry standard of 1,000 used in polling today) with quotas on the region where the interviews were conducted, how rural or urban the areas were, and the gender, age and socio-economic status of the respondents. Gallup predicted Roosevelt to win comfortably.

As you will have guessed – since you have never heard of 'President Landon' – Gallup was right and the *Literary Digest* was spectacularly wrong. The story made George Gallup a household name in America and struck a blow to the reputation of the *Literary Digest* from which it never recovered.

Polling is like tasting soup

Methods have obviously moved on since then, but the principle proved by the story is that a small sample can reveal the opinions of a large population – so long as the sample is representative. The *Literary Digest*'s error was in not ensuring their sample was representative. They ended up with too few poorer voters, who tended to vote for Roosevelt, as they were less likely to read the *Literary Digest* – and also less likely to respond to the poll.

Gallup talked about opinion polling being like tasting whether a pot of soup has enough salt. You don't need to eat the whole pot – if you've given it a good stir, a spoonful will do the job.

How pollsters 'stir the pot' in this analogy – that is, how they make sure the respondents in their poll are representative of the overall population – is through sampling and weighting. Sampling is basically how you choose the people you interview. Pollsters set quotas for things like age, gender, region and social grade, to make sure that for each they have as similar a proportion as possible as is contained in the overall population. So, for example, if half the population of Britain is female, half of your respondents should be female in a poll of British public opinion.[1]

Weighting comes after you have received your responses. Despite their efforts in sampling, pollsters will almost always have slightly too few or too many people in various demographics. To compensate for that, pollsters assign a weight to each respondent, so that if there are, say, too few Londoners in the poll, each of their answers is given more weight than the average response, while if there are too many Scots in the poll, each of their answers is given less weight than the average response.

How Sky Data works

Online opinion pollsters use research panels as the source of their respondents. These are usually made up of people who have clicked on a link to express a willingness to answer polls in exchange for incentives (often points you can accumulate in exchange for prizes). The panels are usually put together for the express purpose of conducting research.

Sky Data uses the database of more than 10 million Sky customers – including Sky TV subscribers but also the likes of Sky internet users – as a form of research panel. We choose our samples from the customer database and weight our data based on similar demographics to those used by other pollsters. But we also use a nuanced geodemographic segmentation system called Mosaic, taking into account income, household composition, tenure, family status, work status, property type, car ownership, population density, technology adoption, education, ethnicity, shopping habits, holidays taken and media consumption.

We conduct more traditional online polls where a link to a survey is sent by email to the selected sample. But we also conduct polls in an entirely new mode, using a relatively old technology – SMS text message.

Polling by text message

If you have ever had an engineer from Sky come and fix your satellite dish or called their helpline, you will likely have received a text message on your phone asking about your experience. Sky sends out vast numbers of these text messages each year and analyses the results, using a platform provided by an external company, Rant & Rave. The same technology, we realised, could be used for extremely fast turnaround public opinion polling – perfect for reacting to breaking news.

> Hi, this is Sky News. We'd like to ask one question about the general election; to take part, please reply 'yes'. Text STOP to opt out of future SMS surveys.

> Yes

> Do you think there should or should not be an early general election on 8 June? a) should, b) should not, c) don't know. Please reply a, b or c.

> A

The methodology in terms of sampling and weighting remains the same as for our online polling, but responses come in extremely quickly – the vast majority of responses will come within a few hours. Working with Rant & Rave, we created a system that is able to provide a statistically robust, nationally representative poll showing the public's view on a story less than two hours after it has broken.

The format requires that the questions be short and simple. Rather than having to click on a link, respondents directly answer the questions by text message.

We then have a dashboard showing the number of responses and how they have answered (though at this stage the responses are not yet weighted). Using this we

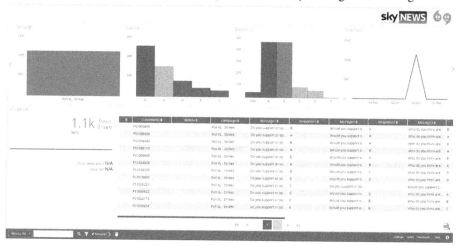

can decide when to close the poll (as a rule we do not publish polls unless we have received at least 1,000 responses) and having a rough idea of how the results might look can let us prepare for how we will tell the story.

Working together with Rant & Rave, we created a system that is able to provide a statistically robust, nationally representative poll showing the public's view on a story less than two hours after it has broken.

Aren't Sky customers skewed?

It's a question we get asked often. The short answer is no – once you have controlled for demographics. Sky customers overall are obviously different in their demographics to the British public overall. However, there are sufficient numbers in the 10 million-strong database to be able to create representative samples. Indeed, the fact that our panel is not made up of people who have specifically expressed a desire to answer opinion polls is an advantage in terms of gathering responses from people who are less politically engaged.

Our findings have been rigorously tested across a range of political attitudinal measures against 'gold standard' academic polls, the British Social Attitudes survey and the British Election Study, verified by leading academics from the University of Plymouth and the University of Oxford.

What's it good for?

The range of methods available to Sky Data allow for both fast turnaround polling to give a top level view of what Britons think, and also more considered, detailed analysis of aggregated data gathered over months in our online polling.

The role of the results also varies. They can be used as original content in and of themselves – for example, in January 2017 *Sky News* ran a week of stories based on a comprehensive Sky Data survey asking how people feel things had changed in the past year – leading off with the finding that people now felt Britain was more racist and less happy as a country than it has been a year earlier.

They are often also used to provide additional detail and context to an existing story. This can be particularly useful as a more representative alternative to vox pops in news packages in providing public reaction to breaking news. An example of this is in two polls conducted before and after

Do you think the country is a more or less happy place than a year ago?

More happy   **Less happy**

8%   **67%**

SOURCE: SKY DATA

then-US President Barack Obama visited the UK and advised British voters to vote Remain in the EU referendum. Counter to the prevailing narrative of the time, the poll results suggested his intervention had been counterproductive for the Remain campaign, with voters less likely to back the Remain campaign following his hardball message regarding hypothetical trade negotiations post-Brexit, warning Britain would have to join 'the back of the queue'.

More detailed analysis of aggregated data allows more nuanced storytelling, looking in greater detail at the factors behind what Britons think and enabling us to mimic political parties and campaigns in mapping where different groups of voters and people susceptible to particular messages are located.

For example, before the EU referendum we published a heat map showing predicted vote in each local authority. This was created by analysing the voting intention of each Mosaic group within each region in our aggregated data. As we also knew the demographic make-up of each local authority by Mosaic group, we could therefore predict an exact voting intention figure for each local authority. This was covered extensively on *Sky News* in the build-up to the vote – and was proven exceptionally accurate when the results came through. We later presented these results at the 'Elections, Public Opinion and Parties' academic conference in association with the Political Studies Association.

Case Study: The 2017 General Election

When Theresa May called a snap election, all indications were that she would romp home with an increased majority. An already healthy polling lead extended to as much as 20 points in the days following the announcement. Labour leader Jeremy Corbyn lagged far behind her in the approval ratings and the Conservatives were far more trusted with the economy than Labour. The same two issues had troubled Labour in the 2015 General Election when the Conservatives had achieved a surprise majority – and Mr Corbyn's Labour lagged behind where they had been in 2015 on both measures.

In 2015, the pollsters got the result wrong, overestimating Labour and underestimating the Conservatives. That was part of a consistent pattern over the decades – when the polls got it wrong, they tended to show higher scores for the Labour Party than were achieved on the day.

Shortly after the election was announced, we conducted an individual poll of at least 1,000 people in each individual region of Britain – Scotland, North East, North West, Yorkshire and Humber, East Midlands, West Midlands, Wales, East of England, South East, South West and London. Within each region, we could then look at how different demographics in each region were set to vote, how they had changed and what it all meant in terms of which seats would change hands.

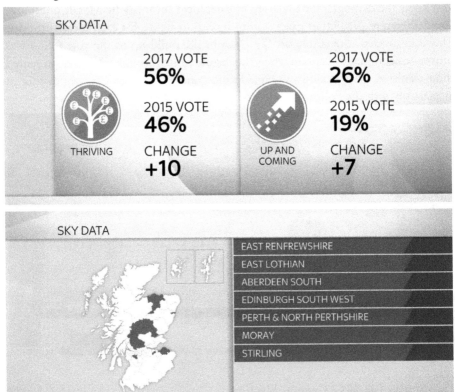

As this was still at the start of the campaign, in line with other pollsters we showed a commanding Conservative lead – but some of the patterns even from this point would still hold true in the final result. Our features included:

- The Liberal Democrats making very little progress, even amongst people who voted Remain in the EU referendum, whom they had been targeting and had gained support from in local elections and by elections previously.

- The Conservatives making big breakthroughs in Scotland at the expense of the Scottish National Party.

- Labour doing far better in the south than the north (particularly the North East) compared with how they did in 2015.

- UKIP's vote share falling to a fraction of that achieved in 2015.

- Labour dominating the vote of people who voted Remain in the EU referendum and the Conservatives dominating among people who voted Leave.

- Graduates becoming more likely to vote Labour, people without educational qualifications becoming more likely to vote Conservative.

- A swing to the Conservatives among less wealthy voters.

The germ of what was to come was there – but very few people expected the huge swing to Labour that was to follow.

Election night

On the day of the vote we conducted a final poll to provide context around why people voted the way they did. The change from the start of the campaign was spectacular. Approval ratings for Theresa May and Jeremy Corbyn were now effectively level. At the start of the campaign, Mrs May's had been +18 (56 per cent satisfied, 38 per cent dissatisfied), while Mr Corbyn's was -41 (26 per cent satisfied, 67 per cent dissatisfied). On the day of voting, they were -7 for Theresa May (45 per cent satisfied, 52 per cent dissatisfied), -9 for Jeremy Corbyn (44 per cent satisfied, 53 per cent dissatisfied).

The issue of healthcare had ended up being the most important issue for voters, with Brexit – on which the Conservatives, Liberal Democrats and UKIP had hoped to campaign strongly – ranked well behind that in terms of impact in deciding how people voted.

And there were huge differences in voting by age, with 18-34s voting 63 per cent for Labour, 27 per cent for the Conservatives, 35-54s voting 43 per cent for Labour and 43 per cent for the Conservatives, and those aged 55+ voting 23 per cent for Labour and 59 per cent for the Conservatives.

It appeared that many traditional Labour voters who had been leaning towards the Conservatives at the beginning of the campaign had returned to the fold – albeit not necessarily with great enthusiasm, with almost as many saying they were voting Labour as the least bad option as because they would make a good government.

All of this was used in the first couple of hours after the exit poll came out at 10pm shocking many with its (correct) prediction of a hung parliament – giving some indication as to what had happened beneath the headline numbers.

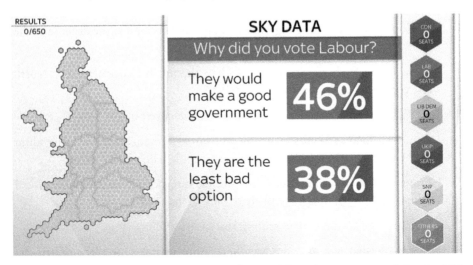

Through the night we also used a similar model to the one we used for the EU referendum heat map to predict what the eventual seat numbers would be based on the results as they came in – helping us project from very early on in the night that the result would be a hung parliament. For each seat we had a predicted vote for each party; as the results came in we adjusted those predictions based on how far off our initial prediction was and the pattern of the results as they came in.

We had several different models running, but by 2am all of them were predicting a hung parliament with the Conservatives on around 318 seats (they needed 326 to win a majority). That remained unchanged from then on, and at 4am we went on air to publicly call the election as a hung parliament.

Achievements and lessons

Sky Data was extremely ambitions from the start – but has proven that an outstanding data journalism capability can be built quickly and to great effect. We were able to break new ground in using a large customer base to conduct traditional polls, introducing representative polling by SMS and in placing Sky Data front and centre of *Sky News'* political coverage.

For all of this we won the 2017 Royal Television Society award for News Technology – and went on to be at the forefront of *Sky News'* 2017 General Election coverage. We will continue to innovate in preparation for the next election – whenever that may be…

Note

[1] Some surveys, such as the British Social Attitudes survey and the British Election Study, do not do this. Instead, a random selection of postcodes are drawn and interviewers call on them in person again and again over months to interview as many of them as possible. This is the most academically pure way to conduct surveys on public opinion, but is far too expensive and takes far too long to be practical for media organisations.

Note on the contributor

Harry Carr is Head of Sky Data. He joined Sky News in 2015 to head up a new initiative that would become Sky Data, directing the project from conception through to centrepiece of *Sky News'* political coverage, winning a Royal Television Society award for News Technology. He also writes and presents about public opinion and politics for *Sky News* and is editor of the weekly All Out Politics podcast with Adam Boulton. Before joining *Sky News*, Harry was a political analyst at Ipsos MORI's Social Research Institute and managed their flagship monthly political polls.

Telling election stories through data

Data journalism played a significant role in *Sky News'* coverage of three major elections over a 13-month period. Hugh Westbrook examines some of the problems encountered – and highlights some of the lessons learned

The 2017 General Election campaign featured a number of personalities whose views dominated the political landscape in the run-up to 8 June. But there was one person who spoke for the nation on the day that Theresa May announced the decision to call a snap poll. When asked for her opinion by the BBC, Brenda from Bristol's aghast 'What! Another one!' summed up the national incredulity at the decision to hold yet another major vote.

Brenda spoke for me as well, but only in part. I knew how much work lay ahead of me as a result of the snap election. The other part of me was full of adrenalin at the excitement of the challenge ahead. My job – looking after the results data which appeared across all of *Sky News'* platforms. No pressure then!

At *Sky News*, the data for an election is central to everything we do. The results programme on TV and our accompanying look-up service on our digital platforms is the core of our offering – and being fast and accurate is all that matters. The snap general election came after an unprecedented run of major elections. This chapter looks at the three elections which took place over the period of 13 months – the EU Referendum, the US Presidential Election and the 2017 General Election – and examines, in particular, some of the specific problems which we encountered with each one, detailing some of the lessons learned as a result.

The database

When *Sky News* was purely a TV broadcaster, the provision of results data was a simpler affair. Data was taken directly from the Press Association and fed to TV graphics, without the concerns over other services using the data and the issues this raises over performance. However, as websites and then mobile began to come to the fore, a new solution was needed to ensure consistency across all platforms and that the service was robust enough to deal with the vastly increased number of users needing to access the data.

The decision was taken to create a central database which allowed for data to come in from both PA and manual inputters, and for that to feed out data to broadcast and digital simultaneously. The vision was that this database would be developed over time to incorporate all the election types which *Sky News* broadcasts live.

After a successful trial for the 2014 local elections, the database was first used for real for the Scottish Referendum in 2014. It was further developed for the 2015 General Election, and in 2016 the elections for the Scottish and Welsh devolved parliaments were included.

This meant that the database was able to deal with all of the major election types held in the UK, except for the Single Transferable Vote system used for the Northern Ireland Assembly. It was felt that building a complex piece of software to show the disappearance of candidates round-by-round was too much technical effort for the on-screen benefit because the interest really lies in seeing the final vote tally and list of elected candidates. It is always important when developing applications such as the election database to consider whether the development work involved provides sufficient benefit to the story being told. If the benefit is only minor, then sometimes a simpler and quicker solution can prove just as effective.

The EU Referendum

The EU Referendum on 23 June 2016 was the first time that a data structure built for one election was reused on a grander scale (see http://election.news.sky.com/referendum). A referendum is a simple election – a list of voting areas, and then a binary choice of two options. On the night, we ran a smooth operation which saw a number of results flow through the system automatically, while our results team was able to monitor the live feeds coming into the building to key in results manually.

In simple terms, a referendum is a small-scale version of a general election. A voting area is like a constituency, simply one that only features two candidates in every place. There is, however, one crucial way in which the data differs. In a general election, winning a constituency matters, and adding up the number of constituency victories gives you the overall result. In a referendum, results in individual voting areas are interesting and are worth reporting, but are actually not significant in terms of the overall result. In this case, the overall total is taken from adding up the number of votes for Yes and No, and that forms the basis for the final result. In reality, more voting areas voting for one side of the debate is likely to lead to that side winning the overall result, but it is not entirely certain. This is because the size of voting areas varies widely in a referendum, based as they are on local authorities. In a general election, the number of voters in different constituencies does not vary so widely.

This discrepancy in size also gave us a technical challenge. We knew that we would get some smaller results very early in the night – Gibraltar, with an electorate of just over 24,000, was always going to be very early, and so it proved by being declared first. Northern Ireland, with an electorate of over 1.25 million, was clearly going to be much later in the proceedings. But late in our planning we discovered that individual totals for the Northern Irish parliamentary constituencies would be made public throughout the night, and we had no simple way to display them. We could not declare them individually since that would have been inaccurate – they were not official voting areas in the election – but our system was only set up to display a complete result, and if you inputted vote totals for Yes and No and submitted that data, then a result would be declared for that voting area as a whole, which would also not be accurate. This meant that if our competitors had a way of adding those numbers into their overall totals, we could be at a disadvantage of several hundred thousand votes on either side, severely impacting our coverage.

The issue was eventually resolved by making Northern Ireland an exception and putting in particular rules around it. We allowed individual vote numbers for Yes and No to be submitted for Northern Ireland and published live to the overall total, but unless an extra step was taken to say that it was an overall result for Northern Ireland itself, no result for the area as a whole would be declared. This meant that we could tell the overall story – and ultimately information about the total number of votes on either side remained paramount – but we did not broadcast any information which was not accurate. The moral of this is that even in an election which seems simple, there is always something unexpected to trip you up. From a software development point of view, it is dealing with these exceptions which takes up a huge amount of the time spent on a project, often far more than is spent on the basic application which satisfies virtually all other criteria.

The US Election

In some respects, a US Presidential Election (http://election.news.sky.com/us-election) is very similar to a referendum. But in its detail, it is quite different. The similarity is purely superficial. The headline story is binary since the likelihood is that you are looking at a straight choice between two candidates. In theory, you could, therefore, assume that your data structure would be similar to a referendum. You would be wrong.

The reality is that this is not a binary election, with a victory in a voting area giving each candidate one vote towards eventual victory. Firstly, there is not a choice of two candidates – independents and others stand across the United States, and while *Sky News* does not name the individual candidates in each state, it does cater for the possibility of a third candidate winning a state by allowing it to be awarded to an independent. In 2016, this became a distinct possibility in Utah, meaning that the database had to allow for an independent to win, and the front-end clients taking the data created an exception for Utah, which meant that if there were an independent victory there, the name Evan McMullin would have been displayed on screen. In the end, this didn't materialise – an example of additional work being done to cater for something which did not occur but which was, nonetheless, necessary.

The other difference from a UK vote is that not all states are equal. Each state in the US has a different number of electoral college votes associated with it, and winning that state gives each candidate that specific number of votes. This is the number which goes into the overall total, meaning that set-up of the database in advance, and triple-checking that the vote number for each state is correct, is paramount for successful coverage.

But again there is an edge case. In Maine and Nebraska, local laws mean that not all electoral college votes from that state are automatically allocated to the winner. They have what is called a split vote, meaning that in theory more than one candidate can be allocated votes from those states. Again, a large amount of complex development was needed to allow the 'split' state to be called and for individual numbers to be added then to the overall total. The development teams were told this was unlikely, and that despite the effort they put into this piece of functionality, it might never get used, which can be quite a hard message to sell. It was, therefore, gratifying for all involved when Maine declared a split result in 2016.

The method used for declaring results was also complex. For a US election, *Sky News* provides all results manually from a dedicated team, and this is based on monitoring of the five main US networks, using them to make a decision on when *Sky News* will be happy to say that a state has gone a certain way. Networks will typically call a state when they are confident their exit polling has told them the result, which means that often they can make these calls as soon as the polls shut. If they can't call it at that point, then they need to wait until sufficient results have been counted in order to make a judgment, and it is becomes a battle across US television to be first with the correct call. The reality of this is that on the hour, every hour, there is a flurry of activity as polls close and calls are made, and then a certain amount of waiting around until the networks are happy.

In the past, *Sky News* has waited until three of the five networks – ABC, CBS, CNN, Fox and NBC – has made its call, and then committed Sky to that result. However, the reality is that once two networks have made a call, then it is likely to be correct, so we switched to two rather than three. The development task was, therefore, to allow information to be broadcast whenever the first network call was made, citing the network, and then switch to a Sky call when the second network call was made. At that point, a Sky call meant that electoral college numbers were fed into the overall total as well for each candidate. The technical complexity around this was to ensure that the numbers were fed in at the right point and individual messages about network calls were no longer sent for broadcast once the Sky call had been made. Much of the testing which needs to be done with a project such as this is about anticipating the problems and practising for them, rather than simply sitting back and testing against data which is simple and has no issues. That does not represent the reality of what might happen.

The 2017 General Election

The good news about the 2017 General Election was that we knew the database could handle it (see http://election.news.sky.com/snap-general-election-24). After all, it handled an election in 2015, and we managed to do some brief testing with the Press Association at the start of 2017 just to ensure our automated feeds were still working as expected. This meant that when the surprise call came, we knew that we had a solid database to work from.

However, that does not tell the story of the work we then had to do to be ready for a multi-platform broadcast. The first task was just to check that the basic journeys for data in and out of the database were functioning properly. We then had to ensure that extra functions such as the ability for people at individual constituencies to type in results and send them through to us were also still operating. Once we knew that the bedrock was working, we could move onto other things.

Inevitably, there were requests for new functionality to ensure that we told the story properly. The first was over Brexit, and a request for us to show how each individual constituency voted in the referendum. This would allow us to then show lists of Brexit supporting and opposing constituencies and then see which way they had voted this time. The first issue with this, of course, is that constituencies were not the voting areas in the referendum, so we had to use a data set which took the referendum data and reallocated it on a constituency level in a way that was regarded by all involved as accurate. Fortunately, Chris Hanretty, of the University of East Anglia, had produced a set of data which was regarded across the media as accurate, and we were able to add this into the database and then output it in the necessary feeds in order to tell the story.

Next, we had to consider the lessening of the UKIP effect, going hand-in-hand with tactical voting. Our database does a lot of work – all it gets fed with for an election for each constituency are the number of votes for each candidate and the size of the electorate. From that it calculates vote share and turnout, and by comparing it with the results from 2015 it can also calculate change in vote share. One of the things we check for is that vote share totals 100 per cent when added up and change in share zero sums when added up – i.e. the rises and falls cancel each other out overall.

This was when we discovered a problem. In 2017, UKIP wasn't standing in a number of constituencies it previously contested. Because our database is based around candidates, and the share and change of share data is not presented if no candidate is present, we were seeing the change in share for UKIP seats being amalgamated into the 'Others' category, meaning that while the change in share totals still zero summed, the story was no longer editorially accurate. Tactical voting – seats like Brighton Pavilion where the Lib Dems had chosen not to stand this time – had the same issue. So we had to make technical changes to provide these change of share numbers for parties which were not standing, and then find a way to display them on TV and digital which made it clear that the parties did not have a share of the vote in 2017, but the share of the vote which they did have in 2015 had disappeared. As well as work for the database team, this also led to extensive testing by all users, as in some cases, this change caused other graphics to malfunction. The law of unintended consequences is one that must always be adhered to when making changes in a complex product such as this – you need to look out for what might have been broken in the process of fixing something else.

And so to Buckingham. On the surface, this is the most straightforward constituency in the country. Traditionally, the Speaker is unopposed, meaning he sails to victory over a couple of minor inconveniences. Great for him, perhaps less great for the somewhat disenfranchised voters of Buckingham. In the past, *Sky News* has taken the view that the Speaker does not belong to a party; therefore, when he or she wins, their allocated constituency victory goes into the 'Other' category. However, after the closeness of the result in 2015 and the inconsistency between *Sky News* and other media, it was decided to change this in 2017 and allocate the Buckingham seat to the Conservative total, while still displaying it as a win for the Speaker.

The pain this caused still hurts! The amount of time it took, the number of times it needed to be tweaked and changed, and the variety of different data feeds it affected all meant that when it was finally completed, about a week before the election, it had taken more time than any other part of the development. For the only result which you could pretty much guarantee beforehand. The most definite result in the election took far and away the most work. There are times when the time you spend on something doesn't seem to be reflected in the end benefit, though in this case, given that accuracy is paramount, it was time well spent.

Conclusion

The *Sky News* election database is a hugely complicated product, with the ability to power fast and accurate results across multiple platforms for a wide variety of elections. This brief analysis of the last 13 months should have demonstrated that alongside the importance of building a robust product which carries out the basic requirements perfectly, a large amount of time will inevitably become dedicated to unlikely eventualities, local specifics and problems which will never materialise. It is always important to factor in the unexpected and plan for problems when embarking on a project such as this.

Note on the contributor

Hugh Westbrook has worked for *Sky News* for 17 years in both editorial and technical roles. He started as a breaking news journalist on *Sky News* active and *Sky News* online and went on to produce a number of interactive graphics, including the award-winning 'Fallen Heroes'. He then moved into a product role and oversaw a number of *Sky News* product launches. He is currently a member of the *Sky News* Products team, with particular responsibility for the *Sky News* elections database.

EU Referendum graphics for BBC television (Act 2)

Jonathan Spencer looks in detail at the BBC's visualisation of the 2016 EU Referendum results, examining critically the major issues confronted by the design team

Context

The heading refers to David Dimbleby's description of the 2017 General Election as 'the third act', the first being the 2015 General Election which returned the Conservative party to government with a majority for the first time since 1992. The second was the European Union referendum held on 23 June 2016. The commitment to hold this vote was in the Tories' 2015 manifesto and was designed to neuter UKIP and the Conservative eurosceptics in one move.

The widely-held belief of many commentators and pollsters was that the then-Prime Minister, David Cameron, thought he would not have to deliver on this manifesto promise as the 2015 election would return another coalition government and the Liberal Democrats would restrict Mr Cameron's movement over Europe. In the event, the Conservatives won an outright majority and Mr Cameron did deliver on the Tory manifesto promise. The Prime Minister, Chancellor and many senior Conservatives campaigned for Remain, though a free vote was given to cabinet members – and Boris Johnson, Andrea Leadsom and Michael Gove were amongst those who opted for Leave. It was a political earthquake when the EU referendum returned a 51.9 per cent to 48.1 per cent majority in favour of leaving the European Union. The result took the Prime Minister and many others by surprise and led to his resignation on the morning of the result.

During any election, the BBC comes under scrutiny to treat the arguments fairly. In a referendum there is only a binary choice for the electorate to make though the arguments are often made with great passion. The BBC, as ever, is committed to covering the issues with due impartiality and has to pick its way through this rather different political terrain.

Brand properties

The BBC wanted to step away from the use of flags since national and supra-national iconography could be perceived to exhibit a bias to one side or the other.

There was also a desire to connect with the 2015 election brand image and develop the hexagon format. For previous events of this nature a small team has worked with key stakeholders to roll out a design solution across the BBC. For the referendum project a large team was brought together to finalise the cross-platform brand. The event included a high-intensity 'war gaming' of both Leave and Remain design solutions – with more than 1,000 concepts considered over three days (all work being done on paper and destroyed at the end of the project).

Both Leave and Remain sides had newly-established logos but the recognition of these was very patchy, so the design team opted for colours: Leave (blue) and Remain (yellow), partially surrounded by a BBC red. The colour selection also nodded to political allegiances, a blue for the Conservatives as a party with a significant eurosceptic element and yellow for the largest broadly europhile party: the Liberal Democrats.

Animation was a key part of the brand property and logo, with Leave and Remain swapping sides between left and right (mirroring the complexity and historic cross-party issues with Europe), briefly creating a question mark and then resolving back to the start position. The animation moved seamlessly from orthographic to perspective views and back again, this playful attitude to the Z plane hiding the serious intent to create a logo equally at home in 2D or 3D environment. The return to the start position made it possible to loop the logo animation. In the course of the animation, the Leave and Remain elements of the logo were almost always surrounded by the BBC red, to contain and provide a frame for the conflicted elements. The idea was that the BBC mediated and provided context for contrasting viewpoints.

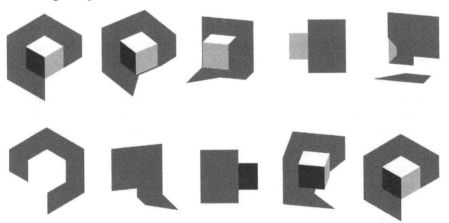

Figure 1: Logo V2 animation loop

The logo went through five iterations during the campaign period and immediate aftermath and the brand was launched with the finished flat logo and an animation that was 90 per cent complete. The team were unhappy with one aspect of the

2D/3D transitioning and the fix could not initially be applied in 3D. But a week or so after launch, a replacement logo V2 was discreetly rolled out to replace the original version.

Two days before the referendum vote, a debate was held between politicians at Wembley Arena. The logo used for the debate's programme titles and stings was our third version and had a slightly different interpretation of the logo and the 2D/3D relationship. We also created a series of infographics to be shown on TV and in the arena which helped to inform and punctuate the debate. For the results programme starting on 23 June, the team rolled out V4 – an enhanced version, visually more fractured by sliding blocks of low specular highly refractive glass through the 3D model animation. V5 was rolled out the following day once the UK had narrowly voted in favour of leaving.

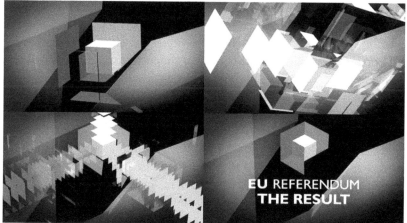

Figure 2: Four frames from the EU Referendum The Result using the V4 logo

Figure 3: End frame from the EU Referendum: The Result using the V5 logo

There was an article in the *Guardian* on Thursday 28 July 2016 regarding a ruling by the now-dissolved BBC Trust on accessibility for colour blind viewers. The ruling related to a complaint raised in 2015 by Kathryn Albany-Ward, founder of Colour Blind Awareness. The complaint focused on the perceptibility of various colours within Jeremy Vine's virtual reality 'battleground' for the 2015 General Election. Because the Vine 'battleground' existed in a virtual set which was lit by virtual lights there was a fall-off of light from the centre of the 'battleground' to the edges. This resulted in different party colours at the edges when compared to the party colours in the centre.

The BBC Trust partially upheld the complaint and made some sensible recommendations that the designers in the *BBC News* visual journalism team were determined to take on board. In the short term, the practical effect of this ruling was to steer the design team towards a binary solution that would be easily accessible to all viewers. This meant that more nuanced solutions were rejected as inappropriate for accessibility reasons early in the design process. The lack of recognition for the logos of Leave and Remain also removed a key support for accessibility. Subsequent design iterations of the trust's rulings have be considerably more successful.

The BBC has limited amount of skilled staff for making complex graphics and programmes. The 2016 EU Referendum was preceded in May by the local elections. The decision was made to use the Elstree set from the 2015 General Election for the 'locals' and leave it in place for the EU Referendum, using a re-light and new animated elements for the screens to give the set a fresh look. To achieve this, the department pulled together two separate but related graphic design teams while the virtual reality elements of the 'locals' were kept to a minimum. This allowed the developers as much time as possible to work with the EU Referendum results programme which was judged the most challenging task.

2016 virtual reality
The move to make the VR graphics more accessible, the lack of audience testing, the technological constraints and the previous experience of the editorial and design teams led the BBC to a slightly less than optimal set of virtual reality graphics for the EU Referendum.

The editorial and design team for the EU Referendum was in a large part composed of experienced producers and designers, most of whom had worked together on a number of UK and US elections before. This collaborative approach makes for a confident mind-set and an ability to work fast and to a budget; it also can lead to a certain rigidity of approach. The television world lacks the useful digital culture of user-testing designs with audiences to find the most effective solution. However, given the relative complexity of the main graphic for the EU Referendum programme it might have been beneficial to test these graphics on audiences either informally or formally.

Given the need to fill the time during an election/referendum night programme between the close of polls and the first results, there is an emphasis on making informative content to entertain and engage the audience in those hours. For the 2016 EU Referendum, the objective of Jeremy Vine's graphic was to use some of psephologist Professor John Curtice's methodology and map the results against the expectations as they came in. The conceptual model which was thought to be the best template was the 2014 Scottish Referendum in which Scotland had been split into 32 counting areas of different sizes, all of which were then dynamically split into Yes or No.

The challenge for the EU Referendum coverage was to do something similar with 382 counting areas. The relative sizes of these areas were also very different, from Northern Ireland with more than 1.8 million electors to the Isles of Scilly with 1,669 (at the time of building the prototype Northern Ireland was to be counted as one area). This amount of dynamically adjustable geometry can cause performance issues for the real time rendering of the graphics. To alleviate the load on the renderers, we took the decisions to use textures rather than geometry. The request from the editorial team was for all of the counting areas to be visible at once. The design team achieved this by imagining the counting areas as square books on a shelf, the total area implied by the height of the spine, so normalisation was necessary to keep all the areas in the realms of the visible.

This made for a very large graphic which, in the virtual world, was not an issue: best practice is to build virtual environments and models in a one-to-one scale. The main aim was to reduce the amount of scaling operations the render engine had to do. Thus, as a result came in the graphic would adjust. In addition, Jeremy Vine's producer, Ben Watt, discussed with Professor Curtice the factors that 'could' define an area as likely to vote Leave or Remain. Professor Curtice was understandably reluctant to share his actual methodology, but gave Ben enough to work with so that we could build a prototype to visualise the likely shape of a possible result.

Our prototype design used UKIP returns as a basic indicator of the order of counting areas from most Leave to most Remain. These were the areas that had fewer graduates, that voted for UKIP and those that had an older demographic were judged more likely to vote Leave. The metropolitan, educated and younger vote favoured Remain. This would give the countryside to Leave and the cities to Remain. This resulted in a similar headache in terms of data visualisation to representing the Labour vote which, in a general election, is concentrated in urban areas. Maps that colour-up in the UK's first-past-the-post electoral system show the English countryside as predominantly Conservative blue with small, often tricky to spot splashes of Labour red in and around population centres. We faced the same issues with our maps in the referendum results programme.

However, unlike the first-past-the-post system, a counting area is not 'won' but rather a vote is of equal weight wherever it is cast. This meant a Leave vote cast in

Gibraltar was still counted towards the Leave total, regardless of the fact Gibraltar voted predominantly to Remain.

However, to keep all the counting areas in shot, some adjustment to the relative heights needed to be made, so the counting areas were arrayed along a flattened sine wave and ordered in relation to their likelihood to vote one way or the other. The idea was that as the night progressed the 'sound cloud', as it became known, would settle and give a national picture with the mainly yellow (Remain) spines dominating on the right of the wave and the mainly blue spines (Leave) on the left. The original design was loosely based on a candlestick chart.

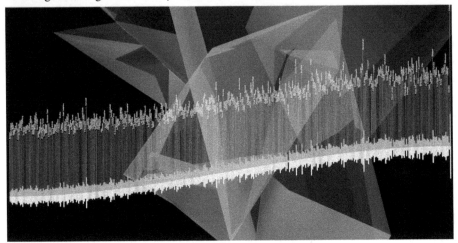

Figure 4: prototype (sound cloud)

Once the design prototype had been built using a combination of Excel and Processing (visualisation software), the concept was handed over to the software developers to build with VizRt. During this stage of the production it was decided that whichever side gained the most votes in a counting area, that colour would be the one displayed on top. This undermined the initial intention to range the counting areas and keep an overall image of either side's performance against the predictions as a large sweep of colour. This sense of 'calling' an area for Leave or Remain appealed to the deep DNA of the election team. The decision to move away from a fixed Remain / Leave order in each counting area was a significant one and set the design on a less subtle, less sensitive path. The editorial desire for winners shown above losers made the chart less coherent from a design perspective.

The integration of maps with the 'sound cloud' graphic followed the same path: areas would be coloured-up for Leave or Remain regardless of the strength of the win for one or other side. This treated the EU Referendum map as a traditional election map using a first-past-the-post methodology rather than a more accurate 'shades of opinion' heat map. On the other hand, it is true people would want to know how their areas voted and that a percentage could and would be displayed.

The adoption of a binary design solution meant the design team could use textures for the counting areas rather than geometry. This had the added benefit of improving performance for the live render engines, removed a practical technological constraint and reinforced the TV design team's preference for a binary design solution.

Figure 5: VR set showing final version of the 'sound cloud' and map on the floor

In recent years, the tradition has been to lay the VR map horizontally flat on the floor to allow Jeremy Vine to use the space and walk over the map from Land's End to John O' Groats. This allows other vertical graphic elements to be combined with the map; in the case of a general election this would normally be the 'battleground'. This combination means that the map is always shot by the studio cameras from an oblique angle which makes it hard to read. This restriction makes the TV designers favour high contrast colour combinations which enhance the legibility over heat maps.

This discussion went back and forth between design and editorial teams without resolution, but the combination of 'election DNA' within the whole BBC team, the desire to find a simple solution that would meet the needs of colour blind audiences and the rendering performance gains led to the decision to treat the Leave / Remain graphics in a simplified binary form rather than using arguably more informative heat maps or chloropleths.

Projections

The BBC projected the referendum results totals on to the outside of Broadcasting House overnight. This was the second time the corporation has used live data and architectural projection in combination, the first was during the 2015 general election. The design was based firmly within the EU Referendum brand.

Full-forms (Twitter bot)

The programme also used full forms to tell the story in individual counting areas. This was done using a 180 degree pie chart with the 50 per cent at 12 o'clock. The BBC can generate these on command and not all of the counting areas will have been broadcast as they were called. So the BBC renders the result and saves it as a still image to a server where it is tweeted out and can be accessed by BBC Nations and Regions for use as they see fit on TV or online.

Conclusion

I designed the 'sound cloud' prototype and, at the time, considered it an elegant solution to the problem of scale. However, since watching the programme and explaining the concept to other audiences, I have concluded it is overly complicated and should have had further user testing. The virtual graphics' saving grace was the use of what was called the 'top shot pie'. This was a smooth transition from the virtual studio with presenter to a very wide (and impossible shot) that displayed the result as a 180 arc.

Figure 6: ZedCam and the 'top shot pie'

This shot used an in-house development tool called 'ZedCam' that give the director a virtual camera able to go beyond the studio walls. The interest in counting areas, and calling them for Leave or Remain, added an emphasis to the geographical debate that was unhelpful after the referendum. The pressures for this were almost all created internally and may have been avoided with more testing of ideas. However, the BBC was not alone in adopting a binary approach to calling the counting areas; most other media companies came up with the same solution. Subsequent discussion of the nature of the coverage and the accurate visual representation of statistics has led me to conclude that the most legible solution could be seen as unacceptably minimal and that the balance between an acceptable level of artifice and clear communications is an ongoing challenge.

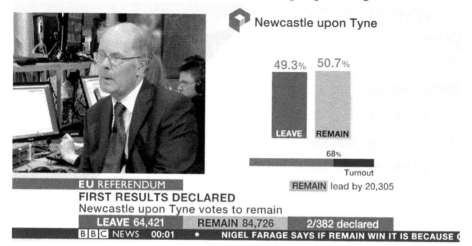

Figure 7: Professor John Curtice with two labelled histograms: an irrefutable combination

Note on the contributor

An award-winning creative director with a track record of visualising high profile big data sets in real time to a worldwide audience, Jonathan Spencer manages the computer graphics team for *BBC News* Visual Journalism. The team's work ranges from creating templated television graphics for the BBC newsroom to the design and creation of election graphics. He has represented the BBC at a number of conferences. Members of the BBC graphic design team, along with Jonathan, are Tony Sinclair, David Hughes, Amanda Constantinou and Mark Edwards.

A brand new *Countdown*: The story of Channel 4's first party data strategy

Technological innovation and the evolution of broadcasting strategy have meant television audience's habits and preferences can now be measured in far more depth. And as Channel 4 begins to unlock the potential of data in its organisation, it becomes even more aware of the tantalising possibilities ahead. Sarah Rose reports

'As the countdown to a brand new channel ends, a brand new countdown begins.' Richard Whiteley's opening words on Countdown, *the first ever programme shown on Channel 4, 2 November 1982*

Introduction

There is nothing a TV audience loves more than a good story. And we have been measuring their consumption of stories for decades now. But this is a story about that TV audience itself and about how technological innovation and the evolution of broadcasting strategy have meant that we can now measure their habits and preferences in far more depth. It is the story of Channel 4's move into first party data. And it is just the beginning. As we begin to unlock the potential of data in our organisation we are well aware of the tantalising possibilities ahead. So this is about our entry into this new era for us as a broadcaster and our discoveries so far.

Once upon a time

Let's set the scene briefly. Channel 4 launched on 2 November 1982. It was designed to bring plurality to the public service broadcasting landscape, hitherto occupied solely by BBC and ITV, with a fresh approach and new voices. The channel was given the unique hybrid status of being publicly-owned while commercially self-funded, with all profits being reinvested in content, and a mission to innovate placed at the heart of its remit. Throughout successive management eras, innovation has run through the lifeblood of the organisation and its strategy.

David Abraham was appointed CEO in 2010 and picked up the innovation baton before he even entered the building. 'Data is the new oil,' he declared, and thus the Channel 4 data strategy was launched. More important than words, a structure was created to put data at the heart of the organisation: Gill Whitehead moved into the newly-created executive role of Director of Audience, Technology and Insight while Sanjeevan Bala was brought in as Head of Data Planning and Analytics. Wider hiring swiftly followed, as well as academic partnerships with University College London which ensured a funnel of young talent was established from the outset. Extending the gene pool of skills was in itself an education for the broadcaster as this was a new breed of employee in television, belonging more traditionally to tech or e-commerce companies. But we have always known Channel 4 needs to adapt to survive. Thirty years since Richard Whiteley's introductory words, another new countdown was beginning.

Channel 4 had been extending its channel line-up since the late nineties and had built up a portfolio of C4, E4, More 4 and Film 4, with 4Music and 4Seven to follow. But the service which enabled the launch of a data strategy was All4, Channel 4's on-demand proposition. Starting life as 4OD in the autumn of 2006, this service was where all Channel 4 catch-up and archive programming was housed. Thousands of hours of content were made available either within a Channel 4-owned and operated app (on smartphones, tablets and smart TVs) or through a closed platform service (Sky, Virgin, BT). The strategy quickly evolved from a pay proposition to an advertiser-funded service. Advertising was sold in catch-up content initially but demand was such that it was soon rolled out to include archive content as well. By 2011, the service was well established and generating almost 400m. views annually. The time felt right to introduce registration and thus to start drilling for David Abraham's oil.

A viewer promise

Crucially, the hallmark of Channel 4's long-developed brand qualities had to be applied to this initiative from the outset. Our reputation for quality of service and editorial compliance and an unbreakable relationship of trust with the viewer were hard-earned attributes which must now serve as the foundation stones for our new venture. So the team focused with most care initially on our 'viewer promise', still considered an example of best in class. Having consulted with the Information Commissioners' Office (ICO), we developed our pact with our audience, based on the two key principles of transparency and control: transparency, in being open with the viewer about which data we were seeking to capture, what we would do with it and why; and control in enabling the viewer to opt out or delete their account easily. Being a television company, it felt most intuitive to convey that with video, so the comedian and 'C4 face', Alan Carr, was brought in to front an entertaining and accessible short film, still used on the site today. As our data strategy evolved, the 'Alan Carr test' became a guiding principle in how we communicated with our audience. Put simply, if Alan Carr couldn't explain what we were doing with our data to viewers, we would hold off from doing it.

The principles of our approach now established, the next question was exactly what data we were going to gather and how. We trod carefully in this respect, asking the minimum questions to enable a credible data strategy. So viewers were asked to enter their name, date of birth, gender and email address. We left postcode as an optional entry, although, given that in excess of 80 per cent of people completed this field, with hindsight we were probably overly-cautious.

But caution was inherent in our approach in those early days. The registration market was still immature and we knew we needed to create a value exchange whereby viewers felt they had a reason to give us their details and would benefit from doing so. So as well as making it clear the recording of personal details meant that we could serve more relevant advertising (the profits from which we, in turn, ploughed back into content), we also introduced programme premieres, exclusive extras and 'money-can't-buy' competitions. We adopted a 'one-step-at-a-time' roll-out strategy, making registration initially optional on archive content only, then mandatory; then optional on catch-up and, finally, mandatory on the whole service. And we tested responses, attitudes and behaviour extensively throughout. We focused on *C4.com* initially, our PC platform, drilled down into viewer responses and then applied our learnings for subsequent platforms. Mobile devices were next, smartphones and tablets on both the IOS and Android platforms, and finally platforms which reached the big screen: Smart TVs, OTT boxes and games consoles. Key to this roll-out was our single sign-on approach, for which we used an external customer management platform. This provided a solution which meant we could register and then identify viewers across the twenty-six platforms we were then carried on. At each stage we kept a close eye on the inevitable viewing drop-off after the implementation of registration. Anything in excess of 15 per cent would have been of concern. Of course, the actual number fluctuated depending on the type of content and platform but, in general, we believe the impact to have settled at well below 10 per cent.

Having established a framework to capture who was watching, we then had to implement a means of tracking what they were watching. Here the drive for quality prevailed again. We now had viewer information of the highest integrity and we had to match that with viewing measurement to the same standard. We put in place a digital measurement framework which specifically tracked all viewer interactivity in a consistent manner, irrespective of the different quirks of each device. This meant we were tracking viewer behaviour and not the individual characteristics of the platforms they were watching on.

Working in the cloud – and open source technology

While undoubtedly a rich resource, the database we were building was nonetheless posing challenges. We were collating literally billions of data points, but they were not yet structured manageably. We needed help beyond our traditional technology set, so we looked – perhaps inevitably – to Silicon Valley. We embraced cloud-based and open source technology, and were one of the first companies in Europe to enable 'elastic computing' which, in essence, allows you to scale up or down the technology you require on a pay-as-you-go model. This gave us the surety of service combined with the necessary flexibility to test ideas rapidly within the business. Being the first to use something creates problems of its own, of course, and we had to fly the Amazon US team over to train our teams as there was no such expertise closer to home.

More traditional research, our natural skillset, played its part too. For our tracking of viewer behaviour to be of real applicable value, we also needed to add contextual colour to that behaviour, essentially adding the 'why' to the 'what'. We, therefore, recruited an 8,000-strong viewer panel, named Core 4, from within our registered base and used them to better understand attitudes, motivations and lifestyle interests, as well as to test programme ideas and brand concepts.

So we had gathered our viewers' details, were tracking their content consumption habits and had dug into their motivations. The next chapter in this narrative is what we then actually do with all this information. And this is where our story divides into two main strands which inevitably – because of the very model on which C4 is based – intertwine and are mutually supportive: the commercial and the creative.

The commercial story

The mechanics of the TV advertising market have always relied on audience data, centrally measured by BARB, the renowned gold standard of TV measurement. BARB's nationally representative panel of 5,500 households underpins the trading of around £4 billion of media value every year. Advertisers have long bought linear audiences segmented by age, gender and socio-economic grouping. But with the gathering of first party data – and, crucially, with the means of execution to leverage it meaningfully – these trading models can be revolutionised. We set out to do exactly that.

Again we started cautiously, testing the effectiveness of demographic targeting with seven blue chip advertising partners. Put simply, demographic targeting in an on-demand service with registration data means you can serve advertising to an audience who you know belongs to a particular demographic. This avoids the wastage inherent in the linear broadcasting model so enables the sales house to charge a higher CPM (cost per thousand). Happily our early test campaigns worked. Brand awareness and click-through rates doubled, ad recognition soared and the campaigns proved to be significantly more efficient than when served on a non-targeted basis. Our strategy was working and advertiser demand was increasing.

More ad innovation followed: interest-based targeting was next, drawing on the additional lifestyle information from our Core4 panel and other externally-sourced surveys, and enabling advertisers to target groups such as 'fashionistas' and 'home bodies'. Next we launched bespoke products such as Ad Elect where either a viewer opted to see their chosen version of an advertisement or we used data to serve the most relevant version for them. Ad Journey enabled the sequential targeting of ads, telling continuous stories to the same viewer on multiple platforms. Ad 4 You went one step further by inserting the first name of the registered viewer into the ad. Coca Cola was the first advertiser to use this, inserting the viewer's first name on a Coke bottle resulting in an astonishingly high 59 per cent of viewers who saw the advert to take some positive action as a result. Burberry went further, displaying a monogrammed perfume bottle with the registered user's initials which could be bought by a single click and delivered the following day. And in spring 2017, we progressed from video personalisation to audio personalisation, creating the ability for advertisers to use the registered viewer's name in the voiceover of the advertisement.

The pace of innovation has been breathtaking. But it has also been essential, as television sales houses are now competing in an internet-enabled world increasingly dominated by the Digital Giants (Facebook, Google, Amazon and Apple) who use their own rich data to increase their revenues inexorably. Amidst that market noise, broadcasters the size of Channel 4 need their message to resonate clearly and consistently: premium content in a premium environment underpinned by data of the highest integrity. Underlining this positioning, we ensured we were regularly audited externally, to increase advertisers' confidence in us. But the results they were seeing on their own campaigns also helped and demand grew. By 2016, 10 per cent of our revenues were from digital sales, vastly disproportionate to the relative scale of our digital viewing.

So the data-driven commercial story is well underway. Contextual advertising is next on the carousel of innovation. Drawing on metadata from our programming and complemented by a knowledge of who is watching, this initiative will allow ads to be positioned in slots highly relevant to specific moments within the content surrounding them. Importantly, the ability to insert addressable advertising into our linear feed beckons enticingly. Questions then arise as to what extent the market wants all advertising to become addressable and what residual value television will retain as a builder of brands, delivering mass audiences in one hit. But when we are debating whether to reign back on our use of data we will know how far we have come.

The creative story

And so to the creative strand to this narrative. Much has been written about the interplay between creativity and data. We take a simple view: it should enhance but not dictate. So we continue to evolve ways of liberating data within our wider business, informing not just our scheduling and commissioning strategy but also our marketing and media planning. The potential is huge. But our main focus to date has been on the All4 product itself. In March 2017, having by then gathered more than 15 million registered users (including over half of all 16 to 34-year-olds in the country), we launched the first true iterations of data-driven personalisation within the user experience: taste segmentation and individual recommendations.

Taste segmentation

It is not credible – even desirable – to deliver more than 15 million different emails or curated content collections, so we needed to group our user base more manageably. No longer needing to rely solely on age or demographic, we decided to divide viewers by taste. The trick was to serve our audience programmes we knew they would like, based on their viewing history, but also to introduce them to titles which stretched them, validated by the viewing of other people with similar tastes to them.

So we created nine taste segments. Why nine? That felt manageable for now. Because – and this was key to our approach – we wanted to retain a Channel 4 taste palette and content curating role, a human complement to the data-driven modelling. We termed this fusion approach 'smart curation', an antidote to the prevailing 'wisdom of crowds' approach elsewhere. An editorial team takes the segmentation output and overlays a human touch, preserving Channel 4 brand values, upholding our public service remit and striking an editorial tone which feels familiar but reassuringly surprising. The viewers don't know which segment they belong to nor, indeed, that they have been segmented at all. They just receive content appropriate for them – through promotions, content collections or tailored emails. As we are able to track their responses to this content, we can, in turn, tweak the algorithms driving it. It's early days but we are already seeing a clear viewing uplift within the live segments. This represents a significant increase in engagement with our product which, in turn, increases the monetisation opportunity.

Recommendations

We also set our data scientists to work on developing algorithms to drive recommendations on a more individualised basis. This modelling predicts what viewers may like based not just on their own history but also what time of day they are watching and on which device, again drawing on behaviour we see across our base. We tested these recommendations tirelessly with real users to help understand what 'good' recommendations from C4 look like. Good is, of course, hard to define; it's a strange amalgam of relevant and inspiring. We are learning not to be too obvious or narrow, not just to show the most popular; to add an element of serendipity, but not one that discredits our other suggestions. We are discovering that the cadence of recommendations is also important. The first few build trust and interest; the next can stretch a bit more and the last can be a wild card. Again it's early days, but there is no doubt that, applied sensitively, data science innovation drives consumption of public service content, viewing loyalty and growth.

Coda

And so, from the kernel of an idea about implementing registration, to a growing suite of targeted advertising products and an All4 user experience personalised at its core, with a lot of awards picked up along the way, our story comes to the present day. Critically, and perhaps to an extent none of us could have foreseen, our market context has evolved during this period such that David Abraham's clarion cry in 2011 to own our own data feels ever more relevant. He declared on his arrival:

> I believe that it is essential for the future of Channel 4 – and of PSB in general – that we ensure that the data that exists around content we generate with our creative partners is not simply controlled and commercially exploited by other platforms, whoever they are. We don't intend to compete directly with the social networks that already exist, but as a public broadcaster, nor will we allow ourselves to be enveloped by them either.[1]

As debates rage about ad viewability and fraud, about measurement metrics and data leaks, the position we adopted of premium data in a premium environment is serving us well. The Digital Giants swirl around us, part threat, part opportunity, but the retention of sovereignty over our own customer data strengthens our hand and shores up our survival.

The countdown to C4 becoming a truly digital organisation is well underway. Our next conundrum is to progress more internal application of our data science – e.g. finance business processes, HR analytics, forecasting and airtime optimisation – as well as continuing to respond to consumer behaviour and technological advances. Real time data from IP delivery is imminent, personalised linear schedules are surely inevitable and a gradual adoption of greater AI and machine learning will be essential to keep pace with our competitors. All these will form the next chapters of our data narrative. Now we have started mining the oil, we intend to flow it not just through our internal operations but also through our future strategy and vision for C4. For our public service remit to innovate, and our desire to connect with and delight our audience, will always be where this story begins and ends.

Note
[1] Abraham, David (2011) *What We're 4*. Speech given at Royal Television Society, 23 May.

Note on the contributor
Sarah Rose is Channel 4's Director of Consumer Insight, responsible for the channel's award-winning data strategy and for the way viewer insight is used within the business. She joined C4 in 2006 to launch its on-demand service, 4OD, and in 2010 became Director of Commercial and Business Development, responsible for all non-ad sales revenues. She previously spent 10 years at ITV where she was latterly General Manager of ITV Digital Channels.

Section 4:
How the picture varies across the globe

Martin Moore

Data journalism is now a central feature of many newsrooms across the world and has become integral to news verification, to investigations and to the visualisation of news stories. Yet the extent and nature of its use varies significantly in different countries. In the US, for example, it is well established and inherent to the work of organisations like *ProPublica* and *FiveThirtyEight*. In China, it is used chiefly to visualise stories and to provide news audiences with useful and relevant information. In Russia, it supports investigations and can help provide evidence of corruption, though is hampered by access to data. Outside newsrooms, there is also a growing international digital community of journalists, experts, interested amateurs and others who are using open data and digital tools to document modern conflicts, to authenticate images and to challenge claims.

Digital propaganda and disinformation have been central to the conflict in Ukraine. Verifying information in this environment is fraught with difficulty, as Eliot Higgins writes. The quantity of information is vast and the claims made are often false, misleading or disingenuous. Yet, there are many informal communities online sifting through the information to make sense of it. *Bellingcat*, a site Higgins and others founded, attempts to organise some of this informal analysis and make the findings more broadly accessible. It has used the *Checkdesk* platform, for example, to build up a dataset of verified Russian geolocated vehicles in Eastern Ukraine. Similarly, it used the platform, *Silk*, to create dynamically generated maps of verified sightings of military equipment and tanks. These tools and methods are now being used during other conflicts and for verification in other spheres. Higgins shows how, by using open source data and making the verification process more transparent, it may be possible to navigate our way through the fog of digital war.

Kathryn Hayes next charts the development of data journalism in Ireland. Through a series of interviews with journalists and academics, she describes both the advances that data journalism has made in Ireland – particularly since the strengthening of the Irish Freedom of Information Act in 2014 – and its constraints and setbacks. The innate conservatism of the Irish government and Irish news outlets, coupled with the investment of resources required, has limited the growth and implementation of data journalism in the country. Where there have been successes, the journalists responsible have often gone to larger news outlets – particularly in the UK, or started their own ventures. If data journalism is to take off in Ireland, Hayes writes, there will need to be a cultural shift both at news organisations and within government.

Beyond the literary tradition

In Russia, the development of data journalism has been slow. This is not just a consequence of censorship – contemporary and historical – but due to the literary tradition of Russian journalism, as Anastasia Valeeva writes. There are, however, various Russian news data initiatives. Valeeva looks at three: *Novaya Gazeta*, the independent news outlet founded in 1993, *Meduza*, the digital-only outlet based in Riga, and RBC, the largest non-state media group in Russia. At *Novaya Gazeta*, Valeeva finds that data tends to be used in quite a traditional way. Journalists trawl through the digital information, as they would have trawled through paper documents in the past, to find stories and back-up theories. At *Meduza*, there is more emphasis put on 'statistical investigations' using data, particularly via their dedicated 'Razbor' or analysis team. At RBC, public and private company data is layered on to open data as part of investigations – for example, into competition for tenders on government contracts.

Data journalism came relatively late to China, write Sixian Li and Shifting Ding, emerging only since 2013 – and taking diverse directions. Li and Ding illustrate this by looking at the reporting of the Spring Festival Rush – the largest domestic annual migration in the world. In 2014 and 2015, CCTV chose to use three-dimensional animation – based on migration data – to show the movement of people. By contrast, sites such as *Sohu* and *Xinhuanet* visualised travel data to help people plan their transport and their routes. *Netease* took another approach, mining the data to look at the rising cost of train fares during the period. Though not yet as detailed or interactive as the use of data in the US and UK, by sites such as *FiveThirtyEight* and the *Guardian*, Chinese news sites are now well aware of data's potential.

Ten principles for data journalism

Damian Radcliffe and his students look at three case studies of data journalism in the US and derive ten general principles from these. The first case study cites best practice in the use of graphics to explain data at *ProPublica*, *FiveThirtyEight* and the *Washington Post*. Data is used, for example, to illustrate where political 'dark money' goes, to show the decline of crime in Latino areas since the 2016 election and the impact of President Trump's budget cuts. The second case study, on the use of evidence in health and science journalism, assesses the extent to which 'digestible, comprehensive and interactive data' has become central to the authority of news stories in these fields. The third and final case study shows how data can be used to help dissect and explain the success of sports teams – citing analyses of the Golden State Warriors basketball team.

In her research, Erin Coates discovered that many data visualisations actually confuse rather than help readers. Journalists therefore need, Coates writes, to make their readers more graphically literate as well as simply visualising data. Her chapter then sets out Alberto Cairo's seven steps for enhancing graphical literacy. These include avoiding common mistakes in the representation of data, the danger of over-interpreting data and giving data the space it needs. Most importantly, Coates concludes, journalists need to be sure they are representing their data fairly and ethically.

The digital environment may be transnational but there are clearly distinct national approaches to data journalism – as the chapters in this section illustrate.

Crowdsourcing conflict and beyond

Communities are appearing on social media and in discussion forums who cooperate and share information with each other. According to Eliot Higgins, of the investigative organisation, *Bellingcat*, these efforts can be harnessed by researchers trying to gain a better understanding of conflict and process large amounts of information into useful data

The rise in the use of social media and widespread adoption of smartphones has led to a massive growth in the amount of information being gathered and made available from conflict zones. While much of this information is useful, the sheer volume of information and scattered nature of where this information is shared often results in conflict researchers being overwhelmed. It is also not merely a question of finding and organising this information but of verification and analysis to produce reliable and useful results.

This has been particularly apparent with the conflicts in Syria and Ukraine, where millions of images are being shared by thousands of sources on platforms including video-sharing websites such as YouTube and LiveLeak, blogging sites like *Blogspot* and *LiveJournal*, social media sites and a range of discussion forums.

With the rise of open source investigation in the public sphere, an increasing number of individuals have begun to examine this content. Debates about these efforts on social media and discussion forums have created communities who cooperate and share information with each other, and these efforts can be harnessed by researchers trying to gain a better understanding of conflict and process large amounts of information into useful data.

These communities are often very informal. An example is the community that has appeared on Twitter around finding the exact location of airstrike footage from various countries. The community is made up of individuals who observed each other's activity on Twitter and, seeing that it was related to interests similar to their own, began to follow each other and discuss their mutual interest. These are individuals from a range of countries and backgrounds brought together by their shared interest in one narrow avenue of analysis.

Challenging Russian claims in Ukraine

In the early stages of the conflict in Ukraine there were many claims of Russian vehicles and troops arriving in Eastern Ukraine to join the battle against Ukrainian government forces. Russian President Vladimir Putin denied the presence of Russian forces, but claims continued to persist. On social media and discussion forums, private citizens in Ukraine shared photographs and videos they had taken of separatist forces and these images were discussed on those same platforms, with keen amateurs and professionals identifying the arms and munitions featured.

This often resulted in startling findings. Weapon systems only known to be used by Russian forces, or known not to be in service in Ukraine, began appearing in images claiming to show separatist-controlled areas in Eastern Ukraine. However, simply confirming the type of vehicles shown was not enough; verifying the location of these images was key, and these communities began to geolocate the photographs and videos showing these vehicles.

Already data points were being created for each image. Date, location and vehicle type were all being established, but these discussions were happening on many different platforms by communities who were unaware of each other's efforts. Data was being produced by communities that ultimately only served to inform those same communities of what that data meant.

Meanwhile, among the media and policy-makers, there was still uncertainty about whether or not the claims of Russian troops and vehicles in Ukraine were true. The investigative organisation *Bellingcat* recognised this problem still existed and that there were communities gathering this information and doing their own analysis. The question was, then, how to turn the information gathered by those communities into data that the media and policy-makers could trust.

Key to this was ensuring as much transparency as possible for the entire process. The videos and photographs used were almost entirely from open sources, so the original sources of the images were almost always available and shareable. The discussions also took place on social media platforms and forums mostly viewable by anyone, while for geolocation of images open source images from Google Earth, Yandex Maps and other sites were used. No conclusions were being made on the word of anonymous sources and the entire process of analysis could be completely transparent.

Nevertheless, all of this information was still scattered on a number of different platforms. *Bellingcat* addressed this by using the *Checkdesk* platform (now known at *Check)* developed by *Meedan*, which is intended to allow the collaborative verification of information. Using this platform, it was possible to create an entry for each video or photograph which could then be discussed by users in comments below the post. Finally, a status could be set for each entry to show whether it was unverified, verified or false.

In practice, this meant each entry would have links to discussions about that entry added in the comments of that entry since as many images had already been discovered and geolocated. Crucially, each entry would be reviewed by the *Bellingcat* team to confirm that accuracy of the geolocation and identity of the vehicle shown.

This resulted in a dataset of verified images of geolocated vehicles in Ukraine. This included vehicles not used by the Ukrainian military but known to be used by the Russian military such as the Pantsir-S1 anti-aircraft system and T-72B3 tank. To make this information accessible and useful to other interested parties, *Bellingcat* created an online database using the platform *Silk*. This allows users to import a database on their online platform that then creates dynamically generated output, such as charts and maps. Each entry that makes up the database and is used to create visualised output can then be explored by other users.

Users of the *Bellingcat Silk* database could not only see a dynamically generated map of vehicle sightings but find in each entry a link to the *Checkdesk* entry for that entry, where they could see the process of verification and the confirmation it had been double-checked by *Bellingcat* members. For each entry it was possible to go from the individual data point in the larger dataset hosted on *Silk* and track it back through the verification process to the point of origin of that image. Efforts by a range of communities has been distilled into useful, verified data. In addition, this did not require *Bellingcat* team members to reach out to the communities to investigate this information but harnessed their pre-existing efforts.

Another result was the recognition that the efforts of those communities, through the work of *Bellingcat*, encouraged individuals to continue their efforts, which attracted more individuals to those communities. This resulted in more volunteers being available to verify images, which could be drawn on in future projects.

As the dataset grew, different types of images were examined by the growing communities. Sightings of military vehicles in Russia were also collected, geolocated and verified, and this allowed researchers to compare vehicles in Russia to vehicles recorded in Ukraine. Initially the database had been used to document vehicles only known to be used by Russia appearing in Ukraine; now it was being used to match vehicles seen in Russia with vehicles seen in Ukraine. This went beyond merely matching the types of vehicles seen but matching markings, damage and other features that could confirm the vehicles were identical and, therefore, the same vehicles in Russia appearing in Ukraine. Again, crowdsourced, expert verified efforts had found more evidence of Russia's involvement in the conflict in Ukraine.

Exposing Russian lies over Syria bombings

Another similar effort involved Russia's bombing of Syria, beginning in September 2015. From the first day of their bombing campaign, the Russian Ministry of

Defence uploaded videos filmed by their air force as they performed attacks on targets in Syria. Most of these videos claimed to show ISIS targets being targeted, but a number of governments claimed that Russia was targeting non-ISIS forces, a claim dismissed by the Russian government.

From the moment these videos were shared on the Russian Ministry of Defence's YouTube channel (https://www.youtube.com/channel/UCQGqX5Ndpm4snE0NTjyOJnA), open source investigation and verification communities began to geolocate the videos. Aerial views of the attacks could be matched to Google Earth satellite imagery, clearly showing the exact location of these attacks. As with the Russian vehicles in Ukraine project, *Bellingcat* published the videos on *Checkdesk*, verified the geolocations and created a *Silk* database showing the locations of these attacks and whom they claimed to be targeting.

Nearly all the videos posted online by the Russian Ministry of Defence in the opening weeks of their bombing campaign claiming to show ISIS being targeted were, in fact, geolocated to territory outside of ISIS control. Importantly, the Russian Ministry of Defence provided their own map of ISIS control, so it was possible to use both the Russian Ministry of Defence's own videos and their own map to show they were lying about the targets featured in the videos.

It is a simple statement to say that the Russian Ministry of Defence is lying about its claims, but when each example that is used to make that statement can be tracked back to the point of origin, verified and geolocated in as open a way as possible, it creates an incredibly solid foundation for that statement.

The same groups verifying the Russian Ministry of Defence videos also began to examine videos from US coalition forces showing bombing in Syria and Iraq. Using exactly the same methodology, a second dataset was created and it was possible to conclude that, with few exceptions, targets were being reported on correctly.

As an apparent response to this investigation, videos published by the Russian Ministry of Defence of its airstrikes in Syria soon began to be described in more general terms. Instead of the targets being described as ISIS they were, instead, described as 'militants', 'fighters' or 'terrorists'. The locations provided, which previously had been over 100km out in some cases, became more general, describing which province the target was in rather than which town or city it was close to. Despite this, more inaccuracies were detected by these crowdsourced efforts, and soon the Russian Ministry of Defence dramatically reduced the number of videos showing its Syria airstrikes published on its YouTube channel.

Countering ISIS propaganda

In other situations, it can be useful to have a community that can be called on to focus their collective efforts on one image. In May 2016, numerous supporters of ISIS posted pictures on social media from major European cities, displaying messages of support for the group. This social media campaign was in support of an imminent speech from ISIS spokesperson Abu Mohammed al-Adnani.

The intention of the campaign was both to promote the upcoming speech and captivate European populations by showing them that ISIS had support throughout Europe. A typical photograph would show a piece of paper held up, with the hashtag used to promote the campaign in Arabic, while the city or country the photograph was taken in was written in the local language. Various backgrounds were shown, including leaves, the interior of a shop and exterior views. It quickly became apparent that the likelihood of being able to geolocate the exterior shots was high, and *Bellingcat* shared the photographs with its followers on Twitter, challenging them to find the locations.

Four photographs were chosen: from Munster in Germany, Paris, London and Holland. The Paris photograph was located rapidly when community

A photograph taken by an ISIS supporter in Paris that was geolocated to the exact location it was taken through crowdsourcing

members identified a Suzuki sign on a building visible in the background. Even though the sign was out of focus and partly obscured, it was still identifiable and a simple Google search of Suzuki dealerships in Paris led to a handful of results, each of which were viewable in Google Street View. Within minutes, a location was found on Google Street View that matched the Paris photograph and by rotating the camera 180 degrees on Google Street View it was possible to identify the likely location of the photographer.

With the Munster photograph, it was somewhat more complex. A bus was visible but out of focus, so the line number could not be made out. It was clearly taken by a T-junction, with multiple lanes in either direction, but there were many locations like that in Munster. However, one member of the community knew that an advertising pillar visible in the photograph would likely be on an online database that allows advertisers to search for advertising spots across Germany, so a search on that website could identify the locations of advertising pillars in Munster. This quickly narrowed down the search locations, and it was then a matter of finding those advertising pillars next to T-junctions in Munster. All of this took less than half an hour and the location was positively identified.

The London image was located after a local who saw the tweet with the geolocation challenge recognised the location in question. The location was provided with a simple geolocation using Google Street View imagery and Google Earth, confirming the location of the third photograph.

The first three photographs were located within an hour of the challenge being issued. The fourth photograph from Holland took longer as the ISIS supporter who took the photograph lied about the location but, again, a local who recognised the area pointed to the correct location which was verified with Google Street View imagery.

All of this information was provided to local police forces, and the online discussion around the photographs generated interest from the media. As a result, the coverage of the photographs was not as the ISIS social media campaign had hoped. Rather than headlines about ISIS being everywhere in Europe, the headlines focused on the idiocy of ISIS supporters in Europe who gave their locations away by posting photographs on the internet.

Backing Europol's campaign on child abuse

Crowdsourcing is also not limited to conflict and terrorism. In the summer of 2017, Europol created the 'Stop Child Abuse, Trace an Object' campaign requesting help from members of the public to identify items they had cut out from child abuse images. While they provided no details beyond the images, the stated aim of the campaign was to identify the locations/countries each object originated from. The items included shopping bags, partial items of clothing, packages of various commercial products and a heating boiler.

This campaign was quickly picked up by members of the Reddit community 'What is this thing?' where members help identify strange and unusual objects shared by both community members and visitors looking for help. Examples range from the remains of a badly damaged airbag device recovered from the wreckage of a burnt-out car by firemen who were unable to identify it, to various knick-knacks recovered from attics across the world.

The community quickly organised around the Europol campaign, creating a dedicated Reddit thread where each item had its own discussion. Within days the majority of items had been identified, with users providing reference images for each item and links to websites which sold some of the items in question. Taken further, it would have been possible to contact the manufacturer of each item and discover the countries that each item was shipped to. While Europol did not provide information about the photographs, crucially whether the photographs were related, it was possible to establish many of the items were sold in western and northern Europe, and the shopping bags belonged to a number of different retail chains operating in certain countries.

Conclusion: The challenges for researchers

What is extraordinary about this is not that the request was made, but that there was a pre-existing community ready to take up the challenge rapidly of identifying a set of random items presented to it by law enforcement. As demonstrated with examples from Syria and Ukraine, there are growing communities fascinated with crowdsourcing, applying a range of skills and knowledge to their pursuits.

We see examples where we have both directed crowdsourcing, such as the Europol example, and undirected crowdsourcing, such as the examples of Russian airstrikes in Syria. People are not only willing to give their free time for such work but find it enjoyable and rewarding, and harnessing these efforts is not seen as exploitative but a positive way for ordinary citizens to contribute to efforts they believe in. The challenge for researchers is learning how to discover and engage with these communities.

Note on the contributor

Eliot Higgins is the founder of *Bellingcat* and the *Brown Moses Blog*. He is an award-winning investigative journalist and publishes the work of an international alliance of fellow investigators using freely available online information. He has helped inaugurate open-source and social media investigations by trawling through vast amounts of data uploaded constantly on to the web and social media sites. His inquiries have revealed extraordinary findings, including linking the Buk used to down flight MH17 to Russia, uncovering details about the 21 August 2013 sarin attacks in Damascus and evidencing the involvement of the Russian military in the Ukrainian conflict. Recently, he has worked with the Atlantic Council on the report, *Hiding in Plain Sight*, which used open-source information to detail Russia's military involvement in the crisis in Ukraine. Eliot is a Visiting Research Fellow at the Human Rights Centre of the UC Berkeley School of Law. *Bellingcat* was awarded the European Press Prize for Innovation in 2017.

Gaining momentum? Data journalism in Ireland

Ireland cannot develop data journalism's potential without media organisations rethinking business models and risking short-term pain for long-term success, argues Kathryn Hayes

Introduction

Irish newsrooms lag significantly behind their US and UK counterparts when it comes to wide-scale engagement in data-driven projects. Despite concerted efforts by some notable pioneers, a lack of sustained interest and support from larger media organisations; appropriate skillsets and training in newsrooms together with a lack of access to usable data have all hindered any consistent momentum. Among the first early adopters was *The Irish Times*'s Data Project launched in 2015 and considered an important digital front by the newspaper aimed at giving its readers more 'immersive journalism' (O'Sullivan 2015).

In the same year, the Independent News and Media group (INM), which owns a number of newspaper titles in Ireland including the *Irish Independent*, started to promote its 'digital first' strategy claiming 'the future for their readers is data-led' (Caffrey 2015). Ireland's national broadcaster, RTE, launched its Investigations Unit in 2012 and three years later, together with RTE Digital, produced some high quality, data-driven investigations. Yet the surge in interest in Ireland in 2015 has not been maintained in any consistent manner due to data champions leaving their organisations, highlighting how dependent data journalism is on a small cadre of reporters with specific skillsets (Heravi 2017). The departure of *Irish Times* data journalist Pamela Duncan to the *Guardian* in November 2015 was a big loss for the Irish newspaper's Data Project given Duncan's work on a number of the newspaper's most successful data-driven projects, in particular the investigation into donations to the Sinn Fein political party in America over a 20-year period (Duncan and Carswell 2015). In terms of individual data pioneers, investigative freelance journalist Gavin Sheridan is regarded as a trailblazer for data-driven reporting in Ireland. Sheridan has since gone on to develop a data company and data products.

An 'innate conservatism' in Irish newsrooms is often blamed for the delayed Irish interest along with the deliberate obfuscation of many of the institutions which hold the most valuable data sets in Ireland (Linehan 2015). The culture of secrecy that has dominated the civil service since the foundation of the state must also be considered in any discussion around accessing data in Ireland. It is argued that this legacy continues to hold sway in many quarters: significantly, an amendment of the Freedom of Information Act (legislation enacted to help open up information in 2003) tried to suppress access to data. This was overturned in 2014, when a new FOI law was introduced. The Irish government has also committed to the international Open Government Partnership (OGP), which includes commitments to making public data available in machine-readable and open-API formats, though progress on this has been painstakingly slow.

This chapter, through a series of interviews with journalists working in the national media and journalism academics, explores the state of data journalism in Ireland. Indeed, it's a country where, alongside a history of prolonged struggle with opaqueness in government, a significant number of political and social controversies have been unearthed through original and investigative journalism (Greenslade 2013). Responses from those interviewed suggest that while the landscape for data journalism is improving in Ireland, access to suitably formatted, open and linked data still remains a key challenge along with the availability of journalists skilled in analysing large datasets and a cultural shift in mindset from editors.

Ireland and its culture of secrecy

The turbulent conditions surrounding the birth of the Irish Free State in 1923 – following the Irish War of Independence against the English Crown and a consequent civil war – meant openness and transparency in government were not high on the agenda of the country's new legislator. As an example of the state's efforts at control, the 1923 Censorship of Films Act was one of the first pieces of legislation of the new government. It gave power to an officially appointed censor to keep from the public films which it believed to be 'indecent, obscene or blasphemous' (Censorship of Films Act 1923, Section 7, 2). The Emergency Powers Act introduced in 1939 – on the eve of World War Two – gave the government wide-ranging powers to censor all broadcasts and newspapers. In 1963, the Irish government amended the Official Secrets Act, making it a criminal offence for any civil servant to reveal anything, no matter how trivial, without express permission of the minister responsible. That early pattern of control and secrecy continued following the outbreak of the Troubles in Northern Ireland in the 1970s and the invocation of Section 31 of the 1960 Broadcasting Act which prohibited Raidió Teilifís Éireann (RTE), the national public service broadcaster, from broadcasting anything that could be interpreted as supporting the aims or activities of organisations which 'engage in, promote, encourage or advocate the attaining of any political objective by violent means'. The Section 31 ban, as it was commonly known, was not lifted until 1994. Likewise, the Emergency Powers Act was also not lifted until the same year.

When Ireland did begin to open up, the pace was glacial. Ireland finally introduced freedom of information legislation in 1997, and it was widely seen as a watershed moment in the relationship between citizens and the state in terms of openness, transparency and accountability.

The FOI Act was, perhaps, too successful (Felle and Adshead 2009). After a while, civil servants stopped putting sensitive or controversial information in emails and started using the phone instead (Hennessy 2008). A number of embarrassing exposés of incompetence by ministers and other rows and mishaps, as revealed by journalists following FOI requests, led in 2003 to the introduction by the then-Fianna Fáil-led government of the Freedom of Information Amendment Act. This legislation introduced fees for making requests; extended the time when access to the records of government was available to 10 years rather than five; gave full protection to communications between ministers concerning matters before governments, and introduced blanket bans on information that would be withheld. It was regarded as a 'severe setback' to openness in Ireland (Foley 2015). A year after the amendments were enacted, the use of the Act by journalist fell by 50 per cent (*Irish Times*, 17 May 2004).

In 2014, a subsequent Fine Gael/Labour coalition government reintroduced a strengthened FOI Act, reversing most of the amendments and abolishing fees. The legislation was also extended to cover the police and state financial bodies such as the Central Bank – important in the Irish context following the 2007 collapse of the economy and near collapse of the banking system – in part blamed on weak banking laws and poor oversight by financial regulators.

Unlocking the data

Launching Ireland's Open Data Portal (ODP) in 2014, the Irish cabinet secretary responsible, Brendan Howlin TD, said open data was a core element of the country's first Open Government Partnership (OGP) national action plan. A key output to date of this initiative is the national ODP (see https//data.gov.ie) which provides access to official non-personal government data in open format. The portal has been significantly improved since. By 2017, the portal was linking to some 4,400 datasets from 93 publishers and recent enhancements include visualisations, a 'suggest a dataset' function and a 'showcase' function where developers can showcase apps, websites etc. created using data from the portal.

Open Knowledge Ireland, which is part of the global Open Knowledge non-profit network, sees open data as 'the library of the 21st Century'. Since 2011, it has been working on *opendata.ie* to help citizens access high value, machine-readable datasets generated by the Irish government and public sector authorities.

In 2016, it successfully campaigned for Irish hospital waiting lists to be published as open, accessible data. According to the group, Ireland has a long way to go before open data becomes part of the critical public infrastructure in a permanent, linked and secure manner. Despite these moves towards opening up government data, Ireland is ranked 31st in the 2015 Global Data Index alongside Japan and Latvia. Ireland's overall index ranking is up five places since 2014. However, it still lags considerably behind the UK which is ranked second after Taiwan (see https://index.okfn.org).

In the following sections of this chapter, interviews with Irish data journalists and journalism academics explore the extent to which newsrooms are using data to tell stories; the problems they face accessing datasets and what training, if any, is available to Irish journalists working with data.

Accessing data

Despite notable efforts at opening up Ireland's database – in particular, the manner in which the Central Statistics Office has been presenting data in interesting ways to boost engagement – access to readily usable machine-readable data can be at times limited. The continued practice by some government departments of releasing data in PDF format has frustrated the process. In 2017, *Iris Oifigiúil*, the official journal of Ireland that deals with information such as semi-state appointments, receiverships and notice of elections, was still being published in a structured set PDF format.

Another considerable stumbling block is getting consistent data across all local authorities and government departments. Ireland has 31 local authorities which operate separately, so undertaking a story on a national scale requires 31 separate FOI requests which may be returned in different formats and 'impossible to analyse', according to *Irish Times* digital editor Paddy Logue (2017). Errors in some of the data released has also presented problems for journalists as highlighted by award-winning Irish investigative journalist Ken Foxe. He commented:

> I think there's a lot of data out there and maybe not enough people to analyse it. Some of the data can be a little bit hit and miss. I've received datasets from public bodies, where I've ended up finding errors in them and having to go back to get them corrected. That's frustrating and potentially problematic if, say, I hadn't spotted the errors, which is not my job (Foxe 2017).

Challenges

Among the biggest barriers to wide-scale adoption of data journalism in Irish newsrooms are resources and money, according to Dr Bahareh Heravi, Assistant Professor, University College Dublin:

> Newsrooms in Ireland need a cultural shift and they need to understand the values data journalism can bring to their newsrooms. Training data

journalists is actually not very expensive. As an example the new Data Journalism Professional Certificate programme in UCD costs only €1,600 for two semesters and the hours are designed to specifically suit busy journalists (Heravi 2017).

Dr Heravi was involved in a Global Data Journalism survey which had 206 participants from 43 countries. Only seven of the participants were from Ireland – five from the public and two from Northern Ireland. Four out of the seven considered themselves to have a better than average or expert level knowledge of data journalism, while the other three considered themselves to be average, below average or novice. The survey found that, while journalists in Ireland did not present a very high level of expertise in data journalism or that they may not have dedicated data teams in their organisations (two participants were freelances), they believed data skills were very important, adding rigour and quality to their work.

Education

Universities and third-level institutions in Ireland have become increasingly aware of the importance of data journalism and some journalism graduates in Ireland have received training, albeit introductory. The National University of Ireland Galway (NUIG) has offered a data journalism module in its MA programme since 2015. Dublin City University (DCU) and Dublin Institute of Technology offer data journalism modules as part of their Journalism BA programmes. University College Dublin began a post-graduate professional certificate in data journalism in September 2017, which specifically targets journalists looking to improve their skills. University of Limerick's journalism department has also begun to place emphasis on data journalism in its BA and MA programmes. In May 2017, UL joined the Google News Lab University Network which focuses on increasing data literacy and DJ skills. UL journalism students also secured a number of Google fellowships at leading Irish news organisations, including *The Irish Times, Irish Independent* and *Journal.ie*. The successful fellows are funded to research and write stories and create timely data to frame debates accurately about issues in Ireland and around the world.

Ken Foxe, who also lectures at Dublin Institute of Technology, cautions against isolating data journalism as a separate discipline to regular journalism, insisting skills such as using FOI, ability to access public records and understanding company accounts should be core skills for all journalists, not the domain of only a small group of people (Foxe 2017).

Data pioneers

Investigative journalist Gavin Sheridan, considered a trailblazer in data-driven reporting in Ireland, is the CEO and founder of Vizlegal, a start-up that converts fragmented legal information into structured data and provides tools for the legal and other industries to use this information. He was previously the Director of

Innovation for *Storyful,* and successfully pursued the National Assets Management Agency (NAMA) – the body created by the Irish government in late 2009 in response to the financial crisis and the deflation of the country's property bubble – for failure to provide information under the Freedom of Information Act, which the agency lost in the Supreme Court.

Sheridan established *KildareStreet.com,* a service that tracks activity in the Irish Oireachtas (parliament) and which is designed to allow citizens to keep tabs on their TDs (members of parliament) and senators. Sheridan is also co-founder of *TheStory.ie,* which is a chronicle of his FOI requests to diverse branches of the Irish government and a growing public database of government records. One of the first posts on *TheStory.ie* involved the conversion of word docs and PDFs to spreadsheets, analysing all published donations to TDs from 1997-2008.

Sheridan (2017) agrees that the labour intensiveness of large data projects can be challenging for Irish media organisations seeking to resource such work. However, he argues this is often a result of 'poor management, or unwillingness to adapt to new workflows, or to innovate internally' (ibid).

Changing mindsets

Selling data journalism to traditional media and demonstrating its value is a persistent struggle for journalists and digital editors, in particular given Ireland's innate sense of conservatism. According to Paddy Logue (2017):

> Newspapers are inherently very traditional and very conservative in terms of new things so it is difficult to convince people that a) we should spend resources in terms of reporters and effort of reporters on this and b) spend money on people who have the skills. It is incredibly difficult to get anyone to pay for anything at the moment, not just in *The Irish Times,* it's across the board, especially if it steps outside the traditional reporter/news desk/picture desk territory.

Conor Ryan, a journalist with the RTE Investigations Unit, has worked on some of the broadcaster's biggest data-driven project, including 'Universities Unchallenged', an investigation over several months which uncovered how taxpayers' money was spent in a number of third-level institutions in Ireland. He said:

> The biggest problem with data-driven journalism projects is the lack of results that are coming out of it versus the amount of time that has to go into it. I don't think people are necessarily building infrastructure; they tend to get a data set in, clean it, order it, make a story out of it and then present it and then it's just a one-hit wonder. What I've been trying to do is to get one data set and learn how to match it with another and learn to build on it so you are getting value and what you do is banked. If, for example, you've gone to the bother of cleaning up the tax defaulters' list, make sure it's there so that when

you are doing something else like the Panama Papers you can test one against the other (Ryan 2017).

Convincing cash-strapped news organisations of the potential of data journalism projects is also a challenge, given the size of Ireland and the potential audience reach. According to Ken Foxe:

Data projects in Ireland generally have a maximum audience of maybe four to five million people and they are unlikely to translate for a wider audience. That will always be an issue for labour-intensive forms of journalism in Ireland where questions can very quickly be asked about whether the end result has justified the resources given over to it. It has already led to an effective monopoly on long-form investigative journalism by the public service broadcaster, which is obviously problematic in its own right (Foxe 2017).

Conclusion

There are many reasons why media organisations in Ireland have struggled to access data. New entrants to journalism are not always presenting with the relevant skill sets. However, given the lack of consistent data projects in mainstream media it is arguable as to whether or not these skills are required of staff in all newsrooms or, indeed, to be encouraged by editors given the focus on daily news beats. Some practitioners and journalism educators would argue that training in data analysis is pointless if the ability to see the story is not finely tuned first and foremost (Foxe 2017).

Moreover, the danger in moving data journalism into a separate category to other types of journalism runs the risk of forgetting that journalists in Ireland have been using data as part of their work for decades, albeit in a less innovative way. Also as highlighted earlier (Logue 2017), the physical and sometimes 'philosophical' divides that exist in some Irish newsrooms, with editorial departments regularly located in different parts of the building to graphics departments and analytics teams, must also be addressed if collaboration is to succeed on any largescale, consistent and meaningful level. This may, as suggested above (Sheridan 2017), involve more innovative approaches to managing resources and work flows.

The danger in isolating data journalism as a separate discipline to regular journalism must also be avoided so that core investigtive skills such as using FOI, ability to access to public records and understand company accounts continue to underpin best practice in all forms of journalism. Economies of scale and population size cannot be ignored when comparing Irish media outlets with big hitters in the US and UK (Hayes 2015). But equally, Ireland cannot ignore data journalism's potential even if this requires a cultural shift within the institutions that hold the data and media organisations rethinking business models and risking short-term pain for long-term success.

References

Caffrey, Elaine (2015) *Independent.ie*: A digital first strategy. Available online at http://digitalmarketingstrategy.ucd.ie/independent-ie-digital-first-strategy/, accessed on 9 September 2015

Department of Public Expenditure and Reform (2014) Ireland and the Open Government Partnership. Available online at http://www.per.gov.ie/en/open-government-partnership-ogp/, accessed on 8 September 2015

Duncan, Pamela and Carswell, Simon (2015) Sinn Fein's money, *Irish Times*, 5 March. Available online at http://www.irishtimes.com/news/ireland/sinn-feins-money, accessed on 8 September 2015

Felle, Tom and Adshead (2009) Democracy and the right to know: 10 years of the Freedom of Information Act in Ireland, *University of Limerick Papers in Politics and Public Administration*, No. 4

Foley, Michael (2015) Keeping the state's secrets: Ireland's road from 'official' secrets to freedom of information, Felle, Tom and Mair, John (eds) *FoI: 10 Years On: Freedom Fighting or Lazy Journalism?*, Bury St Edmunds: Abramis pp 186-194

Greenslade, Roy (2013) Irish journalists alarmed at Freedom of Information pricing proposal, *Guardian*, 13 November. Available online at http://www.theguardian.com/media/2013/nov/13/irish-journalists-alarmed-at-freedom-of-information-pricing-proposal, accessed on 8 September 2015

Hayes, Kathryn (2015) Closed shop? Irish data pioneers battle to access information in 'open' regime, Felle, Tom, Mair, John and Radcliffe, Damian (eds) Data Journalism: Inside the Global Future, Bury St Edmunds: Abramis pp 242-253

Hennessy, Mark (2008) Democracy and the Right to Know: Proceedings from the University of Limerick Department of Politics and Public Administration Conference marking the 10th anniversary of Freedom of Information in Ireland, 29 February

Linehan, Hugh (2015) Data journalism: Reinventing news for 21st century digital society, *Irish Times*, 27 February. Available online at http://www.irishtimes.com/opinion/data-journalism-reinventing-news-for-21st-century-digital-society-1.2119160, accessed on 9 September 2015

Interviews

Duncan, Pamela, data journalist, *Irish Times*, interview in person in Dublin, on 26 June 2015.

Foley, Michael, Lecturer in Journalism, Dublin Institute of Technology, interview in person in Dublin, on 26 June 2015.

Foxe, Ken, investigative freelance journalist, Assistant Lecturer in Journalism, Dublin Institute of Technology, interview via email, on 26 June 2017.

Heravi, Bahareh, Associate Professor, Postgraduate Director, School of Information and Communications Studies, University College Dublin, interview via email, on 27 July 2017.

Logue, Paddy, Digital Editor, *Irish Times*, interview via telephone, on 22 June 2017.

Ryan, Conor, investigative journalist, RTE Investigations Unit, interview via telephone, on 20 June 2017.

Sheridan, Gavin, investigative journalist, interview via telephone and email, on 30 June 2017.

O'Sullivan, Kevin, Editor, *Irish Times*, interview via telephone, on 1 July 2015.

Note on the contributor

Kathryn Hayes is a Lecturer in Journalism at the University of Limerick. She has worked as a journalist for 20 years mostly as a freelance in Ireland's mid-west region supplying daily news to a number of national Irish newspapers titles and broadcast media outlets. Kathryn has been contributing to *The Irish Times* from the Limerick region since 2003 and is a regular Limerick stringer for Ireland's national broadcaster RTE. She is currently involved in journalism research as a PhD candidate at the University of Limerick. Email Kathryn. hayes@ul.ie or tweet @hayes_cait.

Investigative open data journalism in Russia

It may be surprising to discover that a considerable amount of open data is available in Russia. Anastasia Valeeva argues that journalists should move fast to make the most of it

Introduction

In a way, investigative journalists all over the world were working with data long before the term 'data journalism' came into prominence. Professional reporters were combing through government statistics, court records and business reports, archives and dusty courthouse basements or obtaining official or leaked confidential documents (Howard 2014: 10). These files were, essentially, data – albeit non-digitised.

Today, when data journalism has become a specialisation on its own, there are other clear similarities between doing journalism with data and producing investigations: both are focused on finding new information, both strive for objectivity and work in the public interest. But where, traditionally, journalists keep their story secret until the moment of publication, with data investigations they need to loosen control over their narrative in two ways: they should trust data and let it tell its own story – and they should share the content with people from other backgrounds to help with the analysis and presentation. This has been noted internationally by journalists and media researchers (Parasie 2015) and particularly in Russia through the interviews made for this chapter.

Another distinctive feature of doing data journalism is being transparent about sources and processes, often publishing the data behind the story. This, again, seems at odds with the traditional culture of journalistic investigation. The fact that professional journalists often do not reveal their sources is, indeed, criticised as a 'fundamental bug of newspapers' (Baack 2015: 6).

To assess the use of open data in journalistic investigations in Russia, I concentrated on three news outlets:

- *Novaya Gazeta*, an independent journal founded in 1993 and famous for its investigations of sensitive areas such as the conflicts in the Caucasus or human rights abuses;

- *Meduza*, a digital-based news organisation whose core team was formed of journalists who resigned from *Lenta.ru* when its editor-in-chief was fired in 2014; and

- RBC, the biggest non-government media group in Russia which comprises an informational agency, news portal, newspaper, magazine and broadcast company. It is particularly noted for its investigations into business and politics.

This chapter draws on a combination of semi-structured interviews, case studies and qualitative content analysis examining both the transparency of journalism stories and complexity of data analysis for the story. I have measured transparency of journalism by seeing if there was a link provided to the source data and if the journalist's own data was put online. Complexity of data analysis is measured by the tools used to produce insight: was it searching for a name in the dataset; performing statistical calculations or running an algorithm? I then move on to discuss the barriers for investigative data journalism in Russia and propose guidelines to overcome it.

Big data investigations at *Novaya Gazeta*

Novaya Gazeta is a newspaper traditionally known for its classic journalist investigations. More recently, it has become famous for using big data and leaked databases in their investigations, as well as open sources and open data in their researching. Significantly, *Novaya Gazeta* joined with the International Consortium of Investigative Journalists and the Organised Crime and Corruption Reporting Project in publishing the Panama Papers in May 2016 and Russian Laundromat in March 2017. These stories are run by an investigative team headed by journalist Roman Anin.

For my research, I wanted to see how much open data was used in the Panama Papers investigation (*Novaya Gazeta* 2016). The open data was never linked to an original source, nor was the database put online. This is easily explained by the very nature of the investigation, but it is also evidence of the level of 'openness' in investigative journalism: it presents the reader with the results without giving access to the raw data.

As for the complexity of data analysis, there were no statistical calculations or special programs employed to establish correlations or discover patterns. Instead, simple 'fishing expeditions' were undertaken, searching in the database, for instance, for the names of people close to President Putin. In effect, journalists at *Novaya Gazeta* were continuing the tradition of old-school investigative reporters when they 'read' the data and searched for proof of corruption through various databases, including open data.

Statistical investigations at *Meduza*

At the online-first media organisation *Meduza*, based in Riga, there is no dedicated data group, but there is a team called 'Razbor' which in Russian means 'scrutiny' or 'analysis'. They work with data in a way which is interesting for two reasons. First, they use data to explain complex issues in step-by-step guides often referencing original data or reports. Second, this team also looks for interesting datasets and analyses them – and their reports are then combined with the traditional reporting done by special correspondents. For this genre, they coined the term 'statistical investigation'.

One of their stories came directly from open data. One weekend, Denis Dmitriev, a member of the 'Razbor' team, had some time to look at the dataset published by the Federal Service of State Statistics on the volume of all food products sold within the borders of the Russian Federation during the 2014 fiscal year. The data was available, albeit in pdf form. Having calculated consumption per capita, Dmitriev discovered, surprisingly, that in one remote region of the Chechen republic people consumed more food than anywhere else in the country. Initially, journalists had two explanations – it was either a secret resort for locals or Chechen officials were 'inventing' their data.

To check, *Meduza* sent a reporter to the region to interview officials and locals. After further analysis of the data, the 'Razbor' team found that the same amount of consumption per capita was repeated across half of municipalities in the republic. This was a solid proof that the data was not collected in a fair and adequate manner – even if the total was true, the way it was divided across regions was artificial. They tried to contact Chechen officials but nobody would pick up the phone (Data Team *Meduza* 2017). But the investigation had a sort of happy ending: after the new data for 2015 was published, the richest region in 2014 was assessed the poorest one in 2015. This is how data journalism can make an impact in Russia: encouraging officials to pay a little more attention to the data they publish.

As for transparency, *Meduza* always provides a link to the original data and always creates its own dataset, though still does not give online access to it. In terms of data analysis, journalists employ the basic understanding of statistical analysis, but do not use computer programming to provide the insights. *Meduza* supports every story with visualisations, but the most important part for them is journalistic reporting.

Open data investigations at RBC

RBC, part of the RosBusinessConsulting media group, has become famous for its investigations in recent years. In particular, reporter Ivan Golunov has built up a reputation for his exclusives based on in-depth work with procurement data and documents.

Golunov not only carefully reads the procurement documents to find the signs of corruption, he also works with the data by sorting, filtering and analysing it. For instance:

RBC has studied all the tenders of the Moscow City Hall under the 'My Street' programme [a complex improvement scheme for the streets of Moscow planned for 2015-2018]. In 22 out of 31 cases, winners offered a reduction in the initial price in the range of 5.26-5.82 per cent. Of these, eight winners offered the same reduction of 5.2631 per cent (RBC 2015).

These investigations have a distinct data aspect since they analyse tender documents *en masse* trying to see the bigger picture – who wins most tenders for a project, who are the key players on the market. The link for the original data is always provided, but not for the database the reporter has compiled to draw his conclusions.

When asked if his investigation could benefit from developers' input, Golunov replied that 'they could automate the work that I am doing manually now' (Golunov 2017). Programmers are not yet seen in the Russian newsrooms as fully-fledged members of the investigative team. The same applies to designers: at RBC, the use of infographics is more an add-on than an essential ingredient of the storytelling. This is partly explained by the nature of the Russian media where no distinct data teams have emerged yet. But part of the answer lies in the journalists' determination to keep their control over the storytelling.

Guidelines for stronger data journalism in Russia

Better data

To tell better data stories, journalists need better data in the first place. Whereas in terms of financial transparency Russia competes with frontrunners such as the UK and the USA, there is a crucial deficiency in the areas of social well-being such as health, science, education, crime, ecology. For the data that is available, too often it is impossible to download in bulk. This denigrates the whole idea of 'open data' and leaves journalists continuing with their same routines: reading open data manually.

Data literacy

For many journalists in Russia, working with open data means getting information from Russian statistical websites, aggregators and registries. Ivan Begtin, open data expert, comments:

There is a terminological misunderstanding here. We confuse open data with the data from open sources. If journalists use open data, they usually use it in a dispersed way, compiling data for a specific investigation (Begtin 2016).

To harvest the fruits of open data, you need to realise its potential: open data gives an opportunity to work with structured information using digital means. Don't read the data, analyse it. In this way we can find the hidden stories. Getting people with relevant skills into the team and understanding the added value of their research is essential.

Culture shift in the newsroom: Transparency, presentation, investment

Developers coming from the open source culture can bring a culture shift to the newsroom and push for publishing the data and the source code behind investigations, making it replicable and available for anyone to explore. The same goes for designers who should not simply create illustrations for a story but be co-authors of the investigation, shifting the narrative away from text-only mode.

To implement all these initiatives, investment of time and money is necessary. This is hard when the resources in the newsroom are already shrinking, but change can happen if editors understand the specifics and added value of data investigations.

Conclusion

There is growing evidence of a developing open data ecosystem in Russia, animated by bottom-up initiatives, with some support from the state agencies. However, it is important to remember that no politician or NGO can substitute for journalists in the role of data storyteller. Objective, independent analysis of public data in the public interest, away from any political opportunism, is possible only with a newsroom infrastructure that upholds professional ethics.

Investigative journalism in Russia uses open data at the moment for 'fishing expeditions' and picking out pieces of information. Strong investigative units in various media are slowly growing their data literacy but still prefer to keep text as the main medium of communication controlling the narrative, not sharing with other specialists such as statisticians, designers or developers.

I, therefore, argue that journalists should work with data in systematic ways and open up their work to colleagues from the other backgrounds. I believe this will empower and enrich investigative journalism in Russia.

References

Baack, Stefan (2015) Datafication and empowerment: How the open data movement re-articulates notions of democracy, participation, and journalism, *Big Data & Society*, Vol. 2, No. 2 pp 1-11

Begtin, Ivan (2016) director at Infocultura NGO, interview with the author

Howard, Alexander (2014) *The Art and Science of Data-Driven Journalism*, New York: Tow Center for Digital Journalism, Columbia University

Golunov, Ivan (2017) journalist at RBC, interview with the author

Meduza (2016) 27 May. Available online at https://Meduza.io/feature/2016/05/27/kak-dmitriy-medvedev-manipuliruet-dannymi-o-naselenii-dalnego-vostoka-faktchek, accessed on 11 June 2017

Novaya Gazeta (2016) 3 April. Available online at http://krug.novayagazeta.ru/12-zoloto-partituri, accessed on 11 June 2017

Data Team *Meduza* (2017), interview with the author

Parasie, Sylvain (2015) Data-driven revelation? Epistemological tensions in investigative journalism in the age of 'big data', *Digital Journalism*, Vol. 3, No. 3 pp 364-380

RBC (2015) 19 October. Available online at http://www.rbc.ru/investigation/society/19/10/2015/561b6c739a79474587968837, accessed on 11 June 2017

Note on the contributor

Anastasia Valeeva is a data journalism trainer and open data researcher. She has researched the use of open data in investigative data journalism as part of her fellowship at the Reuters Institute for the Study of Journalism, Oxford. She has taught data journalism at Data Bootcamps in Montenegro and Germany, Data Journalism Summer Institutes in Kyrgyzstan and Albania, and at the Higher School of Economics, Russia. E-mail: anastasiya.valeeva@gmail.com, twitter handle @anastasiajourno.

The Spring Festival Rush: How data journalism is applied in China

Sixian Li and Shiting Ding examine reports from various types of Chinese media about the Spring Festival Rush and offer a detailed, critical overview of data journalism in China

Introduction

Along with the internet, big data significantly impacts on all aspects of contemporary societies. Both Fang Jie, a lecturer at the Renmin University of China,[1] and Shen Hao, a professor of the Communication University of China,[2] define data journalism as a new way of reporting news based on data capture, data mining, statistical analysis of data and data visualisation.

Chinese media began to explore the field of data journalism in 2013. Since then, following years of experimentation, Chinese media have developed their own indigenous style of data journalism. There are three main categories: the first is data journalism in the traditional media such as CCTV; the second appears on news channels and on web portals such as Netease, while the third appears on new media platforms of traditional media organisations such as the Data Journalism Channel of *Xinhua.net*.

A particularly important development occurred in 2014 when the *Evening News* of CCTV ran a series titled *Reporting the Spring Festival Rush with Data* showing that rural labourers working in metropolitan areas were returning to their home towns at the beginning of the Spring Festival. This was the first time that details about these migrations were collected and visualised on the Baidu map, the counterpart of Google Maps in China.

The Spring Festival Rush – or Chunyun in Chinese – is a period of around 40 days (from the fifteenth day before the Chinese New Year) of extremely high traffic loads on the roads and railways at the time of the rural workers' annual vacation. It has been called the largest annual human migration in the world, involving millions of rural Chinese families and, not surprisingly, it receives enormous coverage throughout the country's media. In an attempt to make their reporting more understandable and attractive, the Chinese media have explored numerous

190

ways of applying data to the coverage. In the following sections of this chapter, the authors will analyse some typical reports about the migration from the three types of Chinese media identified – and consider the future for data journalism in the country.

Traditional TV: Focusing on the social function of media

During the Spring Festival period in both 2014 and 2015, CCTV broadcast a series reports called *Reporting the Spring Rush with Data*. In the first year, the report relied on data collected in real-time by the Baidu map to visualise the flow of people during the period. Significantly, the presenter was surrounded in the studio by data and interacted with the data through their body language in the animated 3D virtual environment.

Reporting the Spring Rush with data[3]

In 2015, the programme used extra information about individual rural workers and mapped the data about the numbers of people at airports, train stations and bus stations of metropolitan cities down to county train stations and bus stations to help the viewers decide which route to take.

News channel of internet portal: Mining data for economic information

On the eve of the Spring Festival in 2017, *Netease* data news portal presented a special programme titled *Read the Numbers: How Can Anyone Get Home without a Train Ticket During the Spring Festival?* This report analysed the data from the

Ministry of Railways of China about the volume of passengers travelling on the trains and roads during the Spring Festivals from 2001 to 2016. The report also highlighted government moves to raise the price of train tickets. Because the growth of railroad construction had been slower than that of highways, there were fears of over-crowding on the trains. But the programme showed that the higher prices failed to drive down the demand for rail travel during the Spring Festivals in those years.

Early in 2013, the sub-channel of *Sohu News* called *Matrix* published a data report, *The Change in the Price of Train Tickets over Years*. Using data provided by *Xinhua.net* and the Railway Ministry, it showed the fluctuations in the railway ticket prices during the Spring Festival Rush in graphs. And the report also pointed out that the high-speed train had played an important role in the daily lives of ordinary Chinese through comparing its price (extremely favourably) with that of other countries.

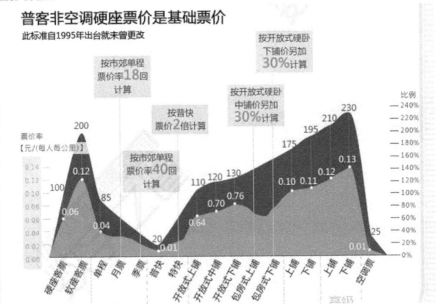

The changes in the price of train tickets over the years[4]

The *Matrix* also produced an interactive page called *Missing Data: People Who Don't Go Home During the Spring Festival* in 2012. This page used data from *Xinhua.net, People.cn, Guangzhou Daily* and other news media, focusing on people who did not go home during the Spring Festival, and showed – in an interactive animation – the reasons why they made that decision. Readers could browse the page and click to read a pop-up screen highlighting various categories: occupation, working hours, job content, etc.

Missing data: People who don't go home during the Spring Festival[5]

The state-owned new online media: Serving the citizen better

The traditional media, such as *Xinhua.net* and *People.cn* are building on a long tradition of high quality news production. But today, with the help of the internet, they are expanding their activities. During the Spring Festival period in 2017, *People.cn* launched a specially themed section on the rush and started an illustrated news section to report on this huge event. *People.cn* sorted out the ten most common categories of information needed by the Spring Festival travellers and presented them in graphs to enhance the understanding.

Ten most common categories of information needed by Spring Festival travellers[6]

For example, in the report *The Train Tickets will be on Sale Tomorrow and the Ministry of Railway Issues the Official Ticket-buying Strategy*, a calendar indicated clearly the ticket pre-sale period with eye-catching red areas to remind the audience when the ticket-buying peak period began and ended.

Compared with the *People.cn, Xinhua.net's* reporting of the Spring Festival Rush was more diversified. The reports were not limited to details about train tickets. The topics of a series of reports titled *From Spring Festival Big Data to Our Country and Your Home* were chosen from the most frequently read news and hot key words on the aggregation app *TOUTIAO* (*Headlines*, in Chinese) during the Spring Festival Rush period, and re-presented them with more information mined from the data to provide a value-added service for its audience.

For example, just before the Spring Festival of 2017, *TOUTIAO* showed that 'travel planning' was a hot key phrase. Then *Xinhua.net* published a web-page titled *The Spring Festival Rush Illustrated and Questing Home Route with Confidence* based on the information about ticket sales, the timetables and the most popular routes from the China Railroad Corporation to help the audience plan their best routes back home. *Xinhua.net* developed a page titled *The National Railway Crowding Before the Spring Festival*, showing the different numbers of travellers on the national routes by differently weighed lines.

Passenger numbers on the national railway before the Spring Festival

Data journalism in China: Opportunities ahead

What can be seen from the above analysis is that reports about the Spring Festival from the various types of Chinese media focused on different topics when using data. But some managed to become more user-friendly by carrying informative reports about such issues as ticketing strategy and passenger numbers.

Each media used data visualisations in different ways. For instance, CCTV made good use of three-dimensional animation in its virtual studio to make all the data more vivid and understandable. Other media outlets such as *Sohu* and *Xinhua.net* used basic tools such as a histogram, pie charts and curve plots with different shapes and colours to visualise data more effectively. On the other hand, the Data Blog of *Netease* focused on mining data for analysis and correlating it to identify possible trends to help their audience select their best course of actions.

Data mining and analysing the statistics are often the first two steps in the production of data journalism, which makes the source of data extremely important. In general, the sources of information in China's three major types of media are diverse and include the government, authoritative websites both at home and abroad, newspapers, magazines, the Ministry of Railways, the Ministry of Transportation and so on.

Data journalism in China is in its infancy. Yet data can now be retrieved and collected at relatively low cost – and this offers huge opportunities to all media (both traditional and new) in terms of better serving society.

Challenges

First, following the analysis of the Spring Festival Rush coverage in the three major types of media in China, it is clear that they all failed to place their contemporary coverage of the Spring Festival Rush in its proper social and historical context. The stories carried by the Data Blog of *Netease* and the *Matrix* attempted to correlate data about the national pricing policy, the railway infrastructure supply and passenger capacity during the Spring Festival. But the analysis lacked appropriate objectivity since little reasoning was offered to support the conclusions and the audience was permitted little interaction with the data.

Foreign counterparts, on the other hand, have carried reports by data journalists far more effectively. The report *How to Change an Election* on the US news website *FiveThirtyEight* in 2016 showed the support ratio for both Democrats and Republicans in each state using a dynamic data map and five interactive charts representing the support ratios of five national ethnic groups. Users could pull the coordinates in the diagram to change the bipartisan support ratio of a national ethnic group and find its impact on the national election. During the 2016 Rio Olympics, a report about the men's 200 meters swimming race, in the London *Guardian*, presented information in an original and dynamic way. Chinese data journalists can clearly learn from *FiveThirtyEight* and the *Guardian* strategies to improve the ways in which they visualise the information – and interact with their audiences.

Second, most of China's media depend largely on data from external bodies and do not have their own databases. However, both traditional and new media are likely to build their own databases in the future, in part through integrating their news production with social media outlets. And this development is likely to encourage feedback from audiences.

Notes

[1] Jie, Fang (2013) *Data Journalism: Theory and Practice*, International Press, Vol. 6 pp 73-83.

[2] Hao, Shen (2016) *Data Journalism: Historical Prospect from the Perspective of Modernity*, *Journalism Bimonthly*, Vol. 2 pp 1-5.

[3] CCTV (2014) Evening news: Reporting the Spring Rush with data, 15 January. Available online at http://tv.cntv.cn/video/C10420/ca0f60b535cf4d5e8a81748963038fb7, accessed on 28 May 2017.

[4] *Sohu News* (2013) *Matrix*: The change in the price of train tickets over the years. 1 January. Available online at http://news.sohu.com/s2012/trainticket/, accessed on 28 May 2017.

[5] *Sohu News* (2012) *Matrix*: Missing data: People who don't go home during the Spring Festival, 11 January. Available online at http://news.sohu.com/s2011/springfestival/, accessed on 28 May 2017.

[6] *People.cn* (2016) Spring Rush: Ten major measures to help people in their travels, 10 December. Available online at http://society.people.com.cn/n1/2016/1210/c1008-28939912.html, accessed on 28 May 2017.

[7] *Xinhua.net* (2016) Focus on data news: National railway crowding before the Spring Festival, 4February. Available online at http://news.xinhuanet.com/video/sjxw/2016-02/04/c_128702289.htm, accessed on 28 May 2017.

Notes on the contributors

Sixian Li is a postgraduate student of School of Television of Communication University of China majoring in broadcast and television, supervised by Prof. Junqi Yan. Her interest lies in sports communication and management and her recent research looks at how to communicate effectively in sport through media. Contact details: 627082681@qq.com.

Shiting Ding is a postgraduate student of School of Television of Communication University of China majoring in Journalism and Communication and she is supervised by Prof. Junqi Yan. Her interest lies in collecting and editing of news media and her recent research looks at sports reporting in new media. Contact details: shimlyding@163.com.

Data journalism in the US: Three case studies and ten general principles for journalists

Data journalism is a well established storytelling method across different news media in the United States. Analysis of this landscape (together with three detailed case studies) allows us to determine elements of best practice, Damian Radcliffe and his students at the University of Oregon argue

1. Politics

For the average American, the world of politics can be difficult to navigate and even more treacherous to understand. Indeed, the field is often filled with an abundance of buzzwords and technical terms. For example, many people understand the power of lobbying in politics. However, there is usually a disconnect between this abstract understanding and actual knowledge of how money moves more widely in the system. To bridge that gap, a variety of publications – including *ProPublica, FiveThirtyEight* and the *Washington Post* – have all begun to use data-driven storytelling to bring readers into the loop.

ProPublica unravels the complexities of campaign finance and voter fraud

ProPublica is a Pulitzer-winning non-profit outfit – known for its interactive, data driven work – which produces high quality investigative journalism and public interest stories. In February 2014, it ran a report showing the complex way that Charles and David Koch spread their wealth in politics. 'How dark money flows through the Koch network'

There have been fewer than **1,000** substantiated incidents of all types of election fraud documented out of more than **1,000,000,000** ballots cast in elections since 2000.

Image from ProPublica *report: 'How voter fraud works – and mostly doesn't'*

includes an interactive map depicting how money flows out of the Kochs' non-profit networks (like the TC4 Trust and Freedom Partners) and into the pockets of partisan organisations such as the National Rifle Association and Tea Party Patriots (Shaw, Meyer, and Baker 2014). Initially, the map is overwhelming and difficult to understand. By hovering your mouse over the different areas, however, you can begin to see exactly how – and where – the money flows.

More recently, a November 2016 story examined a hot electoral topic: how voter fraud works. 'How voter fraud works – and mostly doesn't' (Cagle 2016) uses graphics to explore what voter fraud looks like across the country. The article is primarily graphics-driven, using minimal text to provide context. A feature called 'Fraud cards' allows users to flip over cards that show documented cases of voter fraud labeled by state and year.

FiveThirtyEight tackles crime and immigration

Another website using a data-driven model for much of its reporting is *FiveThirtyEight*. Created by Nate Silver and owned by ESPN, it focuses closely on polls and data for politics, economics and sports blogging. In a May 2017 article, 'Latinos in three cities are reporting fewer crimes since Trump took office' (Arthur 2017), data is used to analyse a decrease in crime reporting within predominantly immigrant Latino communities.

The article posits that recent immigration reforms by President Trump are the chief cause of this, and uses statistics and graphs from various cities with high Latino populations to back the claim. The use of graphs within the article helps the reader grasp the sharp declines that have occurred in a more tangible way.

The *Washington Post* unpacks Trump's budget proposals

Meanwhile, a 2017 online article from the *Washington Post* stands as an excellent example of a traditional print publication using data journalism in the digital medium. 'What Trump cut in his agency budgets' (Soffen and Lu 2017) displays a series of graphs and charts representing President Trump's proposed budget for the US government. The proposal called for massive cuts in several departments and an increase for the Defense Department, garnering much media attention and political strife.

For each affected department, the *Post* uses a chart to illustrate the increase – or decrease – in its budget with blocks, coupled with a graph showing the change in budget over the past year, a description of what programmes are being cut from the department and the impact of the new budget. This shows the possibilities of turning data into charts and graphs to improve the storytelling. The visual elements make the budget more understandable to the reader, as opposed to being bombarded with a wave of numbers and text.

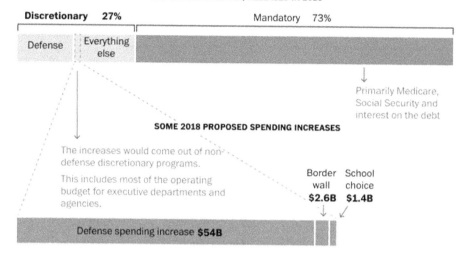

Proposed budget changes, the **Washington Post**

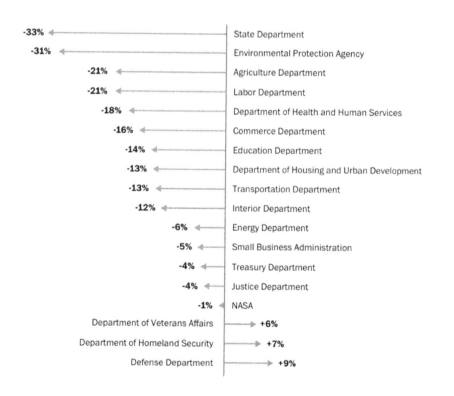

Proposed changes to the Defense Department budget, *the* Washington Post

The piece also has interactive features to enhance the page's user experience (UX). It has a drop-down menu at the top that takes people down to the selected department of their choosing, as well as a comments section at the bottom that is automatically updated but can also be paused with the click of a button. This allows the reader to express their opinions more efficiently and interact with the online community and/or find their desired information.

Combining a clean, easy-to-use layout with concise storytelling, the page demonstrates the *Washington Post's* understanding of the importance of the user's role in effective data-driven journalism.

2. Health and science

Both mainstream and specialist media continue to provide considerable coverage of health and science related stories. However, in an era of instant information, there is a risk of complex findings being misrepresented or misunderstood.

The American Council on Science and Health and Real Clear Science joined forces to show – as reflected in the infographic – trustworthiness across three measurements: the implementation of science journalism, the amount of evidence they provide in their stories and how compelled the readers are by the stories. Their research, and ours, suggests that utilising digestible, comprehensive and interactive data to complement a story is crucial to the success and validity of accurate scientific reporting.

Without clear evidence, science journalism loses its credibility and becomes little more than a sensationalised opinion piece stripped of any true value. In today's increasingly bipartisan world, hard scientific data may be one of the last slivers of journalism that audiences can believe in.

Damian Radcliffe

Infographic: The Best and Worst Science News Sites[1]

Fox News: Veganism

In a 2016 article, *Fox News* challenged some of the assumptions identified by advocates of veganism – which supporters argue is both environmentally friendly and more environmentally sustainability – citing a research study which explored the impact of different diets on agriculture and land cultivation (Fox 2016).

Contrary to what a data story should entail, the article contained no statistics, and the link the provided by Fox did not lead to the actual study, but a report on the Quartz website.[2]

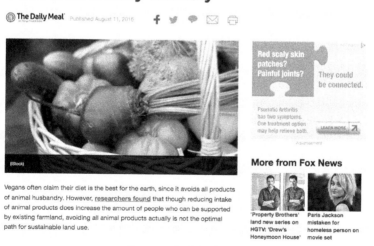

Screengrab of Fox News story

It's left to Quartz to cite and link to the original research – an open access scientific journal, *Elementa: Science of the Anthropocene* – as well as to produce reporting which includes important data and statistics from the study. In failing to cover adequately a topic that could lend itself as an ideal data-based piece, *Fox News*, in this instance, provides a clear example of how news outlets are failing to provide evidence-based journalism.

FiveThirtyEight: Eat like 'The Rock'

In stark contrast to the conservative *Fox News*, the data-heavy online publication *FiveThirtyEight* aims to inform almost strictly through numbers. The website is known for its analytical concentration on sports and politics, although it has branched out from these fields. One intriguing example of this can be seen in its 2015 piece on the diet of Hollywood actor and former pro-wrestler Dwayne 'The Rock' Johnson (Hickey 2015).

The story breaks down Johnson's diet and presents the information in a way that is easily digested by any audience. In one paragraph, the article hyperlinks to four different sources providing information on average caloric intake, price of food and pounds of cod consumed.

> The average American man in his forties consumes 2,734 calories daily, according to data from the USDA. Johnson eats roughly 1,000 calories a day in cod alone. Annualized, Johnson eats about 821 pounds of cod per year. According to FishChoice, Pacific cod goes for $1.75 per pound, meaning Johnson spends roughly $1,400 per year on cod. As all our cod consumption slowly progresses past sustainable levels, let's all consider Dwayne Johnson uniquely responsible.

Screengrab from article about the daily diet of Dwayne 'The Rock' Johnson

Beyond the basics of citing sources, *FiveThirtyEight* sets itself apart from text-heavy publications with clean and easy-to-understand visuals and infographics to complement its data. As seen in the chart, the numbers are easy to interpret because of the familiar and simple layout; the author, Walt Hickey, lets the data do the talking.

MEAL	CALORIES	CARBS	TOTAL FAT	SATURATED FAT	PROTEIN	MEAL MASS
Meal 1	810	38g	15g	4g	77g	24oz
Meal 2	594	84	3	1	56	25
Meal 3	1069	125	28	7	72	27
Meal 4	909	121	18	8	62	28
Meal 5	769	89	25	9	70	22
Meal 6	816	115	4	1	73	28
Meal 7	398	14	18	6	50	15
Other	225	5	3	0	47	0

NUTRIENT	THE ROCK	AVG. US. MALE IN FORTIES
Calories	5165	2734
Total carbs (g)	566	317
Total fat (g)	109	107
Sat. Fat (g)	33	35
Protein (g)	480	105

The *Guardian*: 'Raw milk: A superfood or super risky?

The Guardian is a well-established daily newspaper that covers science and health, often effectively using data to aid the story-telling process. A recently published article titled 'Raw milk: A superfood or super risky?' explores the potential health benefits and dangers of drinking raw, unpasteurised milk – which almost 5 per cent of people in the United States now consume (Simmonds 2017).

> A US food safety official once compared drinking raw milk to "playing Russian roulette", and the Centers for Disease Control and Prevention (CDC) says raw milk illnesses have spiked as more people drink it. Between 2009 and 2014, raw milk and raw milk cheese caused the vast majority (96%) of all illnesses linked to contaminated dairy products. Considering far fewer people consume it, that makes unpasteurized dairy 840 times more risky than pasteurized, the CDC says. The recent deaths of two people who ate raw milk cheese made in New York underscored the sometimes deadly consequences.
>
> Eight years ago, Michele Jay-Russell, a microbiologist at the University of California at Davis, helped start a website called Real Raw Milk Facts to counter what she describes as a "very sophisticated misinformation campaign" lauding the benefits and downplaying the dangers.

Screengrab from article featured in the **Guardian** *online*

While she does not utilise infographics and tables to the extent that *FiveThirtyEight* does, Simmonds still does a thorough job of letting the data and sources have their presence known. Through use of key stats – including the size of the market and the likelihood (based on past data) of getting ill from eating raw, or contaminated dairy products – Simmonds is able to pepper her story with figures which provide important context for her wider piece. The debate over drinking raw milk is ongoing, but the *Guardian* makes it clear that this traditional use of data-informed reporting won't go sour anytime soon.

3. Sport

Being considered the greatest of all time is something every player and team strives to be. But how do you prove your greatness? One way to do this is through data. And luckily, sports fans – as well as teams – love data.

The National Basketball Association (NBA) has historically been one of the most competitive sporting leagues in the world, but that changed after the Golden State Warriors hired Steve Kerr to be their head coach in 2014. The Warriors were previously one of the worst franchises in the NBA's history, but now they have a team that some pundits (Schwartz 2017) claim could be the greatest team ever to play the sport. How does data support this claim? Three different publications – *FiveThirtyEight*, *SB Nation* and the San Jose *Mercury News* – have each argued for the Warriors' historic superiority, using different data to help advance and evidence their claims.

FiveThirtyEight

FiveThirtyEight.com rose to fame after founder Nate Silver correctly used data to predict the outcome of the 2012 US election, down to every vote in the Electoral College and each congressional district. Now, along with political data journalism, *FiveThirtyEight* is a leader in sports data journalism.

FiveThirtyEight has created its own dataset, 'Elo', to show how teams have been performed throughout their history. *FiveThirtyEight* describes how it works: 'The only inputs are the final score of each game, and where and when it was played. Teams always gain Elo points for winning. But they get more credit for upset victories and for winning by larger margins. Elo ratings are zero-sum, however.'[3]

By using Elo, *FiveThirtyEight* shows how the Warriors were historically one of the worst teams in the NBA's history.

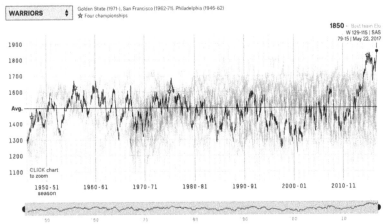

Image: Long-term performance of the Warrior, FiveThirtyEight

When narrowed down to the last decade, the Warriors' rise to power in the league is evident.

Recent performance of the Warrior, FiveThirtyEight

SB Nation

As *SB Nation* has shown, the Warriors also have two players who are statistical anomalies: Stephen Curry and Klay Thompson. Curry is one of the best three-point shooters to play the game (three-points are the most points one can score in a single shot). Curry and Thompson were ranked first and second for made three-pointers in the 2015-16 season (Cato 2016).

Steph Curry without an assist, **SB Nation**

Moreover, Curry's shooting is not only dominant from just beyond the three-point arc (23.75 feet from behind the basket), but he can also make shots from deeper down the court (Cato 2016b).

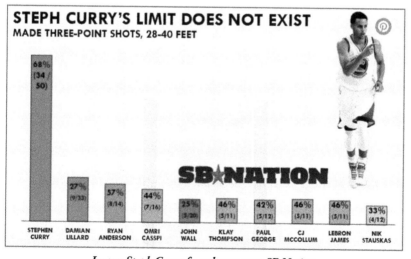

Image: Steph Curry from long range, **SB Nation**

Basketball is a team sport, but when a team has two of the best shooters the game has even seen, it is no surprise a team can be so dominant. *FiveThirtyEight's* Elo has ranked the best teams to ever play,[4] but the current Warriors team has yet to be part of it as the play-offs have yet to conclude. (Note the team subsequently went on to win the NBA Finals in mid-June 2017).[5] Last season's Warriors lost in the NBA Finals to the Cleveland Cavaliers and that Warriors team is still ranked third behind two of Michael Jordan's NBA-winning Chicago Bulls.

Mercury News

A big contributor to scoring in basketball is assisting, a pass that directly leads to a basket.[6] The Warriors are the least reliant on isolation basketball— a technical term that means a team chooses not to pass the ball (Slater 2016). In the 2017 season, as demonstrated by several videos on the San Jose *Mercury News* website, the Warriors have had assists on 71.2 per cent of their made baskets, which is 6.1 per cent better than the next best team.

A lot of the credit for the Warriors' success is also revelaed in a statistic that is not normally kept: screens. Screens are when players plant both feet to block an opponent from getting to a player on the opposing team. *FiveThirtyEight* has documented the Warriors' surprisingly dominant success at screens, crediting it to the team's lethal attacking play (Herring 2017).

The Warriors set screens differently than any other NBA team

The Warriors' ballhandlers **run fewer pick and rolls** than any other team...		... and finish fewer of these plays **with their roll men** ...		... but set far more **off-ball screens** per game.	
TEAM	PLAYS/GAME	TEAM	PLAYS/GAME	TEAM	PLAYS/GAME
⋮		⋮		1 Warriors	14.4
26 Grizzlies	14.4	26 Bucks	6.3	2 Mavericks	9.2
27 Kings	14.3	27 Raptors	6.2	3 Wizards	8.7
28 Bucks	14.0	28 Heat	6.2	4 Pacers	8.3
29 76ers	13.6	29 Suns	5.4	5 Hornets	8.0
30 Warriors	12.1	30 Warriors	4.4	⋮	

FiveThirtyEight — SOURCES: NBA, SYNERGY SPORTS

Image: from 'The beautiful chaos of the Warriors' offense' **FiveThirtyEight**

All in all, the 2016-17 Golden State Warriors may well be the best team to play the game of basketball. It's not just the data that suggests this, their 2017 triumph in the NBA Finals may just be the start of an extended period of unprecedented on-court dominance by a brilliant team.

10 key principles for data story-telling

Based on our reading across these three thematic areas – and detailed research into coverage provided by seven different journalistic outlets – we were able to identify a series of important principles which all journalists using data should seek to abide by. Many of these values are not just applicable to data storytelling; indeed, they should already be an established part of the journalist's craft, but these principles are worth reiterating nonetheless, not least because – based on our reading and research – these core values are all too often overlooked.

1. **Don't beat readers over the head with numbers**. Data should be used to illustrate key points and help bring a story alive. The data itself is seldom the story, the implications of it need to be unpacked and explained.

2. **Decide which tools allow you to tell a story best**. Journalists have access to a plethora of means, including graphs, infographics, charts, tables and interactives to help tell a story. The value derived from each of these tools will vary depending on the story you wish to tell and the key data that you want to focus on.

3. **Determine if you should develop a house style**. When looking at sports stories, we found that each publication favoured a different way of incorporating data. The *San Jose Mercury News* tended to weave stats into stories, *SB Nation* showed a preference for bar graphs, whilst *Five ThirtyEight* had a larger propensity for tables and complicated graphs.

4. **Determining your approach may be influenced by both the story you want to tell *and* the data literacy – and preferences – of your audience**. Either way, your data-driven stories should be well designed so that audiences do not struggle to understand what's being shown or how to interact with the data. For complex visualisations that may mean including some instructions (an idea too often overlooked by journalists), as well as links – including downloadable data files – to the original sources used in these efforts.

5. **Don't link to blog/press releases, link to the actual study**. These types of editorial shortcuts are often in evidence. But, in the hyperlinked economy, there is no excuse not to take your reader to the original source of the conclusions – and data – you are reporting on. Enable them to continue the journey – and check the veracity of your claims for themselves.

6. **Provide proper attribution of your sources**. Data-driven stories need to show their sources and avoid unattributed assertions. Unfortunately, especially in the health sphere, this is all too common. Journalistic assertions are often made without links to the evidence which can (one hopes) back them up. Don't fall into the same trap.

7. **Ensure your links work.** Linking to broken sites, or incorrectly inserting the correct address of a URL, is sloppy. If journalists don't care enough about their work to get these basic elements right, is it any wonder that they fail to inspire confidence in some of their audiences? Doing these core tasks well is important, failure to do so merely helps erode trust in the profession.

8. **Make it relatable and digestible.** Data-driven story-telling still requires good writing and a story news sense. Data requires context and explanation. Be sure to provide it.

9. **Don't overwhelm your audience.** You don't have to provide all of your data at once. Most stories work better if you decide the key elements to include, and where the focus should be: you don't have to include every statistic you have access to. Be selective – whilst also being objective – with data in the same way as you would any other source.

10. **Good data journalism is harder to find than you may think.** Data-driven storytelling includes many elements such as images, charts, graphics, visuals, stats and interactives. Finding – and reviewing – examples of great (and even not so great) work by other outlets (as we have sought to do here) can inform and inspire your own efforts, as we all strive to improve our craft and be the best journalists that we possibly can be.

Notes

1 http://www.acsh.org/news/2017/03/05/infographic-best-and-worst-science-news-sites-10948.

2 https://qz.com/749443/being-vegan-isnt-as-environmentally-friendly-as-you-think/.

3 Fischer-Baum, Reuben and Silver, Nate (2015, updated 2017) The complete history of the NBA, *FiveThirtyEight*, 21 May 2017, last updated 12 June 2017. Available online at https://projects.fivethirtyeight.com/complete-history-of-the-nba/#warriors.

4 Fischer-Baum, Reuben (2016) After all that, The Warriors aren't even the second-best team ever, *FiveThirtyEight*, 20 June. Available online at http://fivethirtyeight.com/features/after-all-that-the-warriors-arent-even-the-second-best-team-ever/.

5 http://www.slate.com/blogs/ring_don_t_lie/2017/06/13/the_golden_state_warriors_are_2017_nba_champions.html.

6 http://www.nba.com/canada/Basketball_U_on_Assists-Canada_Generic_Article-18072.html.

References

Arthur, Rob (2017) Latinos in three cities are reporting fewer crimes since Trump took office, *Five ThirtyEight*, 18 May 2017. Available online at https://fivethirtyeight.com/features/latinos-report-fewer-crimes-in-three-cities-amid-fears-of-deportation/, accessed on 28 May 2017

Cagle, Susie (2016) How voter fraud works – and mostly doesn't, *ProPublica*, 3 November 2016. Available online at https://projects.propublica.org/graphics/voterfraud, accessed on 28 May 2017

Cato, Tim (2016) These 3 charts prove Stephen Curry's having the best shooting season ever, *SB Nation*, 29 February. Available online at http://www.sbnation.com/lookit/2016/2/29/11134406/stephen-curry-greatest-shooter-all-time-graphs-charts-stats, accessed on 28 June 2017

Fox (2016) New study reveals vegan diet not so environmentally friendly, *Fox News*, 11 August. Available online at http://www.foxnews.com/health/2016/08/11/new-study-reveals-vegan-diet-not-so-environmentally-friendly.html, accessed on 29 May 2017

Herring, Chris (2017) The beautiful chaos of the Warriors' offense, *Five ThirtyEight*, 19 May. Available online at https://fivethirtyeight.com/features/the-beautiful-chaos-of-the-warriors-offense/, accessed on 28 June 2017

Hickey, Walt (2015) Dwayne 'The Rock' Johnson eats about 821 pounds of cod per year, *Five ThirtyEight*, 7 April 2015. Available online at https://fivethirtyeight.com/datalab/dwayne-the-rock-johnson-eats-about-821-pounds-of-cod-per-year/, accessed on 29 May 2017

Schwartz, Nick (2017) Skip Bayless says the 2017 Warriors have a chance to be the greatest team ever, *Fox Sports*, 23 May 2017. Available online at http://www.foxsports.com/nba/gallery/skip-bayless-golden-state-warriors-best-team-ever-finals-cavaliers-052317, accessed on 27 June 2017

Shaw, Al, Meyer, Theodoric and Barker, Kim (2014) How dark money flows through the Koch Network, *ProPublica*, 14 February. Available online at http://projects.propublica.org/graphics/koch, accessed on 28 May 2017

Simmonds, Charlotte (2017) Raw milk: A superfood or super risky? *Guardian*, 30 May. Available online at https://www.theguardian.com/lifeandstyle/2017/may/30/raw-milk-health-superfood-safety-goop, accessed on 30 May 2017

Slater, Anthony (2016) The Warriors are on an impressive, Kevin Durant approved streak of 30-plus assists, *Mercury News*, 20 November, updated 24 November. Available online at http://www.mercurynews.com/2016/11/20/the-warriors-are-on-an-impressive-kevin-durant-1approved-streak-of-30-plus-assists/, accessed on 28 June 2017

Soffen, Kim and Lu, Denise (2017) What Trump cut in his agency budgets, *Washington Post*, 23 May. Available online at https://www.washingtonpost.com/graphics/politics/trump-presidential-budget-2018-proposal/?utm_term=.5e3e6f3c45eb#dept-19, accessed on 28 May 2017

Note on the contributors

Damian Radcliffe is the Carolyn S. Chambers Professor in Journalism at the University of Oregon, a Fellow of the Tow Center for Digital Journalism at Columbia University, an honorary research fellow at Cardiff University's School of Journalism, Media and Culture Studies and a fellow of the Royal Society for the Encouragement of Arts, Manufactures and Commerce (RSA).

He is an experienced digital analyst, consultant, journalist and researcher who has worked in editorial, research, teaching, and policy positions for the past two decades in the UK, Middle East, and USA.

University of Oregon students: Aaron Alter, Romario Garcia Bautista, Eric Schucht and Sam Smarglassi (politics); Ryan Eberle, Hannah Morrow, Tyler Smith, Mack Veltman and Natalie Waitt-Gibson (health and science); Nick Baxter, Jonathan Booker, Cameron Derby, Shawn Medow and Zach Wilkinson (sport) led the research and writing of this chapter, with students drafting the research, writing and analysis of each thematic section. The '10 principles' section stemmed from a classroom discussion about the takeaways from the research work undertaken by the group.

Effective and ethical data visualisations

Visual storytelling needs to be in sync with all other forms of storytelling by staying grounded in truth and ethics, according to journalist and researcher Erin Coates

Introduction

Data visualisations and data journalism are the current buzzwords, even if computer-assisted reporting and visuals have been around for a while. A quick search on Google trends shows that interest in data visualisation has grown over time in such countries as the United States, the United Kingdom, Canada and Germany, to name a few. There are still some people who assume data visualisation means still-image infographics. In reality, data visualisations and the interactive capabilities that have come with digital advances have made the jobs of data story-tellers much easier and more effective.

Interactive data visualisations have created a new way for journalists to tell a story. With the overwhelming amount of data available, these visualisations make it easier to compare different data sets. The data available on different topics from vaccination rates to mass shootings in the United States could have a real impact on a reader's comprehension of complex topics. This is where interactive data visualisations come into play. Journalists, designers and computer programmers team up to create new ways to tell stories based on data so the audience can learn from it and draw their own conclusions. With more newspapers and magazines moving into online platforms, there is a growing need for different storytelling techniques to grasp the attention of readers.

I became fascinated by data visualisations after Nicole Dahmen, an assistant professor of visual communication at the University of Oregon, spoke to my data journalism class. Following her lead, my thesis looked at whether the salience of controversial topics was affected by the use of data visualisation. I found that, though people did not alter their opinion after seeing the data visualised, the visualisations themselves seemed to confuse them. From this I concluded that we journalists have a job to do if we are to make our readers 'graphically literate' when it comes to data.

Alberto Cairo's steps to becoming 'graphicate'

Alberto Cairo, the Knight Chair at the University of Miami, calls the ability to interpret graphs and data visualisations correctly 'graphicacy'. Ineffective and misinterpreted graphics are dangerous and it is imperative that our audience be able to understand them. The following are Cairo's seven steps towards developing graphical literacy – or teaching journalists and the public to be 'graphicate' (Cairo 2017) outlined in his keynote at the Microsoft Data Insights Summit in June 2017. Building from his lead, I have supplemented his steps and added examples:

1. Is your data measuring what you think it's measuring?

Mining through data in search of trends and stories takes time. Clean data sets have numbers that should not lie, and there can be more than one story in any significant data set. However, it is important to note that what you believe the data is measuring could be completely different from what it actually is measuring.

The American Press Institute recommends being as sceptical as possible and investigating the data for sources of bias, hidden variables and anything else that could lead you to the wrong conclusion. According to Samantha Sunne, of the American Press Institute (2016): 'You can't do a single project with just data and not journalism. Hitting the pavement, making phone calls, talking to sources are always necessary.' The only way we, as journalists, can understand data is by conducting interviews with experts who will be able to explain why we are seeing various trends and what the data is showing.

2. When exploring your data, always visualise it

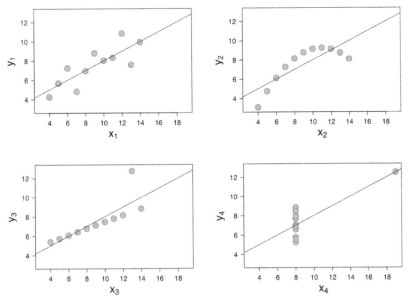

Image source: https://en.wikipedia.org/wiki/Anscombe%27s_quartet

Relying on summary statistics leaves out the possibility of features in the data that could potentially go unnoticed. Visualising the data provides a sense of what trends are present in the data. Cairo used the example of Anscombe's quartet, which shows four datasets with almost identical summary statistics, yet appear quite different when graphed. Statistician Francis Anscombe constructed these datasets in 1973 to show how important it is to graph data before analysing it.

As you can see, these four data sets with similar mean, median, mode etc. appear radically different when they are visualised. Merely relying on these summary statistics could lead us to get the story wrong and fail to notice the trends in the data.

3. A visualisation must always represent the data proportionally

There are many ways to misrepresent data graphically and there are many media entities who do so. Common graphic mistakes include: not starting at a zero baseline, a vertical scale that is too big or too small, mislabelled graphs – and missing data. 'There is a very basic rule in data visualisation which is that graphics that use height or length to represent your data, like a bar graph, need to have a zero baseline. If they don't have a zero baseline, you are distorting the data' (Cairo 2017).

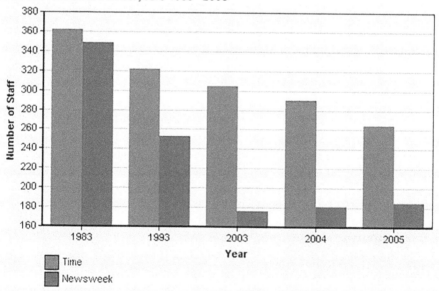

*Image source: https://web.archive.org/web/20060929104732/http://www.journalism.org/
node/1472*

The team at *Perceptual Edge* uses this example to show two different problems with this bar graph. To start, the wrong kind of chart has been chosen to show the change in staff over time. Bar charts are better used for categories and line charts for trends. Bar graphs are supposed to show the quantity of what is in each category, and by not starting at the zero baseline the audience's perception of how many people are in each newsroom are skewed. The second issue with this bar graph is that it does not show a continuous range of time. When comparing the staff size over time, it would be better to have a uniform time interval to show changes and trends, not just in particular and arbitrary years.

4. A visualisation shows only what it shows and nothing else

One of the many problems of data storytelling comes from over-interpreted data. The age-old saying that correlation does not necessarily mean causation serves true in data storytelling as well. There may be underlying variables in the data set which need to be uncovered by journalists and revealed to our readers.

In terms of data visualisations, our audiences can also over-interpret what they are seeing. Something I found in my personal research is that people are able to understand and read graphs better if they are properly labelled. As interactivity in online visualisations increases, we also need to teach our audience how to interact with the data, avoiding the pitfalls of wilful misinterpretation or cherry-picking results to satisfy a presumption.

5. A visualisation must always include the right amount of relevant data

Simplifying information does not always make it clearer to our audiences. Visuals should clarify, not simplify. Sometimes it is necessary to increase or decrease the amount of data shown. The context of the data set should also be taken into account because isolating a visualisation can mislead the viewer to draw the conclusions without all of the necessary information.

For example, the *Wall Street Journal* produced a project titled 'Battling infectious diseases in the 20th Century: The impact of vaccines.' This set of graphics is interactive, providing more information as the viewer scrolls over each square and reveals data based on state and year. The visual serves as evidence to the authors' claim that 'the number of infected people ... generally declined after vaccines were introduced' (DeBold and Friedman 2015).

6. Build narratives and test your visualisation

One of the most effective ways of showing data is by telling a story with it and using visuals to provide evidence. To accomplish this, Cairo begins with text: he writes a very long sentence and then illustrates it. Once the sentence is formed, it can be broken up into different pieces and subsequently visualised. This can be achieved in a number of ways, but it might take multiple visuals or charts. Squeezing all the information into one chart could confuse the audience. In 2015,

Ben Wellington, from the *New Yorker*, created a data story titled 'New York's noisiest neighborhoods' based on complaint types.

Wellington starts with a glance at the data, before moving into different charts that show the time the complaints were made compared to the number of complaints separated by day and the distribution of complaint types based on the time of the day. From there, he provides an overview of the neighbourhoods and how many complaints were made before using a map to show the different neighbourhoods and which complaints were most common. A reader scrolling through this story can easily see where he is drawing his information from and make conclusions on the data because of the evidence the visuals provide.

7. Visualisations are tools. Therefore…

Use them to expand audience knowledge. According to Alberto Cairo: 'The software tools are only the beginning, the principles are much more important' (Cairo 2017). There are many visualisation tools available to data journalists as well as computer languages that can help us create the right visuals. Despite all of these tools, it's important to stick to the roots of good storytelling and make sure we use the data truthfully. There is a challenge today of bad data, bad visuals and even false news. We need to represent the information we present ethically and truthfully.

Using data visualisations ethically

Data journalism makes it possible for data to be analysed and visualised without extensive knowledge of information technology. Interactive information graphics are visual representations of information with verbal and visual elements. The main characteristics of these graphics are interactivity and multimedia and their value is based on their ability to display complex information (Weber and Rall 2012). In their research, Wibke Weber and Hannes Rall interviewed different media companies, according to which every person on the data visualisation team sees themselves as a journalist so they can collaborate accordingly.

The challenge that needs to be addressed in the media is 'how to create visually appealing images without compromising journalistic integrity?' (ibid: 351). Data journalism and data visualisations take time to collect and organise data, and even though time is limited for news coverage, it is important to prioritise accuracy before speed. Charles Blow, a former graphics director, commented:

> Show only what you know. Which is like we're not going to – if there's a breaking news of the Osama bin Laden's capture. We're not going to reproduce what happened inside that complex; we don't know it. But we know where it was, we know the shape of the complex, we can point to the general areas where we know that something happened, but we don't show that thing happening (cited in ibid: 354).

The goal of every journalist who creates visualisations should be the same: show only what is known and do not assume or extrapolate.

Bongshin Lee, Nathalie Henry Riche, Petra Isenberg, and Sheelagh Carpendale proposed that the visual data storytelling process 'summarizes the main roles and activities that visualization storytellers engage in as they turn raw data into a visually shared story, along with the types of artifacts that result from these activities' (Lee et al. 2015). The first component of the visual data storytelling process is exploring and analysing data to choose a collection of data excerpts to create the story. Constructing the story is the second component, assembling the data into a storyline that is 'interesting, illuminating, and compelling' (ibid: 86). In this step, it is important to draw connections between the different data pieces and formulate the message that will be conveyed through the visual data story. The third component is the process of delivering the story while keeping the target audience in mind. What the audience understands through the storytelling experience is the perceived story from the visual data story (ibid: 87).

In *Narrative Visualization: Telling Stories with Data*, Jeffrey Heer and Edward Segel investigate various case studies of narrative visualisation and discuss how to use data to tell stories. These researchers talk about how storytellers, especially online journalists, are 'increasingly integrating complex visualization into their narratives' and the most sophisticated of these 'focus on data exploration and analysis' (Heer and Segel 2010). The case studies chosen for research mainly come from online journalism and identify a few techniques that can be applied when creating these visualisations. One is called visual highlighting and uses the colour, size or boldness of the visual elements to tell the viewer where to look. Multi-messaging is another tool that provides related but different information to the viewer in elements such as frames or panels. The presentation in multi-messaging guides the viewer through the data explaining certain patterns and highlighting key events. Single-frame interactivity pertains to the interactive items in a single frame without taking the viewer to a different 'visual scene'. Basically it encourages the user to explore the data through the single view provided for them (ibid: 1143).

Effective data visualisations and why they work

The PEW research center published an interactive graphic on the movement of European Union migrants within the EU. One reason this visualisation is successful is that it has multiple dimensions, allowing the viewer to explore the data on their own within the confines of a single image. The second element of Jim Stikeleather's 'The three elements of successful data visualizations', published in the *Harvard Business Review* (2013), is setting up a clear framework. This visual does this by having a short description of what the data shows above the visual and set text with two drop-down menus giving the audience the option to explore the data further. The full sentence also tells a story for the audience to easily understand what the data says, which is Stikeleather's third element.

As of 2015, **5,330,000** people who were **living** ▾ in **Germany** ▾ , or about **7%** of its current population, were born in other EU countries.

Country of birth	EU migrants ▾
● Poland	1,930,000
● Romania	590,000
● Czech Rep.	540,000
● Italy	410,000
● Austria	260,000
● Greece	220,000
● Croatia	210,000
● Hungary	170,000
● France	150,000
● Netherlands	140,000
● Bulgaria	110,000
● UK	100,000
● Spain	100,000
● Portugal	100,000

Note: The figures in this interactive feature refer to the total number (or cumulative "stocks") of migrants born or living in European Union countries, not the annual rate of migration (or current "flows") of migrants between EU countries. At the time of the production of this interactive, the UK was still part of the European Union even though the country voted on June 23, 2016, to leave the EU. Read More >

Image source: http://www.pewglobal.org/interactives/origins-destinations-of-european-union-migrants-within-the-eu/

Conclusion

Data visualisations are useful tools that journalists should be employing to develop stories and increase understanding of topics as our knowledge of the technology increases. Although these new tools are powerful, it is also important not to leave our audiences behind in this data phenomenon. There are still many who can't interpret and understand numbers or graphics. It is our job as journalists to guide our audiences through the data, creating narratives whenever possible, so that they can understand our claims backed up by the information displayed to them.

Visual storytelling needs to be in sync with all other forms of storytelling by staying grounded in truth and ethics. In his keynote, Alberto Cairo compared data visualisations to a hammer because they are tools that can either build or destroy. Journalists need to hold each other accountable especially in this time where many people do not consider the media trustworthy and the demand for constant news puts pressure on organisations.

References

Cairo, Alberto (2017) *Data visualization from truthful art to universal language.* Keynote speech at Microsoft Data Insights Summit, Washington State Convention Center, Seattle, 12 June

DeBold, Tynan and Friedman, Dov (2015) Battling infectious diseases in the 20th century: The impact of vaccines, *Wall Street Journal,* 11 February. Available online at http://graphics.wsj.com/infectious-diseases-and-vaccines/

Lee, Bongshin, Riche, Nathalie Henry, Isenberg, Petra and Carpendale, Sheelagh (2015) More than telling a story: Transforming data into visually shared stories, *IEEE Computer Graphics and* Applications, Vol. 35, No. 5 pp 84-90

Segel, Edward and Heer, Jeffrey (2010) Narrative visualization: Telling stories with data, IEEE Transactions on Visualisation and Computer Graphics, Vol. 16, No. 6 pp 1139-148

Stikeleather, Jim (2013) The three elements of successful data visualisations, *Harvard Business Review.* 19 April. Available online at https://hbr.org/2013/04/the-three-elements-of-successf

Sunne, Samantha (2016) The challenges and possible pitfalls of data journalism, and how can you avoid them, *americanpressinstitute.org,* 9 March. Available online at https://www.americanpressinstitute.org/publications/reports/strategy-studies/challenges-data-journalism/

Weber, Wibke, and Hannes Rall (2012) Data visualization in online journalism and its implications for the production process, *IEEE Xplore,* International Conference on Information Visualisation. Available online at http://ieeexplore.ieee.org/document/6295837/?reload=true

Wellington, Ben (2015) Mapping New York's noisiest neighborhoods, *New Yorker,* 17 January. Available online at http://www.newyorker.com/tech/elements/mapping-new-york-noise-complaints

Note on the contributor

Erin Coates is a journalist who specialises in local news and human-interest stories. As a recent graduate from the University of Oregon's School of Journalism and Communication, she completed her thesis on the implications of data visualisations and plans to continue her research on a larger scale as she pursues data storytelling.

Section 5:
Into the future...

John Mair

Data journalism has fought its way on to the pages and screens of the modern media: the genie is now firmly out of the bottle. But it needs new skills to 'do' DJ. How do we find those skills and teach them to new generations of current and wannabe data journalists?

This section examines the future of data journalism education and how to plan for it. Bahareh Heravi, of the University College Dublin, Ireland, looks to a recent worldwide survey of those practising data journalism for answers. Her own solution is simple: teach data journalism as part of the core curriculum on all university journalism courses. That way lies some possible compensation for the 'data deficiency' in too many practising and aspiring journalists. Data, in her view, should be up there with story finding and shorthand as the cornerstones of the curriculum.

Professor Marie Kinsey and Petar Milin teach at the Sheffield University School of Journalism Studies, one of the more prestigious in the UK. One is a data scientist, the other a former BBC and IRN radio producer with wide experience in and out of the academe. In their chapter, they argue for combining the two disciplines into a synthesis that will benefit both. The wannabe data journalists must first learn some of the 'theory' of data science algorithms, stats modelling – and all that put together with their hack skills: curiosity, research and verification. They should learn to treat statistical data with as much of a sceptical eye as any other form of data. To misquote Louis Heren's famous aphorism: 'What is this lying data set and why is it lying to me?' Pure data may be a myth but only those who have the tools and can unpack it can get to 'the truth' or close to it.

Jonathan Stoneman has trained hundreds of data journalists over the last six years – around 700 at the BBC alone. His journalism training experience qualifies him as something of an expert in the world of DJ education. In his chapter, 'Training data journalists of the future', he is optimistic and yet despondent at the same time. He writes: 'Guessing what the future will look like is a waste of time. It will be what it will be' so 'Prescribing in detail what the data journalist of the future will need is a fool's errand.' But he has a clear idea that data journalism has a definite future: 'It is here to stay – a key resource for journalists and one which is likely only to increase in importance.' And the way to find out just how important it will have become is through data on those who have the DJ skills and when and how they are using them. 'The next step should be to track the relationship between data journalism training and journalistic output – to keep a record of what training led which journalist to publish what story, using which particular tool or technique. That data will give a much better idea of what is working, what the balance between soft and hard skills is – and what direction data journalism training needs to take next.'

And finally, as we look to the future for journalism and data journalism in particular, who better to guide us than Professor Paul Bradshaw, of Birmingham City University, the Christopher Columbus of DJ in the UK and called by some 'the Jeff Jarvis of British journalism'. Bradshaw sees technology as the future for the 'second wave' of data journalists and outlines a ten point plan (a very twentieth century tabloid device) for the future. His master plan is based on interactivity and reader/viewer interaction with the curated content of professional journalists. He quotes as a good example *The New York Times* and their interactive content which allows reader to see how close or far way they are from some social trends.

In Bradshaw's brave new DJ world the reader or viewer has changed from a passive consumer to an active participant shaping the news through using new tools. Whether this interactivity is just electronic 'nerdism' or activist obsession is open to question. But he does see a bright new future: 'For most of the 20th century we could only arm our audiences with information and hope that they use it wisely. Online we can give them the means to do something with it, too – and we have only just begun.' So there we have it. The sometimes clumsy past of data journalism – the prehistoric CAR – to the present and widespread usage on all platforms to the future. That may be uncertain but one thing is for sure – it will be driven by both data and journalistic curiosity. Hopefully.

Teaching data journalism

Assessing the current state of data journalism education, Bahareh Heravi proposes a way forward for developing data skills in journalism programmes and beyond

Introduction

Data journalism is a relatively new term, yet there are multiple definitions at play. Before we delve into a discussion of data journalism and pedagogy in this chapter, I'll specify my usage: I define data journalism as finding – in data – stories that are of interest to the public and presenting them in the most appropriate manner for public use and reuse.

Similar to any other journalistic work, data journalism puts the tenets of journalism first: it is about the investigation, the story, and communicating that story to the public. In data journalism, data is the source, and computational methods and applications are the tools to aid journalists in their work.

The rapid emergence of data journalism in newsrooms, and the challenges this poses, calls for a review of the educational offerings for journalists. The limitless amount of data generated every day, the vast number of available data sources, and the abundance of data and computational tools and applications available, demand new skills and training. To facilitate the demand for 'upskilling' in the data realm, we must pay attention to how journalists are trained. For the purposes of this paper, I will focus on data journalism in a higher education/university context.

Two main teaching categories

Teaching data journalism is often conceived of as teaching data to journalists and rarely the other way around, i.e. teaching journalism to data specialists. I will follow this distinction, and for the purpose of this article, I divide the teaching of data journalism in two main categories: teaching data to *already-journalists* and teaching data to 'to-be journalists'.

Teaching data to already-journalists is often at the postgraduate level through professional certification programmes or individual courses where existing journalists, or journalism graduates, can enhance their data skills. Examples are the Lede programme at Columbia's Graduate School of Journalism, or the postgraduate professional certificate programme in data journalism at University College Dublin. The latter specifically requires that the participants have a degree in journalism or have worked as professional journalists.

Teaching data to to-be journalists is different in that it aims to incorporate data into journalistic pedagogy from the beginning. In this case, a complete programme is designed around teaching both journalism and data at the same time. These are often undergraduate programmes or Master's programmes where both journalists and non-journalists are accepted. Examples are Cardiff University's Computational and Data Journalism MSc and Columbia University's dual degree (undergraduate) programme in Journalism and Computer Science. Both programmes teach journalistic as well as data skills as part of their curricula.

We return to these two categories later in this chapter. In the following section, I briefly consider what data journalism programmes are available and what courses are being taught around the globe in this area.

What is out there?

Berret and Phillips (2016) studied 113 American Journalism programmes, accredited by the Accrediting Council on Education in Journalism and Mass Communications, to find computer-assisted reporting (CAR) and data journalism programmes. They report that nearly half these programmes offer no course on data journalism-related subjects. Out of the 59 programmes which do offer data journalism classes, 27 offer just one course, usually foundational, and 14 offer two courses. Only 18 of the 59 programmes are reported to offer three or more courses in this subject. They further report that the courses offered are 'largely introductory and the need is still largely for the basics, such as knowing how to use a spreadsheet, understand descriptive statistics, negotiate for data, clean a messy data set, and then interview it to find a story' (ibid: 9).

In a separate ongoing study, I compiled a dataset of data journalism courses and programmes globally. Setting aside the details of this study's methodology or research results, it became clear that the US has the largest offerings in data journalism-related courses and programmes while in Europe only a scattered number of such courses and programmes exist. Table 1 provides an overview of the number of data journalism-related subjects globally.

USA	Canada	China	Ireland	Netherlands	UK	Australia	Italy	Europe
153	4	3	4	3	3	2	2	1

France	Germany	Hong Kong	South Africa	Spain	Sudan	Switzerland	Thailand	Turkey
1	1	1	1	1	1	1	1	1

Table 1: Number of data journalism-related courses and programmes in various countries

The data suggests that, out of all European countries listed in Table 1, only the UK (three universities), Ireland (one university) and Spain (one university) offer data journalism within a self-contained programme, with more than one course dedicated to data journalism or offerings of postgraduate programmes in data journalism. The rest of the countries in Europe only provide one or two courses in this area.

When it comes to instructors of these data journalism courses and programmes, in line with the study underlining Table 1 and of Splendore et al. (2016), Berret and Phillips (2016) report that many journalism programmes do not have a faculty member skilled in data journalism. The faculty breakdown differs by region – the dataset behind Table 1 suggests that while most American programmes are taught by professionals, in Europe many university programmes in data journalism are taught by academics, with professional journalists providing occasional training.

Data journalism skills

A systematic approach to planning a data journalism programme requires learning about the skills that prospective students already present and the skills they would find most useful to learn. To understand these aspects, I used data collected as part of the Global Data Journalism Survey 2017 (Lorenz 2016, Heravi 2017). As part of this survey, we asked participating journalists about their educational background, existing skills and skills they expressed interest in acquiring for their future work. This study (3 December 2016 to 10 May 2017) was open to anyone who worked as a journalist or a data journalist in the previous year. Some 206 journalists from 43 countries participated in the survey with 181 respondents filling it out to completion (Heravi 2017). In the remainder of this section, I present the partial results concerning data journalism education, from the initial survey results previously reported in Heravi (2017).

While the survey was open to all journalists, 86 per cent of participants considered themselves to be a data journalist. The survey results, we believe, are potentially biased towards journalists who have some interest in data journalism as they were more likely to participate in the survey to begin with. Despite the high percentage of participants reporting themselves as data journalists, in terms of data journalism proficiency, only 18 per cent rated themselves as experts in data journalism, while 44 per cent of respondents identified as having a better than average knowledge in data journalism and 26 per cent identified as having average knowledge in the field. Some 13 per cent identified as novice or below average level of expertise in the field. Only half of our participants (50 per cent) had formal training in data journalism.

In terms of education level, 97 per cent had a university degree, with 40 per cent graduate (bachelor) level, 54 per cent postgraduate and 3 per cent with a doctorate or above degree.

Studying the academic background of participants, 62 per cent were formally educated in Journalism at the university level. While Journalism was by far the most prevalent higher education degree, it was followed by Politics (15 per cent), Computer/Information/Data Science/Engineering (12 per cent) and Communication and Language/Literature, each with 10.5 per cent. Some 26 per cent of respondents said they were educated in 'other' degrees.

In terms of formal training in knowledge areas used in data journalism, most of our participants demonstrated a high degree of formal training and proficiency in journalism, with smaller and varying degrees of formal training in the more data oriented and technical aspects such as data analysis, statistics, coding, data science, machine learning and data visualisation (Heravi 2017). This breakdown of formal training in various related fields between our participants is depicted in Figure 1.

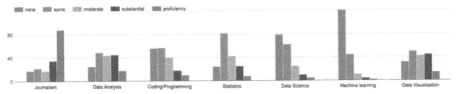

Figure 1: Level of formal training in related knowledge fields

What data skills are journalists interested to learn?

A remarkably high portion of participants in the survey (98 per cent), expressed interest in acquiring further skills to practise data journalism, with 81 per cent indicating they were *very* interested. Some 42 per cent said they were interested in formal higher education degrees in this area. However, if the training offered were to be shorter-term or more flexible, a striking 74 per cent of participating journalists expressed interest in formal training in higher education, e.g. a postgraduate certificate or higher education diplomas.

In terms of specific data skills journalists are interested to acquire, data analysis presented itself as the top skill, with 64 per cent expressing they were interested in learning about it. This was followed by learning 'how to programme/code' at 63 per cent and visualising data at 51 per cent. These top three data skills were followed by another three skills: 'how to clean data', 'how to develop data-driven applications' and to learn 'how to check if data is reliable', with more than 48 per cent of journalists expressing interest in each.

In summary, these results show that most participating journalists had formal higher education training in Journalism and related areas but these same journalists lacked training in data skills. Shorter, targeted higher education programmes would be the most attractive offering for increasing their skills in data, and many expressed a desire to make such improvements. The most important topics to be taught, according to the survey, are data analytics skills, followed by coding skills. Indeed, these figures signify how important training, and particularly data journalism training, is when it comes to formal higher education training.

What to teach?

As mentioned earlier, data journalism is about journalism first, and then it is about data. Hence, the first skills that any student must have are journalistic and investigative skills. After these, the most important topics to cover would be familiarity with data and data sources, an understanding of the life-cycle of data journalism projects, skills for data wrangling and, most importantly, data analysis skills, including sufficient knowledge of statistics. More advanced data visualisation, programming and other advanced topics may follow.

To discuss this in more detail I will return to our two groups: the 'already journalist', and the 'to-be journalist'.

The 'already-journalists'

'Already-journalists' are individuals who have trained in journalism and possibly have worked as professional journalists. They are familiar with the news production cycle and the aspects involved in 'doing' journalism: finding story leads, securing sources, verifying information, storytelling, writing and so on. Individuals in this group often require training in the data aspect and not much training in journalism. They may have further specific requirements in terms of the structure of the courses, as well as class timetables, in order to fit with their professional lives.

To this end, the first course any journalist interested in data journalism should take is an introductory course to data journalism, to understand the various aspects of working with data. Such a course could start with the possibilities inherent in working with data, including critical questions around the nature of 'empirical' work. The course could begin by examining exemplary data stories to unpack their components and determine what makes them stand out as compelling and convincing stories. Basic technical skills also need to be surveyed: learning where to find data, the basics of collecting and cleaning data, entry level statistics and how to use tools such as Excel or 'off-the-shelf' data-visualisation tools (e.g. Datawrapper, Infogram or Tableau). By the end of this course, the participants should be able to create data stories of their own, even if these stories are basic in their statistical analysis or contain rudimentary visualisations. An example of this type of work is evident from my Journalism MA students at the National University of Ireland in Galway (*Newslab.ie* 2017).

Learning the basics of the data journalism cycle enables students to understand the components first, as opposed to pedagogical approaches that throw students into advanced or more technical subjects from the beginning, such as coding, without a clear sense of where these skills can take them. It is important for journalists to know how a complete data-driven story is created, even if they are not visualisation experts, statisticians or computer programmers. By actively engaging in the lifecycle of a data-driven story, they will learn better how to collaborate with programmers or graphic designers. This will also help the journalists to understand the value of each of these steps in a data-centric investigative project, even if in a professional capacity – back in the newsroom – they may not perform some of these steps in person.

Following this foundational introduction, students could proceed to studying data analytics and statistics in more depth (and these skills reflect the desired education listed by journalists participating in the Global Data Journalism Survey). A particularly effective approach to familiarising journalists with data work would be a practice-driven training where they can put the data skills gained immediately into action, incorporating data into other investigations they may be working on professionally, or could use in their professional context.

In summary, I propose the following order for training 'already-journalists' in data-driven investigations:

1. Introduction to data journalism: including learning to find data, clean data, merge data, basic Excel and data analytics and basic data visualisation using tools such as Datawrapper, CARTO, Hightcharts and Tableau.

2. Data analytics, including statistics. Using R as a statistical tool is my recommendation as the students not only learn to run statistics but also they learn to code using R programming language. Two in one.

3. Hands-on practical production of data-driven journalism work, such as a data journalism studio.

4 (or 5). Data visualisation and information design.

5 (or 4). Programming in a language such as Python.

After these five courses, students can continue in any area towards advanced level training.

Thus far, I have focused on 'upskilling' journalists in the emerging areas of data journalism. However, there are many individuals entering data journalism who do not hold a formal background in journalism. The training for these could follow a more varied path, incorporating data skills alongside training in journalism.

The 'to-be journalist'

In contrast to the 'already-journalist' discussed above, these are individuals who are not trained, or do not work, as professional journalists. Regardless of where they are in their careers, they are only starting their journalism career and, in many cases, are just starting their undergraduate education. I split this group to three sub-groups, and briefly propose an approach to training for each below:

A. Starting a BA in Journalism

These individuals, in most cases, are coming straight from high school / secondary school, eager to learn everything about journalism. They are best positioned to learn data skills alongside their training in journalism and this can be accomplished by incorporating data courses into degree requirements or electives. Suggestions for data-oriented courses include: Introduction to data journalism, Advanced data journalism, Data-driven investigative journalism, Introduction to programming, Advanced programming (or a specialisation, such as database programming, interactive/web-based programming), data visualisation, Information design, and Statistics.

B. Holds an undergraduate degree outside Journalism, but in a related area

This group is often educated in degrees that provide complementary skills to that of a journalist, such as English, Politics, and Communication Studies. Individuals in this group may be trained in studying socio-economic phenomena, or trained in non-journalistic genres of writing. The suggested training for this group would incorporate that of Group A above, alongside 'traditional' journalism skills (writing for the news, investigation, sourcing and verification, etc.).

C. Educated in Computer Science, Information Science or Data Science

These individuals come from a technical background: they know about methods in some, but generally not all, of the following areas, depending on their degree: data analysis, quantitative and qualitative methods, and programming. This group often lacks training in writing. What they need, then, is a Journalism degree or programme and an introduction to the tenets of data journalism so they can put their technical skills to work in the specific domain of journalism. It's also important that statistics training is incorporated when an individual's technical training has not included this.

Conclusion

The time to include data journalism in all journalism programmes has arrived. While many journalism programmes still do not cover data skills, many have introductory offerings on the topic and a few have more advanced offerings. As a general observation, journalists and journalism graduates lack sufficient data skills. However, they express interest and the need to further their skills in these areas.

This gap calls for a reform in journalism programmes across the world. Data journalism is an interdisciplinary field and, while I expect that we will see an increase of data offerings in journalism programmes in the upcoming years, we require a broadened approach to data journalism training. This approach must be mature enough to facilitate entrants from the various disciplines that converge to create data journalism professionals.

References

Berret, Charles and Phillips, Cheryl (2016) *Teaching Data and Computational Journalism*, Columbia Journalism School. Available online at https://journalism.columbia.edu/system/files/content/teaching_data_and_computational_journalism.pdf

Heravi, Bahareh (2017) *The State of Data Journalism Globally*. Proceedings of the First European Data and Computational Journalism Conference, Dublin, Ireland, 6 July

Lorenz, Mirko (2016) What is the current status of data journalism? Participate in our global survey to find out, *datadrivenjournalism.net*. Available online at http://datadrivenjournalism.net/news_and_analysis/2017_global_data_journalism_survey

Newslab.ie (2017) Data Journalism, MA in Journalism at NUI Galway. Students' final data journalism project class blog 2015-2017. Available online at http://www.newslab.ie/nuigddj/

Splendore, Sergio, Di Salvo, Philip, Eberwein, Tobias, Groenhart, Harmen, Kus, Michal and Porlezza, Colin (2016) Educational strategies in data journalism: A comparative study of six European countries, *Journalism*, Vol. 17, No. 1 pp 138-152

Note on the contributor

Bahareh Heravi is an Assistant Professor in Data Journalism at the School of Information and Communication Studies at University College Dublin (UCD). Before joining UCD, she was the head of Insight News Lab at the Insight Centre for Data Analytics at the National University of Ireland, Galway. She is the former Lead Data Scientist at *The Irish Times* where she spearheaded *The Irish Times* Data. Bahareh is the Director of the Postgraduate Certificate programme in Data Journalism at UCD and has lectured on data journalism in several other Irish universities and institutions, including the National University of Ireland Galway, Dublin City University and *Irish Times* Training. She is the co-chair of the European Data and Computational Journalism Conference and the founder of Hacks/Hackers Dublin. Twitter: @Bahareh360.

Data literate journalists: The next generation

Petar Milin and Marie Kinsey argue that the next generation of data journalists will need some theoretical grounding in aspects of data science if they are to make effective use of developments in machine learning and statistical modelling. Never has a journalist's traditional scepticism been more necessary

'Data! data! data!' he cried impatiently. 'I can't make bricks without clay.'
Sir Arthur Conan Doyle (1892) 'The Adventure of the Copper Beeches', in *The Adventures of Sherlock Holmes*

The great detective Sherlock Holmes thrived on identifying and piecing together evidence in the fight against crime. At the end of his analysis there always lay a logical story, well argued and well supported by the evidence. But more than a hundred years ago when Conan Doyle was writing, finding data was hard. Now, it seems, Sherlock Holmes' prayers have been answered: we live in the age of data. In the words of the psychologist William James, data is today's 'blooming, buzzing confusion' (James 1890: 488): there is big data and it has its own science, data science. And data now has a new starring role in journalism – not the discovery of data but the methodical exploration and illumination of large and accessible data to find stories.

Of course, data has always played a part in journalism, from the reporting of government budgets to the state of a county's roads. But the developments in the use of big data and within data science have implications for how the next generation of journalists do their job and, therefore, what education they have in 21st century data literacy. Just how important will it be for journalists to have some acquaintance with these new and exciting disciplines? And how much will they need to understand of the possibilities and limitations of data science?

In this chapter, we will distinguish two ways in which data science and journalism can interact – as data communication and data journalism – and discuss each strand in turn. Data communication refers to the journalist's ability to analyse data in a statistically sound way as a prerequisite for reliable reporting. Data journalism or data-driven journalism is the next step: it capitalises on the abundance of data that is created on a daily basis and aims to explore this archived treasure to report something interesting and relevant about it. To achieve this goal, data journalism increasingly relies on a complex mix of statistical modelling and machine learning. And while statistical modelling and machine learning overlap to a large extent, they do differ in their respective goals. The former aims to draw reliable inferences and predictions, while the latter is used to describe stable structural properties and create summaries of large datasets. Statistical modelling embodies a set of assumptions and arrives at the probability of a particular scenario – for example, within economic forecasting. Machine learning is usually considered a type of artificial intelligence that allows computers to learn to recognise patterns and structure in data, often by mimicking human expertise. The challenges within both are appreciating the quality of the original data.

Why data? Why now?

Data journalism is all about data. Yet, this could be the case, for quite prosaic reasons: our *digital footprints* are becoming ever-larger, the data amasses and we start asking ourselves what we can do with it, how we can use it to our advantage? Somehow, we approach big data as we approach most other things in the world – with the desire to learn something (anything!) from it and to put that knowledge to use in adapting to our ever-changing environment.

This situation has brought about a range of intriguing paradoxes and challenges for data journalism. First, it seems that the availability of data preceded the formulation of the questions it could answer and the elaboration of a methodological apparatus that would support answering such questions. So we turned to what was available – techniques from statistics and machine learning in particular – to find answers to questions that remained to be asked. Second, while statistics may have been the obvious choice, it is also deemed treacherous and deceptive; there are 'lies, damned lies, and statistics'. How can a journalist be absolutely sure of the accuracy of the conclusions drawn from a statistical modelling? To make matters worse, voices announcing a cataclysmic future have already emerged. They claim that 'our data' will be used against ourselves: our personal data will be analysed for the purpose of 'unwitting persuasion' (Cadwalladr 2017). To protect ourselves, we distort our own digital traces which will, consequently, impair the data that we may wish to analyse. So why bother with data? This is certainly not what Sherlock Holmes was crying out for.

Telling stories with data

Large scale data analyses have long been present in journalism. According to Anderson (2015), there are prime examples of data-driven long-form reporting (including the use of infographics) right after the Second World War, in the monthly magazine conveniently named the *Survey Graphics*. Anderson (2015) goes on to argue that, in fact, journalistic practice in the US before 1830 relied on records as its primary source of evidence while, in the 1830s, the demands for reports increased dramatically, possibly due to the end of the civil war (see Garcia 1989).

Yet, a prospective data journalist may first need to overcome the problem of the public's distrust in statistics. There are several possible reasons for this distrust. For one, Velleman (2008) notes that statistics is not *deterministic* nor strictly algorithmic in the sense that any of its procedures consist exclusively of predefined steps. There is more to statistics than procedures and Velleman argues that, in many respects, statistics is more a science than a sub-discipline of mathematics as it requires *inference* – a judgment based on a particular statistical method applied to data.

Through a complete 'proceduralisation' of statistical methods, where we follow a number of steps and look for straightforward answers, we lose the possibility to reason and infer and risk drawing incorrect conclusions (especially if driven to find a particular one). With this in mind, Sir Ronald Fisher criticised two other famous statisticians, Jerzy Neyman and Karl Pearson, for making recommendations that were too mechanical; he personally was much more in favour of probing and 'modelling' as continuous processes towards decision-making based on shared information (Abelson 1995). However, the open race between candidate-models for our data may appear as 'playing at the truth rather than seeking it' (Velleman 2008: 8).

Furthermore, statistics might seem somewhat mysterious to the lay person. Velleman uses a quote from *Lancet*'s 2 January 1937 editorial to emphasise this point: 'Statistics ... tends to induce a strong emotional reaction in non-mathematical minds. This is because statisticians apply to problems, in which we are interested, techniques which we do not understand.' There is also a widespread belief that statistics is next to impossible to master and even less so to apply. Just consider how many best-sellers there are promising learning 'without tears' (c.f., Rowntree 1981).

This scepticism about the nature of statistics is unlikely to disappear. Statisticians are not interested in what is certain and definite but in what is probable or likely as a matter of degree. And when asked to draw a conclusion and make a prediction about future outcomes – for example, forecasting the trends in economic growth – often their best-fitting model, given some (possibly big) data, will suggest only a typical instance. And here lies another trap for the discipline: often such a judgment might appear as an over-simplistic portrayal of the diversity and richness of life. As Davies (2017) points out: 'Reducing social and economic issues to numerical aggregates and averages seems to violate some people's sense of political decency.'

But a simplified, averaged, almost uncompassionate description of profoundly important dimensions of our life appears unavoidable with big data. Big data is typically aggregated over many sub-sets and across strata and, as such, is prone to the *amalgamation paradox* (also known as the Yule-Simpson effect: see Wagner 1982; Good and Mittal 1987): trends can change dramatically and tell a different story if different sub-sets of data are combined and then analysed.

Critical appraisal, scepticism and, above all, a non-mechanistic approach to the process of statistical modelling will go a long way towards alleviating the prejudices against statistics. Amalgamation can be dealt with by introducing considerations about causality explicitly (see, for example, Kock and Gaskins 2016). The distinction between statistical modelling and machine learning outlined at the beginning of the chapter highlights how the latter is moving towards relaxing the constraints about when and how data can and should be analysed because it often introduces a 'human' element (i.e., 'expertise'). What remains less obvious is that machine learning is capable of providing crucial and sufficient descriptive flexibility and replacing 'insensitive' numerical aggregates with more fluid and, thus, richer quantitative summaries of the question under scrutiny.

Finding news in data

Rooted in the tradition of investigative journalism and, the more recent computer-assisted reporting (CAR) – arguably conceived in 1967 when Philip Meyer introduced social science research methods to investigate causes of the Detroit riots (Meyer 1973; also see Hewett 2013) – data journalism has steadily become more sophisticated. In parallel with the development of computer and information technologies and the accessibility of large-scale data, data journalism became entrenched at the start of the 21st century. Parasie and Dagiral (2012) argue that the first truly data-driven initiatives were launched around 2005. The real tide, however, came in 2010 when data journalism started flourishing in well-established media institutions such as *The New York Times* in the US and the *Guardian* in the UK (OECD 2010). Five years later, in 2015, the scientific journal, *Digital Journalism*, devoted a whole issue to 'Journalism in an era of big data' (http://www.tandfonline.com/toc/rdij20/3/3).

Curiously, the data-driven approach seems to create an interesting tension with what is considered 'newsy' content. News, after all, is something different, unique and out of the ordinary. Data often only shows us the typical or the average. But statistical modelling and machine learning actually support quests for 'uniqueness' because they can also indicate exceptions: knowing what is typical or average and what is unlikely or surprising are two sides of the same coin.

We would go even further and say that tension is to be expected if not desirable in times of change and growth. Some 25 years ago, the development of computer-assisted corpus linguistics (Biber, Conrad and Reppen 1998) offered the language-related sciences a new methodological toolset. That ended up changing the landscape of the discipline of linguistics itself profoundly by proposing that language analysis is more feasible with samples of real world text collected from their natural context (c.f., Greis and Stefanowitsch 2007). We contend that the same holds for data journalism: instead of a new domain of journalism, it offers researchers and professionals a new set of tools.

This change may well trigger a domino-effect and increase the interest from researchers in Communication Studies and in Media and Journalism Studies, in particular, since these 'data-centric phenomena, by some accounts, are poised to greatly influence, if not transform over time, some of the most fundamental aspects of news and its production and distribution' (Lewis 2015: 321). Already machine learning is having an impact on the way journalists do their jobs with tools that can sort through a story in real time looking for information that can be automatically tagged and annotated, e.g., people and places.

Some theory is useful

Both theories and models are idealisations – simplified representations that capture (most) important aspects or parts of complex systems such as language, sociology and biology. Such a coherent idealisation is crucial in that it fuels research questions and shapes the methods and techniques needed to answer them. In case of journalism, this is not an easy task because, as a profession, it resists clear-cut definitions (Steel 2009; Hanitzsch 2011). Furthermore, it remains disputed whether journalism studies qualifies as a distinctive research (sub)discipline (see Fedler, Carey and Counts 1998; Deuze 2005), as they are, in fact, often viewed from an ideological point of view, i.e., as 'ideologies of narrative and readership' (Conboy 2004; see also Zelizer 2004; Schudson 2001).

Does information theory (Shannon 1949, 1956) help? After all, it is a formal theory of communication and means we can start from the simple and intuitive proposal that journalism is, one way or another, about communicating information that is (highly) surprising or unlikely. Surprise, however, can be part of the message itself, i.e. part of its content, or it can come with the way that message is expressed or coded. While surprising message content is not of immediate interest to information theory (see Shannon 1949: 31), a surprising message encoding goes to the core of the theory (Milin et al. 2009). A front page of a tabloid with flashy pictures and headlines in large fonts may be interesting for being less informative about the content of the message than about the way in which editors chose to convey that content. This is the essence of Shannon's theory: it focuses on how a message is transmitted, leaving aside what it means. Semantic aspects are irrelevant for sending and receiving the message, i.e., for signalling (Ramscar 2017).

So we can conclude that this particular framework seems a likely candidate to serve as theoretical foundation on which to operate the statistical and machine learning apparatus that comes with data journalism (and perhaps data science in general). Information theory scrutinises communication in terms of (formally

233

defined) surprise, uncertainty, perplexity and associated concepts. It can help identify precise hypotheses of why, at a specific point in time, a certain story (from the set of possible stories) is selected to be told in terms of its potential to invoke surprise. It can also be used to explore how and why different news organisations might choose different ways of communicating the same story. Statistics and machine learning, on the other hand, offer natural tools to draw inferences based on high quality data. Such a model can be further used to discuss what is expected and likely and, therefore, help journalists to be more certain about what is possible but surprising. All we need for this are criteria about what should be considered un/likely or im/possible. And it's here that understanding the basics of data science can make for better journalism.

In sum, information theory provides a broad framework for discussing the newsworthiness of data. It also helps us pose specific questions and seek objective answers. At the same time, such a general theoretical framework does not preclude the use of elaborated models of analysis of power relationships (Wodak and Mayer 2001), framing (Goffman 1974) and other productive approaches to study journalism (c.f., Conboy 2013).

The future?

Data journalism is not, and probably never has been, just about data. There are different strands within this dynamic field (Coddington 2015; Uskali and Kuutti 2015) that have enormous implications for how journalists do their jobs and the quality or otherwise of the journalism they produce. Yet, all future data professionals – and data journalists in particular – need a thorough understanding of the processes of distilling information from big data by using data science techniques. Knowing more about the specific algorithms behind machine learning decision-making, recognising statistical processes and assumptions is becoming a marker of the next generation of data journalists especially in understanding the limitations and drawbacks of those techniques. Yet, future generations of data literate journalists will be most particularly helped by a cultivated, well-planned field of research, perhaps rethinking 'first principles' and proposing strong theoretical foundations. Next, we should strengthen its methodological apparatus and, hopefully, re-brand its statistical component to meet, answer and overcome existing criticisms. The future is bright, if not 'with certainty' then at least 'significantly' – in the statistical sense. Perhaps even Sherlock Holmes would approve.

Acknowledgements

We wish to thank Dagmar Divjak for helpful discussions and generous comments on initial versions of the manuscript. We are also thankful to Dmitry Chernobrov who pointed us to a specific literature relevant for this work.

References

Abelson, R. P. (1995) *Statistics as Principled Argument*, New York: Psychology Press

Anderson, C. W. (2015) Between the unique and the pattern: Historical tensions in our understanding of quantitative journalism, *Digital Journalism*, Vol. 3, No. 3 pp.349-363

Biber, D., Conrad, S. and Reppen, R. (1998) *Corpus Linguistics: Investigating Language Structure and Use*, Cambridge: Cambridge University Press

Cadwalladr, C. (2017) Robert Mercer: The big data billionaire waging war on mainstream media. *Observer*, 26 February. Available online at https://www.theguardian.com/politics/2017/feb/26/robert-mercer-breitbart-war-on-media-steve-bannon-donald-trump-nigel-farage

Caliskan, A., Bryson, J. J. and Narayanan, A. (2017) Semantics derived automatically from language corpora contain human-like biases. *Science*, Vol. 356(6334) pp 183-186

Conboy, M. (2004) *Journalism: A Critical History*, Thousand Oaks: Sage Publications

Conboy, M. (2013) *Journalism Studies*. Abingdon, Oxon: Routledge

Davies, W. (2017) How statistics lost their power – and why we should fear what comes next, *Guardian*, 19 January. Available online at https://www.theguardian.com/politics/2017/jan/19/crisis-of-statistics-big-data-democracy

Deuze, M. (2005) What is journalism? Professional identity and ideology of journalists reconsidered. *Journalism*, Vol. 6, No. 4 pp 442-464

Doyle, A. C. (1892) *The Adventures of Sherlock Holmes*, New York: Harper & Brothers

Fedler, F., Carey, A. and Counts, T. (1998) Journalism's status in academia: A candidate for elimination?, *Journalism & Mass Communication Educator*, Vol. 53, No. 2 pp 31-39

Garcia, H. D. (1989) *Journalistic Standards in Nineteenth-Century America*, Madison: University of Wisconsin Press

Goffman, E. (1974) *Frame Analysis: An Essay on the Organization of Experience*, Cambridge, MA: Harvard University Press

Good, I. J. and Mittal, Y. (1987) The amalgamation and geometry of two-by-two contingency tables, *The Annals of Statistics*, Vol. 15, No. 2 pp 694-711

Gries, S. T. and Stefanowitsch, A. (eds) (2007) *Corpora in Cognitive Linguistics: Corpus-Based Approaches to Syntax and Lexis, Vol. 1,* Berlin: Walter de Gruyter

Hanitzsch, T. (2011) Populist disseminators, detached watchdogs, critical change agents and opportunist facilitators: Professional milieus, the journalistic field and autonomy in 18 countries, *International Communication Gazette*, Vol. 73, No. 6 pp 477-494

Hewett, J. (2013) Learning in progress: From computer-assisted reporting to data journalism via freedom of information, open data and more, Mair, J. and Keeble, R. L. (eds) *Data Journalism: Mapping the Future*, Bury St Edmunds, Abramis pp 3-14

James, W. (1890) *The Principles of Psychology*, New York: Henry Holt & Co.

Kock, N. and Gaskins, L. (2016) Simpson's paradox, moderation and the emergence of quadratic relationships in path models: an information systems illustration, *International Journal of Applied Nonlinear Science*, Vol. 2, No. 3 pp 200-234

Lewis, S. C. (2015) Journalism in an era of big data: Cases, concepts, and critiques, *Digital Journalism*, Vol. 3, No. 3 pp 321-330

McCrae, R. R. and Costa, P. T. (1983) Social desirability scales: More substance than style, *Journal of Consulting and Clinical Psychology*, Vol. 51, No. 6 pp 882-888

Meyer, P. (2002) *Precision Journalism: A Reporter's Introduction to Social Science Methods*, Bloomington: Indiana University Press

Milin, P., Kuperman, V., Kostic, A. and Baayen, R. H. (2009) Words and paradigms bit by bit: An information-theoretic approach to the processing of inflection and derivation, Blevins, J. P. and Blevins, J. (eds) *Analogy in Grammar: Form and Acquisition*, Oxford: Oxford University Press pp 214-252

Parasie, S. and Dagiral, E. (2013) Data-driven journalism and the public good: 'Computer-assisted-reporters' and 'programmer-journalists' in Chicago, *New Media & Society*, Vol. 15, No. 6 pp 853-871

Piedmont, R. L., McCrae, R. R., Riemann, R. and Angleitner, A. (2000) On the invalidity of validity scales: evidence from self-reports and observer ratings in volunteer samples, *Journal of Personality and Social Psychology*, Vol. 78, No. 3 pp 582-593

Ramscar, M. (2017) *Memoryless Distributions and the Structure of Natural Language: The Discriminative Nature of Human Communication*. Unpublished manuscript, University of Tübingen. Available online at http://sfs.uni-tuebingen.de/~mramscar/

Rowntree, D. (1981) *Statistics Without Tears: A Primer for Non-Mathematicians*, London: Penguin Books

Schudson, M. (2001) The objectivity norm in American journalism, *Journalism*, Vol. 2, No. 2 pp 149-170

Shannon, C. E. (1949) Communication theory of secrecy systems, *Bell System Technical Journal*, Vol. 28, No. 4 pp 656-715

Shannon, C. E. (1956) The bandwagon, *IRE Transactions on Information Theory*, Vol. 2, No. 1 p. 3

Steel, J. (2009) The idea of journalism, Eadie, W. F. (ed.) *21st century Communication: A Reference Handbook*, Thousand Oaks: Sage Publications pp 583-591

Velleman, P. F. (2008) Truth, damn truth, and statistics, *Journal of Statistics Education*, Vol. 16, No. 2 p. 2

Wagner, C. H. (1982) Simpson's paradox in real life, *The American Statistician*, Vol. 36, No. 1 pp 46-48

Wodak, R. and Meyer, M. (eds) (2009) *Methods for Critical Discourse Analysis*, Thousand Oaks: Sage Publications

Zelizer, B. (2004) *Taking Journalism Seriously: News and the Academy*, Thousand Oaks: Sage Publications

Note on the contributors

Dr Petar Milin is Senior Lecturer in Data Science at the University of Sheffield. Marie Kinsey is Professor of Journalism Education and Joint Head of Journalism Studies at the University of Sheffield.

Training data journalists of the future

Journalists and their editors need to be exposed to the possibilities for original journalism which are opened up by access to, and facility with, data. Moreover, nobody should feel intimidated by rows and columns of data or by numbers, statistics or charts, argues Jonathan Stoneman

In May 2017, a roomful of data journalism trainers from Europe and the USA took only a few minutes to fill a whiteboard in response to the simple question: 'What do you train people on?' The list of programs, coding languages, sites and techniques which today's data journalists are being taught how to use was impressively, but forbiddingly broad for anyone thinking about getting into data journalism.

Asking what aspiring data journalists should be learning is the wrong question. The huge list of programs and coding languages just makes the problem worse. For a start, anyone looking at an extensive list like that today ought also to ask what it will look like in 10 years. What will tomorrow's trainers be demonstrating to new data journalists in 2027? Will everyone be learning R and/or Python? Will spreadsheets be a thing of the past? What will the go-to tools be?

Guessing what the future will look like is a waste of time. It will be what it will be. Of course, the codes and tools list will look very different; the data journalist of today will probably see only a handful of their current list of favourite tools in use in 2027. Prescribing in detail what the data journalist of the future will need is a fool's errand.

What is certain is that the journalist of the future will need to be able to handle data with ease and confidence. It is here to stay – a key resource for journalists, and one which is likely only to increase in importance. What we need to ask more urgently is what *deep* skills a journalist working with data should have – now, and in the future.

For an authoritative guide to what journalists are currently being taught there is *Teaching Data and Computational Journalism* (Berret and Phillips 2016). The authors define data journalism broadly and also look carefully at the content of university courses in the USA. Berret and Phillips divide data journalism education into four key areas:

- data reporting;
- data visualisation and programming;
- emerging journalistic technologies, such as drone journalism, sensor journalism and virtual and augmented reality journalism;
- computational journalism including 'the use of algorithms, machine learning and other methods to accomplish journalistic goals' (ibid). This last skill includes the learning of programs such as Python and R.

Berret and Phillips define a set of guiding concepts for each of these four areas of expertise, with the first listed under 'data fundamentals' as 'finding what no one has known before' (ibid). This vital skill is common to all branches of journalism, of course, but data arguably makes the needle in the haystack easier to find. 'Finding what no one has known before' is clearly a soft skill which is here to stay. Other hard skills required of the data journalist over the coming decade may change or emerge. Hard skills linked to any technology must evolve, and while the ability to, say, code in Python will be very useful, it is the softer skills such as critical thinking, curiosity and tenacity which will remain the keys to success.

Soft skills are harder to teach in a classroom but, without them, no one can really call themselves a journalist – however complicated the coding, mining, scraping, cleaning or analysis that they need to perform. At the end of the process there should be a story which interests, informs and edifies an audience.

So just what is data journalism?
Berret and Phillips' sub-division into these distinct areas is a useful reminder of how many skills and processes have been lumped under the one label – data journalism. Analysing a town or county council's spending needs skills which are far removed from those required to decipher data from a group of sensors, or to come up with and pursue an investigative story idea in which crucial evidence has to be gathered by a bot, by use of Freedom of Information legislation, or by designing and analysing responses to a crowd-sourced survey. Yet these are examples of data journalism and the skills required should, in theory, all be included in the curriculum of a course in data journalism.

The easy, if trite-sounding response to the apparent challenge is simple – don't panic. Experience shows that the journey towards mastery of data journalism begins with a single step. Nobody should try to acquire these hard skills just in order to get started in data journalism (although having them on one's CV can help a new graduate win a place in a newsroom). Putting the answer at its simplest: journalists should learn only what they need to know in order to get the story they are working on.

In conversation in 2013, Aron Pilhofer, then of *The New York Times*, noted that when teaching at conferences he often saw the same people year after year, taking the same classes: 'Excel 101', 'Introduction to SQL', 'Cleaning data with OpenRefine'. They had not used the skills in the intervening months, so they had lost them.

The New York Times is not the only news organisation to find that the most effective data journalism skills are acquired on the job rather than in the classroom. Between 2012 and 2014, around 600 BBC journalists attended a one-day course on the basics of data journalism. Surveyed by this author a year later, only a handful of those who responded could point to stories which had resulted from the training. But, among that handful, were one or two journalists for whom the introduction was sufficient inspiration to get them to go on looking for data-driven stories as a regular element in their work.

Meanwhile, journalists working on *The NY Times* were rapidly gaining skills but doing so on a 'just in time' basis – they needed to acquire a particular skill to get a particular story and then they re-used that skill to secure another story until they reached a new challenge. They would overcome that by learning a new skill. Then they knew how to deploy that skill in pursuit of their next story. And so on. Gradually their personal list of skills, tools and code expanded – but always on a 'need to know' basis. The old adage 'use it or lose it' applies to data journalism skills where new techniques really have to be exploited within days of learning them if they are to be retained.

Sweet music the Simon Rogers way

It may help to take a parallel from the world of music suggested, in part, by former *Guardian* Data Editor Simon Rogers. In January 2013, he posted an article, 'Anyone can do it: Data journalism is the new punk' (Rogers 2013), in which he began:

> This is a chord ... this is another ... this is a third. NOW FORM A BAND. ... It might be 35-years-old, but this will do nicely as a theory of data journalism in 2012. Why? Arguably punk was most important in its influence, encouraging kids in the suburbs to take up instruments, with little or no musical training. It represented a DIY ethos and a shake-up of the old established order. It was a change.
>
> Crucial to it was the idea: anyone can do it.
>
> Is the same true of data journalism? Do you need to be part of a major news operation, working for a big media company to be a data journalist?

If we can stick with the musical analogy briefly: what we are now looking at is something broader than the full-range of punk at its height and nobody can fairly expect the students of the genre to be able to do it all from day one. But they do need to know some chords to get started.

Some of the people we train will leave the classroom and never touch a (metaphorical) guitar again. One or two may head home, grab their instruments and start practising and soon begin to make something musically interesting. Without a basic ease or facility with chords (rows/columns) they will get nowhere; without practice they will not get facility; and all too often their briefly-acquired knowledge of the fundamentals of data analysis will atrophy. Meanwhile, of those who form a band and strum away, some will go on to achieve more and more; perhaps learning a second or third instrument, building knowledge and skills which enable them to write and perform ever more sophisticated songs.

There is, of course, a huge difference between a metaphorical band working on the basis of three swiftly learned chords and the complexities of using data within journalism. The complexities of journalism were neatly spelled out by Jonathan Stray in his book *The Curious Journalist's Guide to Data* (Stray 2016):

> … a story is a narrative that is not only true but interesting and relevant to the intended audience. Data journalism is different from pure statistical analysis – if there is such a thing – because we need culture, law and politics to tell us what data matters and how. A procurement database may tell us that the city councillor has been handing out lucrative contracts to his brother. But this is interesting only if we understand this sort of thing as 'corruption' and we've decided to look for it. A sports journalist might look for entirely different stories in the same data, such as whether or not the city is actually going to build that proposed new stadium. The data alone doesn't determine the story. But the story still has to be true, and hopefully also thorough and fair.

Don't panic – learn what you need!

Back in our world, if the answer to the question: 'How do you learn all this?' is simply 'Don't panic – learn what you need', then educators have to ask instead: 'What *do* we teach journalists about data?' The internet is full of answers – hundreds of results come up in response to a search for 'data journalism syllabus'. On *Journalist's Resource*, one can find a very well-conceived generic syllabus subtitled 'From numeracy to visualization and beyond' (*Journalist's Resource* 2017). Complete with a coherent set of exercises and reading lists, the page sets out the following learning objectives:

- Think critically and deeply about the limitations of datasets and evaluate the strengths and weaknesses of data.

- Assess how institutions may be collecting and using data and the implications of these processes for the public.

- Use and manipulate datasets with ease and comfort, being able to ask interesting questions and explore various angles.

- Deploy basic software and applications of various kinds to analyze and visualize data in creative ways.

- Demonstrate a solid grasp of data storytelling techniques that can help broad audiences understand data.

Basic skills which open journalists' eyes to the possibilities offered by data are vital. Journalists and their editors need to be exposed to the possibilities for original journalism which are opened up by access to, and facility with, data. Basic data literacy and numeracy should be a given. No journalist should feel intimidated by rows and columns of data or by numbers, statistics or charts. Learning how to use spreadsheets should remain a staple of data journalism training for the foreseeable future.

Beyond these two basic building blocks, the *required* skillset is in the eye of the beholder. Aspiring data journalists need the 'deep' skills – curiosity, creativity and critical thinking – to help them pick their way through the landscape shaped by data.

The final objective from the *Journalist's Resource* list above is, to my mind, the most important in that it requires the student to demonstrate 'a solid grasp of data storytelling techniques'. In other words, and rephrasing Bill Clinton slightly: 'It's the journalism, stupid!'

What is 'journalism' and how do you get it?

'Journalism' is an often-misused word, including some almost meaningless uses, but 'journalism' is a state of mind – something you either 'get' or you don't. Just as some people appear to be innately musical – they 'get' it; they understand what makes one chord better than another at any given moment and what makes one song better than another – some people are able to find stories in data by asking 'journalistic' questions while others churn datasets around and around without ever finding anything valuable in news terms. (This is not a problem confined to data-driven journalism – in any news conference there will always be a few journalists who note down what the speaker says accurately without being able to turn it into a meaningful news story.)

For those who 'get' the journalistic part of data journalism, the facility with data is no more than an extension of their normal journalistic instincts – they 'talk' to their data, letting it help them come up with theories about possible stories hidden within. They know how to get meaningful answers from the data and how to join up various dots to find stories others cannot see.

There is a risk that if we simply define 'data journalism' as a core skill we will solve nothing. If someone lacks the journalistic nose for a 'story' then data will be something to be hashed around just as an un-musical guitarist throws out unrelated musical chords, wasting everyone's time in the process. For the un-journalistic, the process of getting the data (perhaps through a long and arduous FOI case), cleaning it, analysing it and then turning it into a visual story results in something which leaves the reader cold, and less informed than they were before they started to read it or to look at the graphic.

The problem is, partly, that some of the virtues of data have been overstated to data publishers and consumers alike. After several decades of growing use of data in journalism we are reaching a crossroads while the publishers of the data have reached a similar point on their side of the coin.

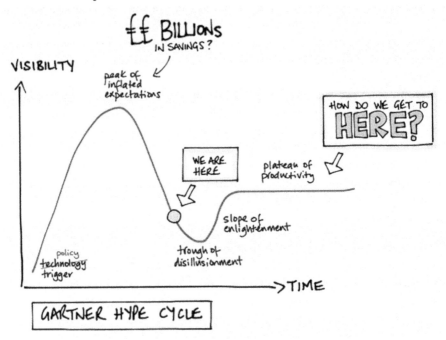

The publishers (government departments, NGOs, local government officials etc) were told opening their data would help bring in savings and efficiency and heightened productivity. These have not materialised – at least, not in the promised quantities. Lucy Knight, Data Lead for Devon County Council, spoke about the adjustments in attitude required at a talk at the Open Data Institute in London in March 2017. Graphic: Knight 2017

Pulitzer Prizes for data journalists?

From the consumers' side, the gap between promise and reality is similarly disappointing for some. Quick early wins for data journalism encouraged some to imagine an amazing future filled with scoops and awards in return for a few clicks of a mouse. Yet much data-driven journalistic works requires huge effort to hunt through gigabytes of near valueless data to find and polish, and then sell to the waiting editor valuable insights or actual stories.

Likewise, among data journalism trainers the ratio of effort to reward is now similarly daunting. More and more people are attending events such as NICAR

(National Institute for Computer Aided Reporting), GIJN (Global Investigative Journalism Network), DataHarvest, and the Centre for Investigative Journalism's Summer Conference in London. But where are the stories? And do they come from the journalists attending those conferences? For every ten working journalists or one hundred attendees relatively few get jobs which will make daily use of these new skills. A tiny proportion of those go on to develop those skills – combining datasets, technology and, maybe, sophisticated visualisation tools – to find and tell complex stories.

To discover what is really working in terms of training, the next step should be to track the relationship between data journalism training and journalistic output – to keep a record of what training led which journalist to publish what story, using which particular tool or technique. That data will give a much better idea of what is working, what the balance between soft and hard skills is – and what direction data journalism training needs to take next.

References

Berret, Charles and Phillips, Cheryl (2016) *Teaching Data and Computational Journalism*, New York: Columbia Journalism School

Journalist's Resource (2017) *Data Journalism Syllabus*. Available online at https://journalistsresource.org/syllabi/data-journalism-visualization-mapping-ethics-syllabus

Knight, Lucy (2017) *Making Open Data Happen in Local Government*, London: Open Data Institute

Pilhofer, Aron (2013) Interviewed by author, May

Rogers, Simon (2013) Anyone can do it: Data journalism is the new punk, *SimonRogers.net*, 24 January. Available online at https://simonrogers.net/2013/01/24/anyone-can-do-it-data-journalism-is-the-new-punk/

Stray, Jonathan (2016) *The curious journalist's guide to data*. Available online at https://towcenter.gitbooks.io/curious-journalist-s-guide-to-data/content/introduction/

Note on the contributor

Jonathan Stoneman worked for the BBC for 20 years as researcher, producer, reporter, editor and finally Head of Training at World Service. Specialising in central and eastern Europe, Jonathan reported for World Service from virtually every country of the former Warsaw Pact in the 1990s before moving on to run the Macedonian and then the Croatian language services. After commuting to Zagreb for several years, Jonathan decided to move into training. There, in an innovative job-share, he ran a training team dedicated to the needs of World Service staff, and generally became fascinated by the art of training journalists. In 2010, Jonathan decided to leave the BBC and become a freelance trainer.

The 'second wave' of data journalism

While networked communications and processing power were key to the emergence of data journalism in the 2000s, new technologies are set to have just as big an impact in the decade to come. Paul Bradshaw looks ahead to this coming 'second wave' and concludes by outlining a set of key principles that data journalists will need to observe

Data journalism isn't doing enough. Now into its second decade, the noughties-era technologies that it was built on – networked access to information and vastly improving visualisation capabilities – are taken for granted, just as the 'computer assisted' part of its antecedent Computer Assisted Reporting was.

It has taken barely a decade for data journalism to settle down into familiar practices and genres. Now we need to move forward. And the good news is this: there are plenty of places to go.

Looking back to look forward

In order to look forward it is often useful to look back: in any history of data journalism you will read that it came partly out of the Computer Assisted Reporting (CAR) tradition that emerged in the US in the late 1960s. CAR saw journalists using spreadsheet and database software to analyse datasets, but it also had important political and cultural dimensions: firstly, the introduction of a Freedom of Information Act in the US in 1967 which made it possible to access more data than before; and secondly, the spread of social science methods into politics and journalism, pioneered by seminal CAR figure Philip Meyer.

Data journalism, like CAR, had technological, political and cultural dimensions too. Where CAR had spreadsheets and databases, data journalism had APIs and datavis tools; where CAR had Freedom of Information, data journalism had a global open data movement; and where CAR acted as a Trojan horse for social science methods to enter the newsroom, data journalism has done the same for the 'hacker' culture (Royal 2010).

Much of the credit for the birth of data journalism lies outside of the news industry: often overlooked in histories of the form is the work of civic coders, technology companies and information activists (in particular, MySociety which was opening up political data and working with news organisations well before the term data journalism was coined). The first data journalists created their roles and practices themselves, but as news organisations formalised data journalism roles and teams, data journalism newswork has been formalised and routinised too.

So where do we look for data journalism's next wave of change?

Rise of the robots

The rise of 'robot journalism' – the use of automated scripts to analyse data and generate hundreds of news reports that would be impossible for individual journalists to write – is one to keep a particular eye on.

Aside from the more everyday opportunities that automation offers for reporting on sports or geological events, automation also offers an opportunity to better 'serve as an independent monitor of power' – one of the 10 principles of journalism outlined by Kovach and Rosenstiel (2007). Lainna Fader, Engagement Editor at *New York* magazine, for example, highlights the way that bots are useful 'for making value systems apparent, revealing obfuscated information, and amplifying the visibility of marginalized topics or communities' (Fader 2016). See, for example, the way that Twitter bot @NYTanon (Lokot and Diakopoulos 2015) tweets every time anonymous sources are used in *The New York Times*.

But is robot journalism a 'discipline of verification' (another of Kovach and Rosenstiel's principles)? Well, that all boils down to the programming: in 2015, Matt Carlson talked about the rise of new roles of 'meta-writer' or 'metajournalist' to 'facilitate' automated stories using methods from data entry to narrative construction and volunteer management (Carlson 2015). And by 2016, observers were talking about 'augmented journalism': the idea of using computational techniques to assist in your news reporting.

The concept of 'augmented journalism' is, perhaps, a defensive response to the initial examples of robot journalism: with journalists feeling under threat, the implied assurance is that robots would free up time for reporters to do the more interesting work. What has remained unspoken, however, is that in order for this to happen, journalists need to be willing – and *able* – to shift their focus from routine, low-skilled processes to workflows involving high levels of technical skill, critical abilities and *computational thinking*.

Computational thinking

Computational thinking is the process of logical problem-solving that allows us to break down challenges into manageable chunks. It is 'computational' not only because it is *logical* in the same way that a computer is, but also because this allows us to turn to computer power to solve it. As Jeannette M. Wing puts it:

> To reading, writing, and arithmetic, we should add computational thinking to every child's analytical ability. Just as the printing press facilitated the spread

of the three Rs, what is appropriately incestuous about this vision is that computing and computers facilitate the spread of computational thinking (Wing 2006).

This process is at the heart of a data journalist's work: it is what allows the data journalist to solve the problems that make up so much of modern journalism, and to be able to do so with the speed and accuracy that news processes demand. It is not, as Wing points out, a way that computers think, but rather a conceptualisation of problems that leans on the creative problem-solving of humans:

> Computers are dull and boring; humans are clever and imaginative. We humans make computers exciting. Equipped with computing devices, we use our cleverness to tackle problems we would not dare take on before the age of computing and build systems with functionality limited only by our imaginations (ibid).

And it is this – not coding, or spreadsheets, or visualisation – that, I believe, distinguishes the next wave of journalists. Schoolchildren are now being taught skills of decomposition (breaking down into parts), pattern recognition, abstraction and algorithm building. And as those children grow up and enter the news industry, imagine how their computational literacy might transform our work.

Nicholas Diakopoulos's work on the investigation of algorithms is just one example of computational thinking in practice. In his Tow Center report on algorithmic accountability, he outlines an approach to reverse-engineer the 'black boxes' that shape how we experience an increasingly digitised world:

> Algorithms must always have an input and output; the black box actually has two little openings. We can take advantage of those inputs and outputs to reverse engineer what's going on inside. If you vary the inputs in enough ways and pay close attention to the outputs, you can start piecing together a theory, or at least a story, of how the algorithm works, including how it transforms each input into an output, and what kinds of inputs it's using. We don't necessarily need to understand the code of the algorithm to start surmising something about how the algorithm works in practice (Diakopoulos 2013: 14).

Problematising computationality

But the next wave of data journalism cannot just solve the new *technical* problems that the industry faces: it must also 'problematise computationality', to use the words of David M. Berry: 'So that we are able to think critically about how knowledge in the 21st century is transformed into information through computational techniques, particularly within software' (Berry 2011: 5). His argument relates to the role of the modern university in a digital society, but the same arguments can be made about journalism's role too:

The digital assemblages that are now being built ... provide destablising amounts of knowledge and information that lack the regulating force of philosophy – which, Kant argued, ensures that institutions remain rational. ... There no longer seems to be the professor who tells you what you should be looking up and the 'three arguments in favour of it' and the 'three arguments against it' (ibid: 8).

This is not to argue for the reintroduction of gatekeepers but to highlight, instead, that information is not neutral, and it is the role of the journalist – just as it is the role of the educator – to put that information into *context*. Crime mapping is a particularly good example of this. What can be more straightforward than placing crimes on a map? As Theo Kindynis writes of crime mapping, however:

It is increasingly the case that it simply does not make sense to think about certain types of crime in terms of our conventional notions of space. Cybercrime, white-collar financial crime, transnational terrorism, fraud and identity theft all have very real local (and global) consequences, yet 'take place' within, through or across the 'space of flows' (Castells 1996). Such a-spatial or inter-spatial crime is invariably omitted from conventional crime maps (Kindynis 2014).

Principles of data journalism in its second decade

These are just some of the contours to the landscape that we are approaching. To navigate it we perhaps need some more specific principles of our own to help. Here, then, are 10 principles of my own, to build on Kovach and Rosenstiel's, which might form a basis for data journalism as it enters its second and third decades.

1. Data journalists should strive to interrogate data as a power in its own right

When data journalist Jean-Marc Manach set out to find out how many people had died while migrating to Europe he discovered that no EU member state held any data on migrants' deaths. As one public official put it, dead migrants 'aren't migrating anymore, so why care?' (Leal 2015). Similarly, when the BBC sent Freedom of Information requests to mental health trusts about their use of face-down restraint, six replied saying they could not say how often any form of restraint was used – despite being statutorily obliged to 'document and review every episode of physical restraint which should include a detailed account of the restraint' under the Mental Health Act 1983 (Holt and May 2016).

The collection of data, the definitions used and the ways that data informs decision-making are all exercises of power in their own right. The availability, accuracy and employment of data should all be particular focuses for data journalism as we see the expansion of smart cities and wearable technology.

2. Editorial independence includes technological independence

Lawrence Lessig made the point over a decade ago that code is law:

> This code, or architecture, sets the terms on which life in cyberspace is experienced. It determines how easy it is to protect privacy, or how easy it is to censor speech. It determines whether access to information is general or whether information is zoned. It affects who sees what, or what is monitored. In a host of ways that one cannot begin to see unless one begins to understand the nature of this code, the code of cyberspace regulates (Lessig 2006).

The independence of the journalist is traditionally portrayed as possessing the power to resist pressure from sources, bosses and business models and the government and law enforcement. But in a networked age it will also mean independence from the biases inherent in the tools journalists use.

From the content management systems in use to the mobile devices that record our every move, independence for journalists in the 21st century will be increasingly facilitated by being able to 'hack' their tools or build their own.

Code creates routes to the information you can access – or builds barriers around it; code affects how well you can filter the information coming to you; code affects journalists' ability to *verify* sources and documents – and their ability to *protect* sources; even to *empower* sources; and code affects our ability to *engage* users

Code is a key infrastructure that journalists work in: if we understand it, we can move across it much more effectively. If it is invisible to us, we cannot adapt it, we cannot scrutinise it. We are, in short, subject to it.

3. Journalists should strive for objectivity not just in the sources and language used, but also the way that tools are designed.

We are now at a crucial stage in data journalism: when we are moving from making stories and tools for other people to making our own tools. As is often said: 'We shape our tools, and thereafter they shape us.' The values which we embed in those tools, the truths we take for granted, will have implications beyond our own generation.

The work of Lawrence Lessig and Nicholas Diakopoulos highlights the role that code plays in shaping the public lives that we can lead; we need to apply the same scrutiny to our own processes. When we build tools on maps do we embed the prejudices that have been identified by critical cartographers? Do we seek objectivity in the visual language used as well as the words chosen?

But it is not just the tools which will shape our practice: the reorganisation of newsrooms and the creation of data desks and the data journalist's routine will also begin to draw the borders of what is considered normal in – and what is considered outside of – the role of the data journalist. Uskali and Kuutti, for example, identify at least three different models for organising data journalism work practices (Uskali and Kuutti 2015): data desks, flexible data projects and the

248

entrepreneur or sub-contractor model. To what extent these models circumscribe or provide opportunities for new ways of doing journalism bears some reflection.

4. Impartiality means not relying only on stories where data exists and is easy to obtain

The increasing abundance of data brings with it a new danger: that we do not look beyond what is already accessible, or that we give up too easily if a story does not seem practical. Just as the expansion of the PR industry in the 20th century led to accusations of 'churnalism' in the media, the expansion of data provision in the 21st century risks leading to 'data churnalism', including the use of automation and dashboards as a way of dealing with those accessible sources.

5. We should strive to give a voice to those who are voiceless in data by seeking to create or open up data which would do so

When the *Guardian*'s 'The Counted' project (see https://www.theguardian.com/us-news/series/counted-us-police-killings) sought to report on people killed by police in the US, it was literally seeking to 'give a voice to the voiceless' – because those people were dead; they could not speak. The Bureau of Investigative Journalism's 'Naming the Dead' project (see https://v1.thebureauinvestigates.com/namingthedead/?lang=en) had a similar objective: tracking and investigating US covert drone strikes since 2011 and seeking to identify those killed.

These gaps in knowledge are examples of 'data deserts' – and neither journalistic solution is an example of particularly complex data journalism: the skills are as basic as keeping a record of every report you can find. Yet this basic process has an important role at the heart of modern journalism: digitising that which did not exist in digital form before.

6. Where we provide personalisation we must still retain editorial responsibility for context and breadth of coverage

If journalism, as Kovach and Rosenstiel argue, must provide a 'forum for public criticism and compromise', what role does personalisation – which gives each person a different experience of the story – play in that? Some would argue that it contributes to 'filter bubbles' whereby people are unaware of the experiences and opinions of people outside of their social circle. But it can also engage people with stories that they would otherwise not read at all.

Data journalists, then, have a responsibility to consider the impact of personalisation and interactivity both in making news relevant to readers and providing insights into other dimensions of the same story that might not be so directly relevant.

This, of course, has always been journalism's skill: after all, human interest stories have been for decades the 'universal' hook that often draws people in to the significant and important. In the 21st century, 'play' may be the universal experience that we increasingly use to connect people.

7. We should strive to keep the significant interesting and relevant by seeking to find and tell the human story that the data shines a spotlight on

For the same reason, data journalists should ensure that their stories are not merely about numbers but people. At Birmingham City University when I teach data journalism, I always tell my students that a good story should do two things: illustrate why we should care, and why it matters. Data helps us to establish why a story matters: it connects one person's story to 100 others like it; without data, a bad experience is merely an anecdote. But without a human story, data becomes just another statistic.

8. The algorithms in our work – both human and computational – should be open to scrutiny

The more that journalism becomes augmented by automation or facilitated by scripts the more that we should consider being open to public scrutiny. If we are unable to explain how we arrived at a particular result, that undermines the credibility of the conclusion. Diakopoulos and Koliska, who have explored algorithmic transparency in the news media, conclude that it is an area much in need of research, development and experimentation:

> There are aspects of transparency information that are irrelevant to an immediate individual user context, but which are, nonetheless, of importance in media accountability for a broad public such as fair and uncensored access to information, bias in attention patterns, and other aggregate metrics of, for instance, error rates. In other words, some factors may have bearing on an individual whereas others have import for a larger public. Different disclosure mechanisms, such as periodic reports by ombudspeople, may be more appropriate for factors like benchmarks, error analysis, or the methodology of data collection and processing, since they may not be of interest to or even comprehensible for many users yet demanded by those who value an expert account and explanation (Diakopoulos and Koliska 2016: 15).

9. Sharing our code also allows us to work more efficiently and raise standards

It has often been argued that transparency is the new objectivity in this new world of limitless publishing. This recognises that, while *absolute* objectivity does not exist (we must always exercise a degree of selection), transparency can help establish what steps we have taken *towards* it. But what is transparency for data journalists? Jennifer Stark and Nicholas Diakopoulos outline principles from scientific research that can be adapted – specifically reproducibility and replicability.

Reproducibility involves making code and data available so a user can rerun the original analysis on the original data. 'This is the most basic requirement for checking code and verifying results.'

Replicability, on the other hand, 'requires achieving the same outcome with independent data collection, code and analysis. If the same outcome can be achieved with a different sample, experimenters and analysis software, then it is more likely to be true' (Stark and Diakopoulos 2016).

Currently the code-sharing site, *GitHub*, is the place where many data teams share their code so that others can reproduce their analysis. It is incredible to look across the *GitHub* repositories of *FiveThirtyEight* or *BuzzFeed* and understand how the journalism was done. It also acts as a way to train and attract future talent into the industry, either formally as employees or informally as contributors.

10. We should seek to empower citizens to exercise their rights and responsibilities

The final principle mirrors Kovach and Rosenstiel's: the obligation on the public to take some responsibility for journalism too. And it is here, perhaps, where data journalism has the most significant role to play. Because where Kovach and Rosenstiel put the onus on the public, I believe that data journalism is well positioned to do more and to actively *empower* that public to exercise those rights and responsibilities.

A *New York Times* interactive which invites the user to draw a line chart before revealing how close they were to the real trend line is precisely the sort of journalism which helps users engage with their own role in negotiating information: a challenge to the very modern problem of confirmation bias.

A tool which allows you to write to your local representative, or to submit a Freedom of Information request, is one which positions the reader not as a passive consumer of news but as an active participant in the world that they are reading about.

For most of the 20th century we could only arm our audiences with information, and hope that they use it wisely. Online we can give them the means to do something with it, too – and we have only just begun.

References

Berry, David M. (2011) The computational turn: Thinking about the digital humanities, *Culture Machine*, Vol. 12 pp 1-22

Castells, Manuel (1996) *The Rise of the Network Society*, Oxford, Cambridge, MA: Blackwell

Diakopoulos, Nicholas (2014) *Algorithmic Accountability Reporting: On the Investigation of Black Boxes*, Tow Center for Digital Journalism. Available online at http://www.nickdiakopoulos.com/wp-content/uploads/2011/07/Algorithmic-Accountability-Reportingfinal.pdf

Diakopoulos, Nicholas and Koliska, Michael (2016) Algorithmic transparency in the news media, *Digital Journalism*. Available online at http://www.tandfonline.com/doi/full/10.1080/21670811.2016.1208053

Fader, Lainna (2016) A brief survey of journalistic Twitter bot projects, points, *datasociety. net*, 26 February. Available online at https://points.datasociety.net/a-brief-survey-of-journalistic-twitter-bot-projects-109204a8d585

Holt, Alison and May, Callum (2016) Face-down restraint continuing in NHS mental health wards, *BBC News*, 21 September. Available online at http://www.bbc.co.uk/news/health-37417132

Kindynis, Theo (2014) Ripping up the map: Criminology and cartography reconsidered, *British Journal of Criminology*, Vol. 54, No. 2 pp 222-243. Available online at https://doi.org/10.1093/bjc/azt077

Kovach, Bill and Rosenstiel, Tom (2007) *The Elements of Journalism: What Newspeople Should Know and the Public Should Expect*, New York: Three Rivers Press

Leal, Natalie (2015) When reporting on data remember that those who don't count aren't counted, *Online Journalism Blog*, 5 January. Available online at https://onlinejournalismblog.com/2015/01/05/reporting-official-statistics-missing-data-invisible/

Lessig, Lawrence (2006) *Code: And Other Laws of Cyberspace – Version 2.0*, New York: Basic Books. Available online at http://codev2.cc/download+remix/Lessig-Codev2.pdf

Lokot, Tetyana and Diakopoulos, Nicholas (2015) News bots: Automating news and information dissemination on Twitter, *Digital Journalism*, September. Available online at DOI: 10.1080/21670811.2015.1081822

Royal, Cindy (2010) The journalist as programmer: A case study of *The New York Times* interactive news technology department. Paper presented at the Anais do International Symposium on Online Journalism, University of Texas at Austin, Texas, USA

Stark, Jennifer and Diakopoulos, Nicholas (2016) *Towards Editorial Transparency in Computational Journalism*, Proc. Computation + Journalism Symposium, Palo Alto, California, 30 September-1 October. Available online at https://journalism.stanford.edu/cj2016/files/Towards%20Editorial%20Transparency%20in%20Computational%20Journalism.pdf

Stray, Jonathan (2016) The age of the cyborg, *Columbia Journalism Review*, Fall. Available online at http://www.cjr.org/analysis/cyborgvirtualrealityreuters_tracer.php

Uskali, Turo and Kuutti, Heikki (2015) Models and streams of data journalism, *The Journal of Media Innovations*, Vol. 2, No. 1 pp 77-88. Available online at https://www.journals.uio.no/index.php/TJMI/article/view/882

Wing, Jeannette M. (2006) Computational thinking, *Communications of the ACM*, March, Vol. 49, No. 3. Available online at https://www.cs.cmu.edu/~15110-s13/Wing06-ct.pdf

Note on the contributor

Paul Bradshaw runs the MA in Data Journalism and the MA Multiplatform and Mobile Journalism at Birmingham City University. He also works as a consulting data journalist with the BBC England Data Unit based in the city. A journalist, writer and trainer, he has worked with news organisations including the *Guardian*, *Telegraph*, *Mirror*, *Der Tagesspiegel* and the Bureau of Investigative Journalism. He publishes the *Online Journalism Blog* and is the co-founder of the award-winning investigative journalism network *HelpMeInvestigate*.

com. He has been listed on both *Journalism.co.uk*'s list of leading innovators in media and the US Poynter Institute's list of the 35 most influential people in social media. In 2016, he was part of a small team that won the CNN MultiChoice's African Journalist of the Year award for a cross-border investigation into Nigerian football agents. His books include *Finding Stories in Spreadsheets, Scraping for Journalists, The Data Journalism Heist, Snapchat for Journalists* and the *Online Journalism Handbook*, now in its second edition.

Lightning Source UK Ltd.
Milton Keynes UK
UKHW02f2104101018

330344UK00006B/668/P